Art and Morality

THE EAST-WEST CENTER—formally known as "The Center for Cultural and Technical Interchange Between East and West"—was established in Hawaii by the United States Congress in 1960. As a national educational institution in co-operation with the University of Hawaii, the Center has the mandated goal "to promote better relations and understanding between the United States and the nations of Asia and the Pacific through cooperative study, training, and research."

Each year about 2,000 men and women from the United States and some 40 countries and territories of Asia and the Pacific area work and study together with a multi-national East-West Center staff in wide-ranging programs dealing with problems of mutual East-West concern. Participants are supported by federal scholarships and grants, supplemented in some fields by contributions from Asian/Pacific governments and private foundations.

Center programs are conducted by the East-West Communication Institute, the East-West Culture Learning Institute, the East-West Food Institute, the East-West Population Institute, and the East-West Technology and Development Institute. Open Grants are awarded to provide scope for educational and research innovation, including a program in humanities and the arts.

East-West Center Books are published by The University Press of Hawaii to further the Center's aims and programs.

Art and Morality

by Nishida Kitarō

Translated by David A. Dilworth
Valdo H. Viglielmo

An East-West Center Book
The University Press of Hawaii
Honolulu

Originally published in Japanese as *Geijutsu to dōtoku*
(Tokyo: Iwanami Shoten, 1923).

Translated from *Nishida Kitarō zenshū* [The complete
works of Nishida Kitarō], 19 vols., 2nd ed. (Tokyo:
Iwanami Shoten, 1965), 3:239–546.

Contents

Translators' Preface

Art and Morality,* here translated in full, was a key transitional work for Nishida Kitarō (1870–1945). More precisely, it was both consummation and breakthrough in the career of this thinker, who during the 1920s and 1930s came to prominence as the foremost academic philosopher of modern Japan. The fifth consecutive work of Nishida's formal academic career as professor of philosophy at Kyoto University between 1911 and 1927, Art and Morality resolved his early philosophical speculation centering around the notion of 'absolute will' as the 'fundamental apriority of the self'. At the same time, the crystallization of ideas contained therein brought Nishida to the point where he felt compelled to "pass through the gateway," as the last paragraph of the work tells us, to a new level of insight that was to influence and characterize his later thought. This development in his thought, known as Nishida tetsugaku (Nishida philosophy), has become the basis of a significant part of original philosophical speculation in modern Japan. After completing Art and Morality, Nishida attempted, in the very next work of his career, to articulate the experience of "the form of the formless, the voice of the voiceless," which, he claimed, "lies at the root of Eastern culture, transmitted from our ancestors for thousands of years." The Kyoto school of modern Japanese religious philosophy is thought to have begun with this turn in Nishida's intellectual development.

Thus, to retrace the progressive steps in Nishida's career, Art and Morality ended one stage in a series of philosophical works characterized by stages, the first consisting of A Study of Good (1911) and

* Geijutsu to dōtoku, in Nishida Kitarō, Nishida Kitarō zenshū [The complete works of Nishida Kitarō], ed. Shimomura Toratarō et al., 19 vols., 2nd ed. (Tokyo: Iwanami Shoten, 1965), 3:239–546.

Thought and Experience (1915); the second, of *Intuition and Reflection in Self-consciousness* (1917), *Problems of Consciousness* (1920), and *Art and Morality* (1923); and the third, illustrative of his mature phase of system-building, of *From the Acting to the Seeing* (1927), *The Self-conscious System of the Universal* (1930), *The Self-conscious Determination of Nothingness* (1932), and *Fundamental Problems of Philosophy* (1933–1934, two volumes). Six more volumes of *Philosophical Essays* were produced in the last ten years of Nishida's life. He died in Kamakura in June 1945.

This prodigious literary career of Nishida Kitarō can be broken into periods in various ways. But it may be helpful to the understanding of his career to view it as a continuing series of stages in self-criticism by this remarkably introspective philosopher. His third book, *Intuition and Reflection in Self-consciousness*, was already a work of self-criticism. In it Nishida rearticulated his own somewhat psychologized notion of 'pure experience', developed in his maiden work, *A Study of Good*, into a phenomenology of 'self-consciousness' that emphasized the unity of being and value, particularly in the experiential dimension of the dynamic—that is, the volitional—self. Following this discovery of the primacy of affectional and volitional a priori in self-consciousness, Nishida involved himself in a long dialogue with Neo-Kantian thought in *Intuition and Reflection in Self-consciousness*. His next works, *Problems of Consciousness* and *Art and Morality*, were progressive refinements of the central position of the self-creativity of the affectional and volitional 'horizons' or 'intentionalities' of experience attained in this early period of his thinking. *From the Acting to the Seeing* was yet another step in this continuing process of self-criticism. In it he presented his new concept of *basho*, articulated as the 'place', or *topos*, of 'absolute Nothingness' wherein the 'true self' is to be found, in an explicitly Buddhistic vocabulary that broke with the Bergsonian and Fichtean voluntarism of his preceding three works. But, in retrospect, Nishida's new concept of *basho* was spelled out between 1927 and 1932 primarily from the point of view of phenomenology and the logic of judgment. His "new logic" finally required a metaphysics of the "social-historical world," defined as the absolute 'place' of the 'mutual determination of individuals'. Original philosophical formulations that nevertheless remind us of certain key values of Buddhist heritage—particularly of the Middle Path, Kegon, and Zen traditions —constituted this further, and perhaps final, phase of self-criticism in Nishida's career. This final position was clearly established and dominant in his writings from *Fundamental Problems of Philosophy* on through his last work, *The Logic of Place and a Religious World-view* (1945).

It is important to underline the fact that Nishida's active literary career exceeded thirty years. Nishida almost never put down his philosophical pen between 1910 and 1945. Since he was never satisfied with the basic form of expression of his thought till about 1934, no work can be overlooked in the evolution of *Nishida tetsugaku*. Nishida himself often wrote of the phenomenon that the work of a creative artist is in actual fact *one* continuously unfolding process over the years of his active career. The nineteen volumes of his own complete works clearly attest to this phenomenon and are essential to the interpretation and evaluation of each of his works.

From this point of view, the most obvious division of Nishida's career into early (1911–1927) and late (1927–1945) periods only serves to clarify the place of *Art and Morality* as a work of both consummation and breakthrough in the evolution of Nishida's Eastern logic of the 'true self'. A key notion of Nishida's philosophy from 1917 through 1923 was that of the 'creative nothingness of the will', which is the source of its own ontological 'being'. In a dialogue with Fichtean, Roycean, Bergsonian, and even Schopenhauerian ideas to a conspicuous extent, Nishida attempted thereby to elucidate the dynamic intentionality of the will as the 'absolute' and 'irrational' source of its own existential immediacy. To Nishida, this 'immediacy' was the very 'ground of the true self' that functions as a qualitative value structure prior to the usual discriminations and dichotomies between knower and known, subject and object, being and value, and so forth. In another light, this was Nishida's way of probing through and beyond the level of (cognitive) apriority defined in Kant's *Critique of Pure Reason* to the profounder dimension of (volitional) apriority set up in Kant's *Critique of Practical Reason*. He deepened the metaphysical basis of this position after 1927 in the form of a doctrine of 'action *qua* seeing', or 'action-intuition', in the *topos* of 'absolute Nothingness'.

Nishida follows the Kantian framework at almost every turn in *Art and Morality*. The a priori, or the act, underlying all other a priori, or acts, of the existential, dynamic self is that of 'absolute will', which is the horizon, or intentionality, of the true self in its concrete immediacy. Each of the chapters rings another change on this guiding idea.

Thus, the focus of Nishida's attention in *Art and Morality* is the experiential *ground* from which and in which either the creative activity of the artist or the moral decisions of the self arise. This ground is analyzed in terms of the *act* of aesthetic expression, the *act* of moral decision, the *act* of reflective judgment, and so forth. But his phenomenological analyses always cause Nishida to return to the consideration of the fundamental source of the expressive and volitional self. It may thus be thought that the work turns on chapter 5, "The Union Point of the True, the Good, and the Beautiful," and chapter 8, "The Subjectivity of Behavior," where his doctrine of the free calculus of the active, concrete self is spelled out in reference to this ultimate ground, or source. In the concluding paragraphs of the work, both Truth and Goodness—both intellectual and moral intentionalities and their underlying a priori—are disclosed as arising in this deeper apriority of 'the self itself'.

It was precisely this 'true self', which is neither subject nor predicate, neither noetic act of consciousness nor noematic object of consciousness, but the *absolute* ground of immediacy of these relative structures, which Nishida rearticulated in terms of the '*topos* of absolute Nothingness' in *From the Acting to the Seeing*. In his later writings, the 'true self' is said to be found in the direction of this middle path—in the direction of this 'place' of absolute Nothingness, or Voidness, the underlying immediacy or self-identity that embraces and grounds all contradictory planes of the self.

It may thus be seen that Nishida's later writings were partly a self-criticism of the tendency exhibited in *Art and Morality* to confuse or uncritically overlap voluntaristic, especially Fichtean, and Buddhistic ideas of the 'true self'. At the same time, *Art and Morality* is important as a witness to the fact that Nishida's later breakthrough to a "logic of the East," which he claimed was neither a subjective Idealism nor an objective mystical pantheism, was achieved only by virtue of his own long odyssey through the language of Western philosophy. He became a spokesman for the logic of the East only after thoroughly immersing himself in the logic of the West, particularly in the Kantian and Fichtean styles of philosophy, to which he was drawn in *Art and Morality*. When later he went on to define Western philosophies and theologies as being essentially characterizable as philosophies and theologies of 'being' and 'form'—in contrast to the Eastern notions of 'Nothingness' and the 'formless'—he was also criticizing a level of ideas that he himself seems to have held in *Art and Morality*.

Thus, the self-criticism of the Fichtean—that is, idealistic, voluntaristic—tendencies of his own thought was the result of a long struggle to fit the proper philosophical language to his underlying, but developing philosophical insight. The emergence of an original, yet intrinsically coherent, interlocking vocabulary may be said to be the mark of a philosopher. Nishida gradually formulated precisely such an original, coherent philosophical vocabulary in the years between 1927 and 1945. *Art and Morality* brought him to the threshold of that achievement. It concluded with a philosophical anthropology and doctrine of creative subjectivity that required a still deeper ground or 'place' of 'self-identity'.

This hard-fought battle by Nishida Kitarō to achieve an original philosophical expression of his insights through a long process of self-criticism of his earlier positions may also be understood in a symbolic, or representative, sense. His long spiritual odyssey tells us something about the process of intellectual assimilation and "modernization" in the field of academic philosophy in modern Japan. Nishida's career grew out of the late Meiji period (1868–1912), during which Japan was assimilating Western values and ideas on a multivariate front. In many ways, his contemporary, the novelist Natsume Sōseki (1867–1916), was his literary counterpart. This process of the "rationalization" of modern Japanese institutions, including philosophical ones, has continued into the Taishō (1912–1926) and Shōwa (from 1926 to the present) periods. Nishida's career is an example of the prodigious energy that has gone into Japan's assimilation of Western philosophical ideas during this century. But the final lesson we draw from Nishida's own career is that the process of internalization of Western ideas and values by the Japanese was accompanied by equally vigorous introspection and criticism of those ideas and values. That Nishida ultimately returned to a radically Eastern and Japanese position seems to tell us something of the creative process of assimilation as a whole in the Japanese case. In this light, Nishida's career reflects the "modernization" of Japan from the perspective of academic philosophy in microcosm. *Art and Morality* was one gate through which modern Japanese philosophy had to pass.

DAVID A. DILWORTH

Art and Morality

Preface

This work attempts a philosophical discussion of the realms of art and morality and their mutual relationships, based upon the ideas I developed in *Problems of Consciousness*, published in 1920. It is my contention that the world of volitional objects lies at the base of the world of cognitional objects and that both art and morality exist as realms of volitional objects. However, I believe that between the two there is a distinction between the given and that which has been constructed, as Kant states in his "Categorical Deduction of Experience." I have thus probed the internal relationship between artistic intuition and moral will in the relationship between intuition and reflection in the volitional self. I am opposed to a view of morality that denies the rich content of humanity, but neither can I agree with a pure aestheticism that considers the beautiful to be directly the good. And, yet, I think that true beauty is not separated from the true and the good and that a superficial art without content is not true art.

The problem of the relationships between the beautiful and the good has naturally involved discussion of the relationships among beauty, truth, and goodness. However, the relationship between truth and reality is still not fully discussed in this work. The objective world of the will of which I speak would seem naturally to mean the world of culture. I have often discussed artistic intuition as the given of such a world. But these terms should still be more strictly defined. As I have stated in the chapter titled "Law and Morality," the truly given is not merely that which inclines to aesthetic structure. However, I think that such a given can best be explained by the example of aesthetic intuition. In the end there may be much misunderstanding concerning my use of the term 'will', which may also be termed the fundamental concept of this work. Before censuring the misunderstanding of others, I must first censure the inadequacy of my own thought; but I should also like to presuppose the points that I discussed to a considerable extent in *Problems of Consciousness* concerning the nature of the will.

NISHIDA KITARŌ
July 1923

Chapter 1

The Essence
of the Beautiful

1

There is no one, confronted by a famous work of art or exquisite natural scenery, who is not struck by its beauty. We do believe these things to be beautiful. However, beauty does not qualify a thing in the same sense that blue or red does; beauty is, rather, a quality endowed by human subjectivity. Aesthetic judgment, according to Kant, is a judgment of feeling; so should not the essence of the beautiful therefore be sought in the act of aesthetic appreciation? But the artistic consciousness is not limited to appreciation. The essence of art must also be traced to the creative act of the artist. Indeed, appreciation, too, may be thought to be grounded on a kind of creative act, as the connoisseur also appreciates a work of art through a vicarious participation in the creative act of the artist. The essence of the beautiful must thus be sought in the subjective act, on the one hand, but we cannot help thinking, on the other, that a *beautiful thing* exists objectively for our aesthetic judgments. Even if aesthetic content is not an existential, or existent, quality of a thing, aesthetic content becomes an object of aesthetic feeling in some sense. We shall be able to elucidate the essence of the beautiful by clarifying this objective quality of the aesthetic object.

The beautiful, needless to say, is not an existential quality of things, for aesthetic feeling is a subjective state aroused by things. But, just as the act of perceiving white is not itself white, a feeling itself is neither beautiful nor ugly. We feel a certain thing to be beautiful and sometimes say that the object of our feeling is beautiful or ugly. There are times, of course, when we say that we have beautiful feelings, but in such instances the feelings themselves have become objects of feeling. It does not follow that an object of aesthetic feeling is entirely subjective simply because it is not the existential quality of

a thing or a relation. For example, a mathematical system is simply
an object of thought and not an objective existence, but it must be
considered as an objective object possessing universal validity. Just
as the mathematician discovers various mathematical principles, the
artist is always newly disclosing the beauty of the objective world. To
articulate the essence of the beautiful, we must clarify the objective
quality of its object in the same way that we must clarify mathematical objects in elucidating the essence of numbers.

If we follow Kant, of course, it can be thought that the
quality of this kind of objective object is based on the universal
quality of the subjective act, and the aesthetic object becomes nothing
more than the structure of our subjectivity in general. Hence, the
aesthetic object becomes clarified as aesthetic feeling, and subjective
qualities, are clarified. However, as objects of pure thought, numbers
are also based on the quality of pure thought, yet the essence of number itself cannot be clarified by a psychological study of mathematical
thinking. To clarify the quality of number itself, we must first clarify
the a priori upon which mathematics is based. The thesis that the
mathematical unit *one* is established as an object of a synthetic act
that can interchange the affirmative and the negative is not a psychological explanation; it can be deduced only through a substantive
analysis of number itself. The quality of number itself cannot be
clarified merely in terms of the development and process of mathematical thinking and its psychological conditions. Psychological explanations cannot avoid being heteronomous with respect to the
explanation of number itself. In my view, the same can be said of the
essence of the beautiful, which can be thought to have its own kind
of universal validity in itself.

If we follow Brentano, who considers the immanence of an object as the special characteristic of a mental act and who distinguishes
acts according to the qualities of their objects, then the clarification of
the qualities of mental acts naturally becomes the clarification of the
qualities of their objects. A mental act and its object possess an inseparable relation, as two aspects of one intentional experience. For
example, if we say that the numerical unit *one* does not change its
quality according to its position, we express its quality as an object,
but if we speak of it as a synthetic act that can interchange the affirmative and the negative, then we express the quality of that act. Not
only are these two aspects unintelligible in separation, but it can
also be thought that the latter, as the a priori of number, rather clarifies the fundamental nature of number. We must also clarify the a
priori of the experience of beauty in this sense, in order to clarify the

essence of the beautiful. Even when we say that something symmetrical is beautiful, we are not merely suggesting that the aesthetic quality is a simple arrangement of lines, for the symmetry obtains in relation to our subjectivity. However, this subjective act is not reducible to the mere movement of eye muscles; it must be something like an act of 'reflective judgment', as Kant calls it, a transcendental act in a dimension beyond the realm of cognitive objects. It must be an internal act that structures its own objective world. If all spiritual phenomena are this kind of structure of meaning *qua* reality, then aesthetic feeling obtains in the intentionality in which linear symmetry lives and acts internally.

I have compared the aesthetic object to number, but the two are not, of course, identical in essence. Number is the object of a mere judgment, while the beautiful is the object of value judgment, which may be said to include the mental act within the object itself. In other terms, the beautiful includes personal content. On this point an aesthetic object is qualitatively similar to a moral object. There can be no moral judgment apart from motive, character, and action; similarly, there can be no aesthetic judgment apart from a subjective state and creative act. Even natural beauty can become an aesthetic object when we project our subjectivity upon it. For this reason it can be thought that in saying that the object is the act itself we can thus think of the object of beauty in the subjective sense, and we can seek the essence of beauty in the psychological qualities of appreciation and creativity. However, there is an inseparable internal relationship between moral judgment and moral behavior. The critical self and the acting self must be one and the same free self, apart from which there is neither moral action nor conscience. In understanding the essence of number, we must clarify the synthetic act that can interchange the affirmative and the negative; similarly, to elucidate the essence of morality, we must clarify this free self. Every moral phenomenon arises in this intentionality. Moreover, this horizon itself of the free self does not allow a causal explanation, since it transcends time and space. The same may be said about aesthetic value judgments, as well. Their object must be the world of the free self. Just as thinking creates the objective world of number, so, too, does free will create its own objective world in its own sphere.

Therefore, to clarify the essence of the beautiful we must clarify the a priori on which the intentionality of the aesthetic object is based. In so doing, we must clarify the essence of aesthetic appreciation and artistic creation and, at the same time, the objective significance of the aesthetic object. But if, instead, we try to find the essence of beauty in a psychological explanation of appreciation and creativity apart from this a priori, we can only fall into an external explanation of the beautiful. Even the theory of the beautiful as the projection of feeling or empathy does not escape this flaw. Moreover, if we seek the objective content of the beautiful apart from this a priori, we have to conceive of its having something like biological life as its ground. And in that way the independent aesthetic intentionality would be lost, and aesthetic feeling would be reduced to a kind of pleasure. However, happiness and unhappiness are mere classifications of the feelings already objectified.

The objective world, which possesses internal necessity and which can require universal validity, must be thought to be based on its own a priori. Just as the self creates its own world by its own self-reflection, so, too, is the a priori an internal power that creates its own world. Every phenomenon in a given intentionality, whether objective or subjective, must ultimately be understood in terms of its own a priori. The independent intentionality established by an a priori exhibits the interrelated polarity of object and act, for the a priori is the union point of object and act. Wundt's discussion of art as a phenomenon of racial consciousness apart from the standpoint of individual psychology can be said to have a perspective emphasizing concrete unity. But art is not merely a phenomenon of racial consciousness; it is a phenomenon of transcendental consciousness.

Of course, just as there is no argument over taste, it can be thought that aesthetic appreciation is always a subjective and individual matter that does not have any universal validity. But such an idea is simply the result of inference, which arises from thinking about feeling as a momentary personal condition. Directly regarding feeling in itself, the fact that feeling itself is directional as an intentional experience must mean that it already includes the demand of universal validity within itself. I think the very fact that we say feeling is a kind of consciousness already implies that it is a transindividual, transtemporal, and transspatial intentionality in its own right. Just as when something appears to be red it possesses an objective demand, as the consciousness of a fact, so, too, does feeling have its own kind of objective reference. Sensation is normative in its sphere, and feeling is normative in its sphere. Even if we say that there is no fact of internal consciousness called feeling, if we nevertheless believe feeling to be one variety of consciousness, then feeling must require its own kind of universal validity. Every phenomenon of consciousness that immanently includes its object must be regarded as including a requirement of universal validity. This requirement of universal validity, which transcends space and time, is a *sine qua non* for the establishment of consciousness. The factual existence of such a requirement presupposes the existence of a transindividual consciousness.

2

I believe that true concrete reality is to be found in the experience of self-consciousness (or self-awareness). In self-awareness the knower and the known are one; the act and the object of knowing are the self itself in this instance. Objectively, the self can be regarded as an unchanging identity that transcends its various acts. Internally, on the other hand, the self can be regarded as an indefinite stream of mental acts from moment to moment. However, within the concrete self this self as object and this stream of acts must be one. That which changes and that which does not change must directly be one. We can think abstractly of the division between act and object, but in concrete experience the two must have an inseparable, internal relationship. The internal union of act and object implies the indefinite development and advance of this experience itself; that is, it implies a process that is creative. The concrete self that thus reflects itself within itself must be an indefinite process. The self conceived statically is the self as a mere object of thought; it is not the thinking self itself.

When we see a color or hear a sound, we say that the color or the sound is part of the external world and that we are made conscious of them through visual or aural activity. However, what is color or sound in the external world, apart from the visual or aural activity? Though the study of physics has provided us with various explanations of what color and sound are, the worlds of color and sound are independent intentionalities to which physical explanation must conform. Physical hypotheses must be changed when they cannot explain this fact of experience. On what basis, then, does the experience of color arise, and how does it maintain an independent intentionality? Why is red distinguished from blue, and why do we recognize infinite shades of color within red itself? We may perhaps say that it is our visual act that does this. But we do not possess the least power to alter color relationships. Colors distinguish themselves. It is what is called seeing things through things. For red to be distinguished from blue, there must be a unity of the two. This unity is both red and blue and at the same time must be thought to be neither red nor blue. And it is precisely this unity that is the perceptual act in the true sense. The mind, which distinguishes black from white, is neither white nor black. Moreover, it distinguishes the two by becoming white and black. The visual act is thus an internal relationship in which colors distinguish themselves, so to speak, and it is the a priori upon which color experience is based. Every concrete experience possesses the two inseparable aspects of content and act in this way.

However, when we have reflected upon this a priori from the intentionality of free will, which is the act underlying every act and the a priori underlying every a priori, the synthesis of these noetic acts creates an independent, objective world. The 'self' is precisely the point of synthesis of such acts. Our seeing a color is the functioning of color itself. The reason we distinguish object and act is that we have reflected on our self, thus objectifying it and attributing various acts to it as center. In these terms, the object may be thought to transcend entirely the determined act of the self. However, an act of the self that has been objectified is merely a determination of a transcendental act. Mental phenomena are established in the intentionality of meaning *qua* reality and are grounded in the internal relationships between objects themselves.

What I have said about the experience of color may also be said of the experience of sound. Indeed, we may apply the same thinking to other experiences, as well. Our empirical world is the infinite synthesis of this kind of experiential content. Each 'self' is an indefinite synthesis of these kinds of acts. In other words, the self is the underlying act that takes such acts as its content. The ultimate unity of internal unities, in which colors distinguish themselves and sounds distinguish themselves, must be a free, creative act that actualizes itself through itself, as the underlying act of all acts. In other terms, it must be the free self. A certain determined act becomes the unity of infinite content with respect to its content. But it cannot yet be said that acts themselves are directly creative. The act that is truly the unity of subject and object, of knowing and acting, and that is infinitely creative by itself must be the free self, which is the fundamental act underlying all acts. Conversely, it can be thought that the content of a finite, determined act is a mere world of possible relationships. A world of reality that is inexhaustible and immovable by our intellects is established only on the basis of the unity of the free self, which is this kind of internal unity of infinite acts.

Therefore, we can think that there are various objective worlds in the intentionality of free will. The purer an act becomes, the more its objective world transcends the psychological act and the more it becomes a purely objective world possessing internal necessity in itself. The representation itself of color, in contrast to the act of perception, is an example of this kind of objective world. A given world established on a finite union of acts cannot avoid being a world of mere cognitive objects; it still lacks the self-awareness of the acts. However, in the intentionality of free will, which is a positive synthesis of infinite acts, we simultaneously possess a purely objective world constructed from the union of the content of infinite acts and a subjective world that takes the union itself of acts as object. The free self, which is this unity of knowledge and action, can objectify itself; the former becomes the world of natural phenomena, and the latter, the world of the phenomena of consciousness. The natural world, which is established on the basis of the synthesis of infinite acts, is also a world of cognitive objects; but the objective world, which arises in a pure act of consciousness, may be thought to be the world of contingent reality, in contrast to what is termed the world of necessary meaning. For the depth of our will is an infinitely unattainable depth; the will is the limit point of an indefinite series of acts.

The true will cannot be reflected upon or determined, for that which can be determined is no longer the will. Our conviction with regard to fact is based on the determination of this kind of absolute will. In mere thought, it might be that this flower does not have to be red, but can be blue. But the redness of this flower is a manifest fact. That which determines this fact is absolute will. As Fichte states, the practical self is at the basis of the theoretical self. What the senses attest to is established through the unity of the absolute will. For a man without volitional experience, there is no reality. In this way, the absolute will takes the world of objective reality as object, on the one hand, while the will possesses a world of subjective consciousness by its own self-reflection, on the other. Each self is the reflection of absolute will; each is the union of infinite acts; each is the act of acts. On this point, the world of consciousness differs fundamentally in dimension from the natural world. The self can both reflect upon itself and possess its own objective world. We are, as it were, the image and microcosm of God. However, our selves are the self-determinations of absolute will. Our freedom is not absolute freedom. Our perceptual acts are a part, but not the totality, of the transcendental act wherein color distinguishes itself. Therefore, no person can experience the totality of color. The system of the totality of color, which is the content of the transcendental perceptual act, cannot avoid being an objective world that stands over against us. The dichotomies between subject and object, and between spirit and matter, arise thereby. Viewed from the domain of intentional acts of our finite selves, the content of the transcendental self can always be regarded as a transcendent, objective world.

Absolute will not only includes the objective world of the two opposing planes of subjectivity and objectivity, but it also possesses its own objective world, the world of the unity of subject and object. This is the world of cultural phenomena. The world of cultural phenomena is the world of the realization of values. As for our individual consciousness, its individual, unique acts, which appear and disappear moment by moment, are thought to be subjective, in contrast to the objective content of such acts, which are common to individual acts that can be repeated many times. But knowing is a variety of acting, and, from the standpoint of the self in which the knower and the known are one, what has been thought of as objective exists in a structure of self-identity; and the self, which is dynamic in itself, is this unity of subjectivity and objectivity. Seen from the acts of our finite consciousness, the natural world constructed by the unity of our transcendental ego may also be thought to be an unchanging, objective world; from the standpoint of the self of absolute will, however, it is merely one content. The nearer our self approaches the plane of the transcendental self, the more the objective world belongs to the unity of the self. Herein arises the world of cultural phenomena.

By culture is meant not the taking of nature as the means of the self, but the seeing of nature within the self. Indeed, culture is the discovery of the self in the very depths of nature. The phenomena of philosophy, art, morality, and religion belong to this horizon of culture. The objective world, which stands on the basis either of one act or of a finite union of acts, since the act itself is not creative, is merely an object of judgment, as the objective world; but the object of the will itself, which is the synthesis of infinite acts, is the objective world of value judgment. The identities of value and reality exist in this horizon. The judging self must be the acting self.

The world of true, concrete reality is an infinite process in which this kind of absolute will develops itself. Consciousness in self-awareness, which can be attested to internally within the self, is precisely the form of such an act on the same level as visual and aural perception. It is the most basic act underlying all acts and constitutes the very core of the personality. Logic and mathematics are established as the objective worlds of reason. But, seen from the standpoint of the total act in which absolute will affirms itself, the world of natural phenomena arises as its objective world, on the one hand, and the world of phenomena of consciousness arises by reflecting on the act itself, on the other; and the world of cultural phenomena that involve the above unity of subject and object arises as the objective world of the will itself.

From such a standpoint, how can our various mental acts be conceived of? From such a standpoint, what kind of meaning do the acts of sensation, representation, memory, imagination, and thinking have, and in what kinds of relationships do they stand? I previously stated that the a priori upon which sensory content is based—for example, the internal relationship in which colors distinguish themselves—is the act of sensation. But we may be able to think that representation is the synthetic act of these kinds of sensory acts. Representation is not a mere union of sensation, but, rather, an act that stands on its own a priori and possesses its own autonomous content. Hence, we can think that space and time are the a priori of this act. This a priori on the exterior constructs a world of perceptual objects, while, at the same time, on the interior it becomes the act of perception. We can also think that the subjective representations of time and space differ from objective time and space; but the latter is the object of the former, and the former is that which has been determined by the latter. We may then conclude that the act of thinking takes representation as its material and also stands on its own a priori and possesses its own content on another level. And we can note, moreover, that the world of sensory content based on the a priori of sensation does not exhibit the opposition and relation between objective and subjective worlds that we find in the world of thought. That which maintains these worlds as one center in the sensory world is probably something like what the physiologist calls reflex action. But this idea, too, is nothing more than an explanation provided from the world of thinking. The world of sensation possesses its own spirit, as it were, and moves directly from sensation to sensation with this spirit as the center. The various qualities of sensation have developed internally in this way. The same can be said of the world of representational content based on the a priori of representation. Moreover, the central motive force of this world may be some kind of spontaneous motion based on instinct. All our perceptions are impulsive. With regard to the world of pure perception, we move impulsively from one perception to another. We may be able to think of the 'space' of the artist as the category of instinctive synthesis that constructs such a world.

What we nowadays term the world of reality, needless to say, is the world of the content of thinking, and the will is the central maintaining force of this real world. Since in this way various representations are unified in the intentionality of absolute will, which is the fundamental act underlying all acts that constructs the world within thinking, and, since sensation is subsumed within representation, the world of personal development, which involves all these horizons, is produced. Our lives and histories can be conceived of in this horizon of concrete experience. Biological phenomena also appear herein.

Now, I think that in the above standpoint of absolute will the immediate synthesis of act and act obtains in the intentionality of feeling, and the objective world in this intentionality of feeling becomes the objective world of art. Herein we discover the world of beauty that transcends the world of objective existence and that is creative in itself. Hence, I have argued that the objective world depends instead upon the union of acts in feeling. The immediate synthesis of act and act—that is, meaning *qua* reality—is the fundamental meaning of consciousness; it is precisely herein that we discover pure humanity. Since the fundamental act of the establishment of this kind of consciousness is the act of aesthetic consciousness, pure humanity becomes the content of aesthetic consciousness. Hence, there can be nothing artistic apart from 'the purely human'. The a priori of art is the a priori of pure consciousness. The understanding of the essence of art must be sought herein.

3

The psychologist considers feeling to be generally composed of mental elements that are on the same level as knowledge; he holds that the qualities of feeling are comprised only of the two directions of happiness and unhappiness and that the various qualitative distinctions of feeling are based on the qualities of the intellectual elements that accompany them. However, I think that feeling is not just one aspect of mental phenomena; rather, I hold that it is the fundamental condition for the establishment of consciousness. If we contend that the reason our mental phenomena differ from material phenomena lies in the internal union of act and act as the intentionality of meaning *qua* reality, then the condition of such a union is concrete feeling, and the content of such a union is the true content of feeling. What distinguishes red from blue must be something that is neither red nor blue and yet becomes both blue and red and establishes the relationship between them. Our act of consciousness is the medium in which blue and red enter into such internal relations. The intentionality wherein colors distinguish themselves is the act of visual perception, and the intentionality wherein sounds distinguish themselves is the act of aural perception.

We cannot objectify these acts in the same sense as we can knowledge. We cannot see seeing, and we cannot hear hearing. However, unless there is this kind of internal unity, we cannot distinguish red from blue; unity itself must be real in consciousness. When we reflect upon it, its content enters into the world of cognitive objects, and nothing at all remains as the content of the act. The two mutually opposing aspects of happiness and unhappiness can only be thought of in the sense of the formal qualities of the union of act and act. In psychology even the term *act* can be thought to be unnecessary. However, something that has no content at all in itself cannot unite with anything else, and in a phenomenon of consciousness the synthetic whole possesses reality, while the elements, in contrast, must be thought of as abstract. The content of knowledge does not determine the quality of feeling; rather, knowledge exists within feeling. The new synthesis of intellectual content means the development of the content of new feeling at its foundation, for the synthesis of intellectual content in the world of cognitive objects becomes possible on the basis of the union of act and act. That which creates new intellectual content is not knowledge, but feeling; in other words, it is the dynamic content of consciousness. As Bergson states, our consciousness is the center that glows within the clouds and mist. The quality of the whole is not established from the union of the qualities of the elements that construct it; it is the inexhaustible base with respect to the elements.

From this concept of feeling, I hold that pure feeling is pure consciousness and not that there is a special artistic consciousness or feeling within feeling. Pure feeling, pure consciousness, is always aesthetic. It is not that the content of feeling is beautiful as mere sensory content. When there is immediate synthesis in the personal horizon—the horizon of absolute will, as pure act in which colors distinguish themselves, that is, in the intentionality of pure visual perception—colors suddenly come to life; they become living colors in themselves—that is, aesthetic objects. When we *become* eye and ear with our entire being, feeling passes over into things and is naturally accompanied by the flow of aesthetic emotion as expression. What the psychologist calls the intensity of sensation already expresses the relationship in the immediate synthesis of acts. Sensation becomes a force in internal unity. Even the beauty of the symmetry of lines functions as the act in which the lines individually live and produce aesthetic feeling through their immediate union. In this standpoint there is nothing that is not beautiful. Even fleshly desires and vices can be made aesthetic. As Arthur Symons states, everyone sees beauty in the human breast, but not in the shoulder blade; everyone sees beauty in the Alps at dawn, but few see beauty in a stagnant marsh. However, these are nothing more than differing forms of the same essential beauty.

As I have said, feelings are beautiful in their pure state. Joy and sadness each has its own kind of beauty. Just as the representation of space is established by the a priori of space, so, too, can feeling be said to be established by the a priori of aesthetic consciousness, which is the union of act and act. As I have also said, happiness and unhappiness are nothing more than classifications of two kinds of mutually opposing qualities when we reflect upon feelings.

However, is there not, then, such a thing as an unaesthetic feeling? And what is impure feeling? Happiness and unhappiness are not mere terms, for we cannot deny that there are such feelings. However, the feelings of happiness or unhappiness, which make personal advantage or disadvantage primary, are adulterations arising through the confusion of another intentionality context with that of pure feeling. When there is a confusion of another intentionality context with that of pure thinking, then our thinking falls into error. Similarly, when pure feeling is confused with the intentionality context of the will, feeling loses its own pure content and becomes the feeling of unhappiness, which is without content. In other words, feeling becomes heteronomous. The heteronomy of conscious acts is one in which the acts of consciousness lose their inherent content, involving a disjunction of the intentional relationship between object and act. That the psychologist places all conscious content under the category of knowledge and that he considers feeling simply as happiness or unhappiness stem from the same way of thinking. For example, greed is an unaesthetic feeling. However, a miser can become an object of art. In this case, greed appears as a pure act, as one pure human characteristic. Its intellectual content that constructs it is included within the act. In contrast, when this emotion becomes an unaesthetic desire, this feeling no longer appears as a pure act; it appears from another intentionality context after having passed into the objective world of knowledge. In other terms, it becomes the content of the will and appears from the world of reality, which is the objective world of absolute will.

There would seem to be two meanings in the idea of transferring the act into the objective world of cognition. One is to objectify ourselves completely. If we do this, the meaning of the act is completely lost. The other is to see the objective world as the place of the actualization of the act, while allowing the opposition of subject and object to exist. When the consciousness of our self—the content of pure feeling—moves the self by the demands of absolute will into the objective world of absolute will—that is, when we have tried to historicize it—the content of the self—that is, of feeling—turns into the content of desire. Thus, feeling can be considered as contentless happiness and unhappiness when the dynamic content of feeling has turned into desire. Impure, unaesthetic feeling always takes the form of desire after the form of pure feeling has been perverted. The reason that the feeling of sensual desire is considered to be unaesthetic is that it most easily changes into the form of desire.

When we reflect upon the content of feeling and reproduce it in the world of cognitive objects, its structural elements are all reducible to intellectual content, its synthetic unity is changed into the content of desire, and the content of feeling itself is lost. In this way the qualities of feeling are divided into the mere qualities of happiness and unhappiness. But feeling possesses its own profound content, which cannot be analyzed. As Bergson states, when we move the hand from point A to point B, it is one simple, indivisible act when seen from within. However, seen from without, it is a curved line from A to B. We may be able to define it by dividing it into an unending number of points and by considering the line as the mutual series of these points. But the hand's movement itself is not merely position and order, for it possesses something beyond that—namely, 'motion' (*la mobilité*). This 'motion' does not arise mechanistically as the necessary result of the synthesis of numberless points. But neither is it something that has unified numberless points after first fixing a goal teleologically. It is the pure internal union of infinite acts. Indeed, the totality is *one* inseparable act. It can be thought that both the points and the order that synthesizes them by taking this act as basis are the foundation of this one act. The object of art must be the content of this kind of creative act, which we may also call 'the flow of life'. In other words, it must be the content of 'time'.

Rodin said to some persons who criticized the ignorance of some noisy swans, "They possess knowledge of lines, and that suffices" (*Ils ont celle* [intelligence] *des lignes et cela suffit*). Knowledge of lines must be knowledge of this kind of content. This view is similar to Fechner's, who has written in the context of explaining aesthetic feeling by means of association that no matter how much pleasurable feeling accumulates in the horizon of desire, it cannot become aesthetic feeling, just as irrational numbers do not emerge from rational numbers. The beauty of an orange in a still-life painting does not arise from its association with an Italian sky, but an Italian sky must be seen within a golden orange, because, as Bergson says, we smell memories of the past within the rose. Even in regard to Fechner's statement that the teleological nature of things supports the beauty of things—as it is said that the uncivilized man regards his tools as a part of his own body—the purposes themselves of the tools constitute a part of artistic beauty, in the sense that our lifeblood flows within them.

Emotions are thought to be complex; but both joy and sorrow are unique, present emotions of the self. In emotion, the memories of the past, the sensations of the present, and the movements of expression must all be immediately one. The associations of the past are important elements of beauty because through them we touch, in the depths of the consciousness of the present, the flow of a profound consciousness that has transcended the present. In the flow of this consciousness the past still lives, even now, as a pure act. As we enter into this flow we generate profound, pure consciousness in ourselves; we create a greater life. This is also the reason that happy events, sad events, and nostalgic memories can all be aestheticized. If recollections of the joys of the past are not merely boasting and if the recollections of the sorrows of the past are not mere resentment, then they are nothing more than joy reflecting the happiness of the present. Mere recollection does not have any aesthetic meaning at all. To see the Italian sky through the color and fullness of the orange and to smell the past within the rose become possible only by our entering into the depths of present consciousness and uniting with the profound flow of the pure act. In material phenomena 'time' is an independent variable; if even our spiritual phenomena are considered psychologically, 'time' is merely such an independent variable. But in immediate and concrete spiritual phenomena, 'time' has content, and 'time' changes through content.

The self of aesthetic appreciation is not the self of mere memory. As Hartmann states, the feeling of beauty is not mere feeling. Many present-day aestheticians explain the establishment of an aesthetic object through the concept of empathy or the 'projection of feeling', but if this concept merely means the union in the world of cognitive objects of our feelings through internal imitation, then there is nothing to choose between it and association. It cannot explain why the world of cognitive objects changes its nature and becomes the objective world of art. My sympathizing with the expressive act of another person means that both he and I are united in the standpoint of pure consciousness, that his and my acts are directly united—indeed, we find a self prior to the division into my self and his self. Such a consciousness of a deeper unity that is beyond the jurisdiction of the laws of natural causality and that is based on a spiritual causality is an internal process of generation. Thus, through this concept of the projection of feeling we understand that this expressive act comes to have a meaning different from cognitive objects. Mere projection, or objectification, of the value feeling of the self would simply be feeling changing its owner.

4

Since many aestheticians, following the lead of the psychologists, consider feeling to be mere happiness or unhappiness devoid of content, they naturally have to seek the content of beauty in other intellectual acts. Thus, the content of perception, representation, or imagination must be considered directly as aesthetic content. Either sensory perception is considered as the foundation of aesthetic feeling, or the feeling of the beautiful is considered as a feeling of expression or as a feeling of the imagination. However, intuition, which truly can be thought to possess aesthetic content, must be an immediate internal union of act and act. A color or sound is not an intellectual object, but the immediate transition from one act to the other, each of which is its own living intuitive function. Therefore, intuition can be considered to be the basic source of the establishment of consciousness, and its content can be considered to be what is given to us. That perception and expression are considered to be the foundation of aesthetic feeling must be in the sense of this kind of intuition. The intellectual content included within perception and representation does not become an aesthetic object; but the content of the union of act and act becomes the content of the beautiful. Even with respect to spatial perception, the content of aesthetic beauty is not objective space, which is an intellectual object, but is a subjective space that continues to function internally as the unifying force of perception itself. The form of actuality (*Wirkungsform*), in which one of Hildebrand's 'factors' is in relation with all other 'factors', must be this kind of thing. Witasek states that aesthetic feeling is a feeling of the content of expression. It is not feeling of the act; but, since his 'act' means an act conceived psychologically, he also expounds the 'unobjective nature' (*Aussergegenständlichkeit*) of the aesthetic quality, stating that beauty is different from symmetry and melody.[1]

The fact that imagination (*Phantasie*) is considered to be the medium of poetic content as something intuitive must be considered to be based on the same reason. In perception each sensory content is immanently united as act, but in imagination both conceptual content and expressive content unite directly in one individual act. This is the reason imagination is usually considered to be intuitive expression (*das anschauliche Vorstellen*). Herein resides the distinction between thinking and imagination. We think of the two as an apperceptive union, but the intentive nature of the imagination lies in the place where their union is immediate. Therefore, no matter how abstract their contents are, when their unity as an act is internally direct we can also have a kind of aesthetic experience. Just as Dirichlet states that he was able to understand mathematics on the occasion of listening to music, we are able to see in mathematics a resemblance to the beauty of music. To seek the intuitive nature of imagination in the sensory nature of its content is to view its external aspect. The intuitive nature of imagination lies in its internal creative nature, as Fichte and Schelling thought. Volkelt considers a kind of release from ordinary reality (*ein Sichloslösen von den Boden der gewöhnlichen Wirklichkeit*) to be the special characteristic of imagination in the narrow sense. Yet the intuitive nature of imagination not only essentially resides herein, but the intuitive nature and vitality of perception must also be based on it.

As stated, intuition of aesthetic content is not passive, but active. In other words, it is not merely an intellectual act; it must naturally involve the act of the will. That which unifies act and act internally must be the intentionality of the will. The content of artistic intuition is something in which act itself directly becomes content. This is the reason that Witasek, in explaining the ideal nature and the unobjective nature of the aesthetic quality, thinks that symmetry and melody are not coextensive with the beautiful. It is not that intuition reproduces the ideal, which is the object of artistic intuition, but, rather, that intuition creates it. The act itself becomes objective. The phenomenon that most present-day aestheticians refer to as the 'projection of feeling', which they consider to be the necessary condition for aesthetic appreciation, must also be understood from such an idea. Regarding the projection of feeling, or empathy,

1. Stephen Witasek, *Grundzuge der allgemeinen Aesthetik* (Leipzig: J. A. Barth, 1904).

it is thought that the thing and the self are opposed to each other and that we 'project' the feeling of the self into things. But I think that there is an immediate internal union of the acts of the self and the other and that there is the generation of a greater self, which we discover as we grow in experience together.

Karl Groos states that things are anthropomorphized through internal imitation and that feelings are projected into things. But, again, I think that such a thing as empathy is, instead, the result of the immediate union of act and act and is the result of a new life's being born, not the cause. When today's self reflects on yesterday's self and thus becomes conscious of its self-identity, our mind unites directly with itself, memory preserves itself and continues to press upon us from the past. Physiologically, the preservation of memory can be thought to be due to the act of the brain cells, but this idea is nothing more than a hypothesis constructed for the sake of explanation. As Amiel states, we are always encircled by the phalanxes of thinking (*les phalanges des idées invisibles*). It is the same even when the spirits of self and other are unified through empathy or the 'projection of feeling'. But it is merely that the form of time has changed into the form of space. The psychologist thinks of instinct as the foundation of this kind of spiritual act. However, instinct is nothing more than something that has projected the will into the background of the natural world.

That which creates our spiritual content is spiritual content. Such a thing as the internal sensation of imitation is simply a symbol of the content of consciousness of the unity of self and other. The sensation of imitation is not merely sensation, but only becomes what it is as something that possesses the content of objective consciousness. Hirn says that when we are children we imitate before we understand and that we understand through imitating, but in the depth of our consciousness, a common consciousness is latent from the beginning. If we hold that the immediate union of sensory content as act is pure perception and that the immediate union of expressive content as act is imagination, then the 'projection of feeling' might also be considered to be the immediate union of will and will. However, these acts are not essentially different; rather, they are ones in which we have concentrated upon differing aspects of the same act. The immediate union of act and act in the transcognitive standpoint is the essence of these acts, and thereby each act can be conceived of as the locus of aesthetic content. The direct union of sensory contents with each other as individual acts, if seen from another aspect, must be what is called the 'projection of feeling'. We must depend upon the 'projection of feeling' even in perceiving the form of things. Vischer says that at such a time muscular perception, such as occurs in 'stroking' (*Entlanggleiten*), must be operative.

The psychologist thinks that a series of 'local indices' (*Lokalzeichen*) of tactile sensation is united by the sensation of movement and that spatial perception is established thereby. But as a concrete perception there is only 'motion' (*la mobilité*), of which Bergson speaks. In this there is something over and above the 'local indices' that have been unified by the sensation of motion; the whole is a single continuity. Creative space—that is, the a priori of space—causes the qualitative changes of tactile perception to be 'local indices' and at the same time causes us to interpret the qualities of muscular perception and articular perception as direction and extension. The space that Kant thought of as the a priori of intuition is the internal creative force that unifies sensory contents as individual acts. Our concrete perception is creative by means of this. It is not that spatial perception is constructed by internal imitation, but that when we feel this way, spatial perception completes itself. It moves from the world of mere cognitive objects to the world of volitional objects. It changes from a passive and abstract state into an active and concrete one. The projection of feeling in such a case is nothing more than the self-consciousness of spatial perception. Just as in self-consciousness the knower and the known are one, so, too, in concrete perception content directly becomes act. This totality can only be expressed artistically as the content of feeling of form (*Formgefühl*). Just as the fact of projecting feeling into the expressive movements of others by internal imitation means the awakening of a common spirit at the base of our hearts, so, too, does spatial intuition become self-conscious. Even the projection of feeling is not essentially the projection of feeling into things. New conscious content emerges therein when everything is united mutually as act. The consciousness of a new content of feeling becomes manifest. Moreover, as content in the dimension of the act underlying all acts—that is, the personal dimension—it naturally comes to possess personal coloration.

Intuition, which is the basis of aesthetic feeling whether it is perception or imagination, is not a simple intellectual act. It must be pure feeling, pure consciousness, which is the immediate union of act and act. Perception or imagination as an intellectual act is merely one aspect of feeling. Subjective feeling is not projected into objective content; rather, there is produced a new objective world in the standpoint of the basic act underlying all acts. This kind of artistic intuition must naturally be accompanied by artistic creativity. Indeed, the act of artistic creation is the state of the perfection of such acts. In *Die Einbildungskraft des Dichters* Dilthey sought the creative act of the poet in the essence of our spiritual life. According to him, in our actual spiritual life both sensation and representation are movements suffused with feeling, and both perception and mental images are living, changing events. They are all one constructive process (*Bildungsprozess*). The constructive process of this kind of spiritual life takes the form of the external will, on the one hand, and the form of the internal will, on the other. But between them lies the broad realm of the constructive act of feeling. Within this kind of constructive act there is also an equilibrium, in which feeling is thought to include reality. But in this experiential context tension is included in feeling itself, and this tension cannot be stopped by the internal or external will. In this case, Dilthey states, "the irrepressible fact casts its shadow on all things," and thereby various images emerge. Everything appears as the result of this act, from the delusions and illusions of madmen and drunkards to the Venus de Milo and Raphael's Madonna. This makes the creative act of the poet similar in quality to the consciousness of dreams and madness. To symbolize this, Dilthey refers to the time when Goethe closed his eyes and imagined a flower: the flower immediately dissolved and produced another within itself, in the form of a rose.

I cannot help being profoundly interested in this passage of Dilthey's. By saying that our consciousness is the internal union of acts in its concrete state—that is, in the standpoint of absolute will—I mean the same as Dilthey's statement that in actual spiritual life all activity is filled with feeling. The passive aspect of such an act (*Tathandlung*) can be thought to be intuition, and its active aspect can be thought to be the 'projection of feeling'. But, as Dilthey states, this act seeks expression that cannot be limited to the will. Precisely this is the essence of the act of artistic creation. Here content that is inexpressible in the form of perception, such as Bergson's 'motion' and the form of the will, seeks expression.

However, I wish to note that Fiedler's *Über den Ursprung der künstlerischen Tätigkeit* (On the source of artistic activity) expresses this idea even more clearly. If we follow Fiedler, a thing does not become the object of our knowledge by its mere existence. We are able to receive only the result of what we have structured into our own world. Hence, we must say, if we carry this idea through more thoroughly, that reality is constituted by the images that are the expressions of the results that we have constructed. Spiritual acts do not stop as events within the mind but must seek expression in the body. Expressive movements are not external signs of spiritual phenomena but are states of their development and completion. The spiritual act and the expressive movement are one act internally. Thus, our language is not a sign of thought but is an expressive movement of thought. Thought perfects itself through language. Our 'world of reality' is nothing more than the world that has been expressed through language. However, our world is not merely one that has been expressed by thought and language. Our spiritual acts are infinite activities, and each possesses its own world of expression. As the act of pure visual perception develops into language, it naturally moves our body and develops into a kind of expressive movement. This is the creative act of the artist (*künstlerische Tätigkeit*). In this standpoint the world of concepts suddenly dissolves, and the prospect of a world of infinite visual perception opens up. I think that the most profound meaning of Dilthey's idea of artistic expression that cannot be limited to either internal or external will can be clarified by this. Dilthey's explanation goes no further than the subjective meaning of the creative act of the artist, but Fiedler clarifies its objective meaning.

However, to clarify the true aspect of artistic creation in the above sense, we must proceed from a profound consideration of the relationship between spirit and body. In the standpoint of absolute will, there is no distinction between the interior and the exterior of the mind. There is only the activity of mind and body as one lived reality. The content of internal unity of acts—that is, of pure consciousness—which appears in this plane, transcends the categories of thinking and is not reducible to the realm of cognitive objects, for we can understand it only by acting in unison with it. Acting is knowing, as in the case of self-awareness.

Bergson, in *Creative Evolution*, attempts an interesting interpretation of the formation of the eye. He points up the contrast between the complexity of the eye's structure and the simplicity of its function. Despite the amazing complexity of its structure, the visual act is one simple event. How, then, does the visual act come to construct the eye? Just as there is something in the movement of the hand over and above its numberless positions and their order, so, too, in visual perception is there something beyond the cells that construct the eye and their mutual relationships. That nature constructs the eye is a simple act like that of raising the hand. When we make a machine, we collect individual pieces, and we put them together in accordance with a certain goal; this involves, as it were, going from the circumference to the center and from the many to the one. But an organic constructive act, on the contrary, begins from one material point and proceeds to widen itself. Moreover, the distinction between the two is not merely an external one. A maufactured product reveals each part of the course of its manufacture. In making a certain machine, the one who produces it first makes the individual parts, then assembles them, and finally puts together the whole machine. The whole corresponds to the whole of the work, while the parts correspond to the parts of the work. The scientist may even consider the eye to be something created in this way. However, while the totality of a vital organ corresponds to the totality of an organic work, its parts do not express the stages of the work. The parts of this organ do not express the means that were employed; they express obstacles that were eliminated. They are not the convex form; they are the concave form. Pure visual perception is a power that attempts to see through to infinity. But this kind of visual perception is nothing but a delusion. The actual visual perception of living things is determined by things; it is a 'channeled vision' (*une vision canalisée*). The eye as a sense organ merely expresses this 'channeling'.

If in the example of moving the hand we consider the hand to have been inserted in some iron filings, our eye is something like the resultant traces. I think that Bergson's idea of the creativity of the visual act touches on the essence of artistic creativity. The fundamental source of artistic creation lies in the élan vital. That which flows forth from the tip of Phideas' chisel and from the tip of Leonardo's brush is the 'flow of life' that has flowed within their bodies from the past of the past. The surge of life that overflows within them can no longer remain within the environment centered around their bodies but creates a new world in their art. Bergson states that, even though the human personality, when young, is extremely rich in potential, it must lose such abundance as it grows. But the rich life of a genius, which he must lose in contact with actuality, finds its outlet in artistic creation. His creativity may take the form of fantasy, but 'the great breath of life' (*le grand souffle de la vie*) is in it. In such an instance, that which unites the artist and his work is internal muscular perception, and a single life force courses through the two.

Therefore, we can also look upon an artistic work as the development of muscular sensation; that is, we can say with Fiedler that an artistic creation is an expressive movement. Fiedler states that the eye not only gives sensation and perception, but that it also moves the external organs of the body, thus causing what is immanent to be developed into external expressive movement. On this point, an artistic work differs fundamentally from a manufactured product. It is not made in accordance with a certain goal; it does not move from the many to the one. Rather, it moves from the one to the many. As Fiedler also states, the one visual act accompanied by its own muscular sensation produces movement in the whole body. Indeed, from the first, it is not merely the act of visual perception the psychologist speaks of. It is a personal act in the experiential horizon of the act underlying all acts. It immanently includes muscular sensation. It is the one 'flow of life'. In this horizon, both the artist and his work become one inseparable act, as in Bergson's concept of '*la mobilité*'. The myriad things surge with life. This is the true meaning of empathy. The objective world of art is the world seen through expressive movement—indeed, the objective world is established thereby—and, as Plotinus states, it is a world that must be understood through silence.

Let me express the above ideas as follows. The world of pure visual perception is the world of concrete, personal experience, in which a visual act develops itself in the standpoint of the act underlying all acts. But if we consider the objective world of transindividual subjectivity—that is, the negative aspect of absolute will—to be the material world, then, just as the development of pure visual perception includes the hand within the pile of iron filings, as Bergson states, so, too, may we think that the act of visual perception advances by cutting through the material world. The body, moreover, is the resultant trace of the totality of life in the material world. The eye is the trace of the advance of the visual act in the material world, for the visual act is not included within the cells of the eye. The cells of the eye and their arrangement are the traces of the advance of visual perception and are the channels through which the visual act flows. Thus, what we usually term the world of visual perception is the world of visual perception for the naked eye, and visual perception opens up the material world to a certain degree. It is, as it were, a sculpture that has been sculpted and a painting that has been painted by means of the power of the eye itself without the use of the hand.

However, as Fiedler states, our ordinary visual world is incomplete as a visual world and is restricted by other objective worlds. A sculpture sculpted merely by the eye or a painting painted merely by the eye is incomplete. The visual act, which is part of the flow of the élan vital, demands infinite development as the basic act underlying all acts. Here the hand of the artist assists at those places where the eye is unable to function. Fiedler also states that the hand, taking over after the work of the eye is finished, causes further development.

At this time, the hand becomes one with the eye; the entire body becomes the eye, as it were. The world of visual perception that has been perfected in this way is the objective world of art. Sculpture and painting are realities that have been disclosed by the eyes and hands of the artist becoming one.

Thus, when the sculptor is sculpting and when the painter is painting, each becomes a process of seeing only. Plotinus states that nature does not create by seeing, but, rather, that nature's seeing is creation. In this way the artist becomes nature itself. If we consider that the visual act itself is the flow of one great élan vital, then art is the overflow of the surge of that greater life that cannot flourish completely within the channels of the ordinary eye. The visual act is a sudden variation (*la variation brusque*) which concentrates on itself alone without waiting for the parallel development of other personal acts. Therefore, it is not that feeling is projected into things, but that everything is basically life and the content of pure feeling in the standpoint of the act underlying all acts, which is the identity of content and power. The sensation of movement, which is thought to be the foundation of empathy, is, on the contrary, nothing more than a reaction of this life toward matter. Even empathetic feeling for the behavior of a tightrope walker means observing him in the same experiential horizon which eye and hand are one. It involves the development of a visual act that cannot be completely realized in the eye. Empathy is not the objectification of the value feeling of the subjective self; it is the development of a concrete life that exists before the existence of subject and object. Visual life and aural life each has its own distinctive intentionality. We can thus conclude that painting and music each possesses its own beauty that cannot be translated into the other medium.

Therefore, the content of art is said to be intuitive. But artistic intuition is not mere intuition; it is intuitive content that has been disclosed through expressive movement. Artistic creation is not mere creation; it is a productive seeing. It is the development of content itself. As in Goethe's experience, from within the mental image of one flower, numberless new flowers emerge spontaneously. The intuition of the artist is an act of formation (*Gestaltungstätigkeit*). We ultimately cannot understand this kind of artistic standpoint, in which intuition becomes creation, if we think of the thing and the mind as independent realities or of knowledge and the will as independent acts. However, concrete reality is the flow of Bergson's élan vital. The direct union of act and act is created in the standpoint of absolute will. Such a thing as Dilthey's idea of tension included within feeling that cannot be stopped by internal or external will must be the pressure of this flow of life. This is not a reality internal to the mind, but a reality that exists prior to the division into mind and things. Here there is no room to insert the blade of conceptual analysis. Its demand is not a fact of the natural world; rather, the reality of the natural world is based on it.

5

Goethe states that we delight in the splendor of the stars in the heavens, which we do not think of making our own (*die Sterne, die begehrt man nicht, man freut sich ihrer Pracht*). Similarly, since Kant, beauty has been considered as 'disinterested' (*interesselos*), and the object of beauty has been considered to be 'phenomenal' (*Schein*). Recent writers like Konrad Lange have sought the essence of beauty in conscious self-delusion (*bewusste Selbsttaüschung*). If we restrict the term *reality* to the meaning of natural-scientific reality, then, of course, we cannot seek an aesthetic object in the world of reality. However, if we consider that the world of reality is the direction of reflection of the absolute self and is nothing more than one abstract plane of concrete reality, then we can attribute reality to aesthetic objects in a sense different from scientific reality. Karl Groos states that the reality of aesthetic objects comes from sensory reality, but that which gives reality to aesthetic delusion is the movement in the organism (*motorische Vorgänge im Organismus*). However, Groos does not recognize a meaning beyond a natural reality and beyond psychological reality in this motion of the organism. Reality given by this kind of sensation of movement, compared to the objective world of cognitive objects, still cannot avoid being a kind of illusion. However, as I have also stated, the internal imitation that generates the world of artistic objects is not the mere sensation of movement; it is the reaction of the flow of life. We cannot have a sensation of movement in the strict sense, but only in the sense of what Bergson terms *la mobilité*. There are only the 'local sign' plus muscular sensation.

A sculpture of an angry man does not completely reproduce the expression and attitude of an angry man; we can say that it assumes its reality as sculpture by uniting directly with the sensory qualities of the sculpted figure. However, I think that, conversely, a man's anger, as in Bergson's concept of '*la vision*', is one expression of the tranquil flow of life in itself. The expression of an actual angry man and that of a sculpted figure are both external shells of this life. Indeed, we can say that the sculpture by a famous sculptor even expresses this truth the better. Of the many expressions that can be seen in an actual angry man, not all are necessary to depict the real substance of the anger. The artist does not imitate reality; he creates a world of life that cannot achieve its full expression within our bodies. He who elucidates the visual act itself as one simple act (*un acte simple, indivisible*), of which Bergson spoke, is not a dissector, but an artist. The very life included within the pupil of the eye of the famous artist creates a world of infinite color and form for us. The world of power that van Gogh saw and the world of color that Gauguin and Matisse saw must be such realities. This world can be seen only through expressive movement. We can think that the artists of present-day expressionism have attained this perspective. I think that the reality of the 'real world' is given by the real nature of such reality. The feeling of reality in sensation is based on it.

Groos gives the following example of the distinction between *Kopie-Original-Illusion* (artificial illusion) and *aufkeimende Illusion* (productive illusion). He considers the case in which two men enter one evening into a room and see a brilliantly constructed suicide. One immediately recognizes its artificiality, and the other is just horrified. Both men have received the same impression, but one of them sees it simply intellectually as an imitation, whereas the other in no way notices its artificial aspect. However, even the man who recognizes its artificiality feels some degree of horror as he looks at the scene and the illusion gradually intensifies, without losing his previous correct judgment. This is the 'productive illusion'. In such an instance both the man who is first horrified and the man who looks at it dispassionately are standing in intellectual positions. However, when the man who thoroughly recognizes its artificiality enters into the 'productive illusion'—that is, when he enters into what Konrad Lange terms 'conscious self-delusion'—he has already withdrawn from the standpoint of intellectual truth and falsehood and has taken a transintellectual position. 'The true' and 'the artificial' in this context become meaningless. An illusion is an event seen from an intellectual standpoint. Delusions and illusions involve differing realities. In the standpoint of transcendental idealism, this world becomes a 'conscious illusion'. When we consciously deceive ourselves, it is no longer deception.

Since Hartmann, the feeling of beauty has been thought of as a kind of 'phenomenal feeling' (*Scheingefühl*). Seeing a play and feeling joy or sadness at it does not mean that we actually are happy or sad. Witasek thinks that, on the occasion of feeling empathy, we do not have a real emotional experience but that we only possess the representation of feeling. In such a case, the 'self' must be the psychological self projected into the world of time, space, and causality; it must be an objectified self. However, this kind of self is not the true self, but the self upon which we have reflected, and not the reflecting self. This kind of self is entirely without content. Such a self is precisely the representation of the self and is not the actual self. Our concrete mental phenomena are not the union of such a self and the content of consciousness. Consciousness is the internal development of content itself, and the unity of such development of content is the self. The content of its unity is the content of feeling. Our true self must always include objective content. Lipps states that the self of aesthetic appreciation is ideal (*ideelles*). But there is no self which is not ideal. Because the self is ideal, it is real. Aesthetic feeling is precisely the truly real feeling (*reales Gefühl*).

A spiritual phenomenon, then, is the identity of meaning and reality and hence is established by the category of actuality (*Aktualität*). The reason we think of aesthetic feeling as phenomenal feeling is that we have objectified the self. At such a time, true feeling has already been lost. If the so-called real feeling is not something like organic sensation, it is nothing more than a form of desire. Hartmann states that the pleasure of aesthetic appearance, which has been filled up by phenomenal feeling, is clearly a real feeling. He further states that this real feeling and the phenomenal feeling are united, just as one who bathes in the sea gives himself up to the sea with a feeling of passive pleasure. But, in essence, there are not real feelings and phenomenal feelings. By Hartmann's standpoint of 'real feelings', feeling is projected into things, things are made to live, and 'phenomenal feelings' are established. This kind of standpoint of the union of subject and object is the standpoint of the true self, for there is no concrete feeling apart from aesthetic feeling. He states that, just as a man dreams of himself in action, so, too, does he who appreciates art find his forgotten self again within the elation of the aesthetic imagination. But there is no such thing as a self that is merely dreamt of (*das geträumte Ich*). As Descartes has stated, the self that dreams is also the self. The standpoint of the true self is one beyond the world of cognitive objects. It is the standpoint of the act underlying all acts, which has transcended the distinction between true and false. The objective world of art is established in this perspective. This is also the reason he stated that the world of art possesses a reality greater than the world of cognitive objects. Even those things that are considered to be empty fantasies and not at all in the world of objective intellectual judgment can become realities in the objective world of value judgment—that is, in the world of culture. Moreover, judgment can be established on the basis of the hypothesis of the consciousness of value. The world that stands on the basis of value consciousness is the most concrete world of reality.

If the aesthetic feeling is the feeling of the true self, in the sense discussed here, and its objective world is, rather, the truly concrete reality, then what is the relationship between the world of the beautiful and the so-called real world? Our individual and personal worlds are parts of the concrete world that is established in the standpoint of the absolutely free self, but our self is not the totality of the absolute self. As Bergson says in *Creative Evolution*, our life is not the totality of the élan vital. An infinite act can be thought to be the countercurrent to the flow of our individual self. Borrowing Herbart's idea, we can think that there must be a struggle against the obstacles (*Hemmungen*) of numberless other representations for one representation to arise in our consciousness. This produces an opposition between subject and object and the distinction between interior and exterior. Bergson distinguishes two kinds of unconsciousness: 'nonconsciousness' (*conscience nulle*) and 'consciousness that has become nothing' (*conscience annullée*). The former is true nonbeing, whereas the latter is the mutual extinction of two opposing numbers of plus and minus. For example, when a stone falls, it is entirely 'nonconscious', for the stone does not know that it falls. Conversely, actions that have become mechanical by habit or the sleepwalking of a somnambulist are things in which representation is blocked by the performance of the action. Therefore, in these instances consciousness truly appears when our performance of the action is inhibited. There was consciousness at the first, but it had been suppressed. Our consciousness expresses an 'inadequation' of the act to the representation (*une inadequation de l'acte à la représentation*). In other words, it is comparable to the aura of potential action that envelops actual action. At the place where there are many potential actions, consciousness, too, is profound. We may say that consciousness is the quantitative difference between actual and potential action.

That we proceed to the scene of action in this idea means that we are uniting with absolute will at the ground of the self. The field of action is the direction of the negation of absolute will. Union with this world becomes the condition of our existence as we stand within absolute will. In this place our act answers action with action, and the act loses its content and becomes merely an action. In contrast to the act, this world arises as the mere objective world, and the material world is nothing more than this kind of world. With regard to the experience of self-consciousness, the act that reflects on the present self and the act that has previously reflected on the self can be considered to transcend past, present, and future and to be united with one another in the standpoint of the self that unites them. Since neither act of reflection is the totality of the self, both acts in this standpoint must be considered to negate their content and to be united with one another as mere behavior. Reality must always have such a scene as its background. The finite is established on the basis of the infinite, and there is such an infinite flow even in the depth of the self. This horizon is the basis of the existence of the self, and at the same time it is a task which is given to be accomplished. The process of absorbing this horizon, its internalization, is the demand of our life, the development of concrete reality.

Our actual life, from instinctive life up to cultural life, is the infinite process of development in this way. The content of artistic consciousness, on the contrary, is the content of concrete reality that internalizes this kind of objective world. The field of action that is the objective world of absolute will is not independently real in itself. In concrete reality knowledge and action must be directly one, and consciousness and unconsciousness must be one, as in self-awareness. The pure content of this kind of concrete reality is the content of artistic consciousness. The content of the will appears at the point where this content directly touches the real world, the field of action. The content of the will, of actual life, is the content of artistic consciousness, which has been determined by the condition of existence. 'Consciousness that has become nothing', which differs from simple 'nonconsciousness', is not something that is hindered by action; it must be something that internalizes action.

'Sensitivity' acquired through discipline is not mere mechanical habit. In the case of a painter painting a picture, he, of course, does not follow conceptual judgment; but his painting is not merely spontaneous movement, either. His movement must have the self-awareness of power. It is not reflective self-awareness, but self-awareness in action. 'Style' is such a self-awareness in action. Aside from the consciousness that is based on the excess of representation with respect to action of which Bergson speaks, there is consciousness that arises by being inhibited by action—that is, by the unity of subject and object. Just as the concrete is the basis and goal of the abstract, so does the abstract exist on the basis of the concrete.

Chapter 2

From Max Klinger's "Painting and Line Drawing"

Art is neither a mere description of reality nor a mere subjective fancy. The so-called real world is not the only world given to us. Indeed, the world constructed by such a concept must rather be said to be the mere surface of reality. In the back of such a world is the flow of a truer reality, filled with a larger life whose depths cannot be fathomed. Precisely this reality is the object of art, and this aesthetic world, like our life itself, is infinitely free and profoundly rich. In music there is truth that can only be expressed by music, and in painting there is truth that can only be expressed by painting. Moreover, if we follow Klinger's ideas, we may also be able to say that in line drawing (*Zeichnung*) there is truth that can only be expressed by line drawing.*

Here the term *line drawing* is used in an extremely broad sense, but it would seem that line drawing has not been thought of in the West as having an independent significance. Either it has been thought of as the preparatory sketch for painting, or it has been used to copy existing painting. However, line drawing has both a meaning and a goal different from those of painting. This fact is clear, for example, if we compare the line drawings of Raphael with those of Dürer. Raphael's line drawings were sketched as preparations for paintings. Even when he made line drawings, he always had an image (*Bild*) in his mind's eye; his goal was the harmony of the image (*Harmonie des Bildes*). No matter how splendid his line drawings were, they were, in effect, nothing more than fragments of paintings. In contrast to this, Dürer's line drawings were complete works just as

* *Translators' note:* Nishida refers throughout this chapter to Max Klinger's *Malerei und Zeichnung* (Leipzig: Insel-Verlag, 1885), 47 pp.

they were. Of course, this does not mean that Dürer did not see color
in his mind's eye, but that he saw a world of even deeper color than
the actual world of color that we see around us. The coloring of this
deeper world truly appears and disappears like a mirage, and we can
barely grasp its forms, movements, and moods. If we try to express it
by actual colors, Dürer's world of deeper coloration immediately
falls back into the world of ordinary reality. The method of expression of the painter who makes this world of more subtle coloration
his object lies only in the method of chiaroscuro.

In each medium of artistic expression there is a spirit peculiar to that material that cannot be expressed by any other material.
Just as the special characteristic of a certain piece of music expressed
in one meter cannot be expressed in another meter, so, too, there
is a motif (*Motiv*) that is expressed by line drawing that cannot be
expressed by painting. The essence of painting lies in the harmonious
expression of a world of colored things. Subjective emotion must conform to this objective harmony. A unified impression is the main goal
of painting. Of course, in *painting* we can distinguish between the art
of form (*Bild*), the art of decoration (*Dekoration*), and the art of space
(*Raum*). Especially with regard to the art of space, there are many
points that resemble line drawing, but the basic goal of painting lies
in its configurations. The aesthetic interest in figure lies in separating
things from their surroundings and expressing their individuality
profoundly and clearly. This kind of expression is only possible
through the medium of color. Color painting must be strictly objective. The addition of subjective fancy merely destroys the figure. In
the art of decoration—and particularly in the art of space—the unity
of the spatial whole of the form and the surroundings differing from
it becomes the main goal. The forms of things must be determined
within space and must possess their meaning within space. Moreover,
the relational unity of such structures is impossible without some subjective basis. Here the poetic elements in painting become enhanced
through line drawing. This is clear if we compare the landscape paintings of such men as Giotto with those of the later Renaissance. Even
in a case of a line drawing of a man that is strictly and particularly
unnatural, if we look at it deeply, it raises us above the vulgar world,
and we feel that we no longer stand before a man of the fleeting world
who was angry yesterday and is laughing now, but stand before an
expression of eternal and noble humanity.

Color is the expression of the joy of this life. Color itself gives
us aesthetic feeling. Even in commonplace things and in tragic things,
color seduces man by its beauty. Color is the exaltation and the vic-

tory of this life. However, while there are extremely happy people who admire and adore the brilliant, moving pageant of this life, there are also many persons who despair of the world and indulge in self-pity and who, defeated in the battle of life, resent other men and are enraged at the world. Can the artist, who takes feelings as life, suppress these impressions? From the contrast between the beauty of such things and the pain and suffering of actual life, infinite images emerge for the poet and the musician. If a civilization does not want to lose these images, there must be plastic arts to express them. Line drawing is one such art. Lessing argued that while the expression of emotion such as that in the Laocoon should be avoided in sculpture it is indispensible in poetry and music. In the latter arts imagination can function apart from reality. There is the same intentionality in line drawing. Line drawing can affect color very much the same way that tone variation and word rhythm affect language. We are able to give free rein to certain spiritual moods only in line drawing. In painting, the air simply gives a bright feeling and the sea a wet, sparkling feeling; but in line drawing a sense of freedom is added to the air, and a sense of great power to the sea.

In sum, the personality of the artist himself can sometimes be better expressed in line drawing than in painting. The artist is able to express his own world and follow his own expression, rather than objective nature. On these points, line drawing can be compared to piano music or to poetry.

Having no aesthetic sensitivity myself, I can neither discuss what value these ideas of Klinger's have, nor through this crude summary properly introduce his brilliant essay, which is so rich in insight. I would simply suggest consideration of the significance of Oriental art in contrast to Occidental painting through his idea. Klinger states that the meaning and raison d'être of line drawing lies in its expressing the images of subjective imagination through the unified impression of the spatial whole, as happens in poetry and music. But in this context, does not the aesthetic intention that constitutes an important element in Oriental line drawing conform to this goal very well? An artist's vision involves his seeing things in the perspective of expressive movement; he sees things through his hand. Only in this standpoint can he see true reality itself, which is the foundation of reality entirely apart from the intentionality of conceptual knowledge. If the spatial unities in line drawing express forms beyond form, we may be able to say that this style of drawing, as it expresses the essence of the artistic expressive act itself so far as it can be touched by such symbols, expresses images that have not yet been born.

Chapter 3

The Content of Feeling and the Content of the Will

1

As one present-day school of philosophy states, if we distinguish between the act, the content, and the object of consciousness, I think we can say that experience, which is entirely concrete in itself, is the immediate internal unity of act and act and that experiential content reflected upon in this standpoint is the content of our consciousness. I have argued that this kind of concrete, 'pure experience' is the content of feeling and of art. But I have also said that the content of the will is the experiential content that appears in the standpoint of the act underlying all acts. Let me now consider the distinction and relationship between the content of the will and the content of feeling. For example, how does love as the object of art differ from love in everyday life? The beautiful is a disclosure of human life and nature, and apart from this there is nothing beautiful. But it does not follow that the beautiful must be regarded as the ideal of behavior; indeed, if we regard the beautiful as an object of desire, then we immediately lose it. The love between Romeo and Juliet is beautiful—as is the love between Paolo and Francesca. However, we do not exactly take these instances as norms of behavior. Nor were they seeking the beautiful as they loved each other. Their love was a severe fact in their actual lives.

Since concrete, true reality is self-developmental, content and act form an inseparable polarity. The functioning of color itself that distinguishes one color from another is the visual act, and the functioning of sound itself that distinguishes one sound from another is the aural act. In the standpoint of the pure act, act and content are one. The act itself may not be an object of consciousness; the knower cannot know the knower himself. However, true concrete reality is

an infinite continuity of acts. The union of act and act is established
in the standpoint wherein we can reflect upon the act itself. This is
what we term a phenomenon of consciousness. The horizon of the
act underlying all acts is the horizon of free will, which we can experience internally; and the reality that is established as the content
of such an act can be considered to be free in its essence. By *free* I
mean what transcends nature or what transcends natural causality.
This is the reason that I have termed a spiritual phenomenon an act
without underlying substance—that is, it is the unity of the act itself.

However, we must allow for various gradations in this kind
of independent, free reality. We must recognize infinite degrees in
the act that takes act itself as content and in the development of that
act and its freedom. Even such a thing as perception is established on
a free, personal basis as a phenomenon of consciousness and cannot
merely be explained as a natural phenomenon. But the person cannot be said to be entirely free in the horizon of perception. For its
creativity is simply impulsive. Turning to the cases of recollection
and imagination, the creativity of the act becomes gradually clearer,
and the contents of recollection and imagination become more personal; but, even in these acts, the person cannot be said to have truly
attained the realm of freedom. Imagination, in the sense usually
expressed in psychology, is freedom vis-à-vis nature but cannot yet
be said to be transnatural, or, more appropriately, to be a freedom
that includes the natural. Only in the act of self-consciousness does
the act entirely transcend the objective world and create an objective
world in itself, and only then does it truly stand in the concrete horizon of the act underlying all acts. The natural world is included
within it and simply constitutes one aspect of it. Pascal's statement—
that, although among all creatures man is only a weak reed, he is a
"thinking reed," and, even when the universe crushes him, he is superior to that which kills him, because he is aware of his own death—
truly proceeds from this insight. The objective world, from this
standpoint, is entirely an articulation of the self; together with its
own articulation, in this instance, the relative self is extinguished and
submerged in the objective world. We bear witness to this in the lived
activity of the pursuit of truth, as well as in aesthetic experience and
in the moral conscience.

I have stated that act and object are one and that act itself is
not yet reflected upon in the standpoint of pure act. But, of course,
strictly speaking, there might never be such a thing as a pure act.
Even in the case in which colors of the same quality are distinguished
merely by their intensity, such quality has not been merely added in

intensity; it can be seen as the opposition of act and act. Every independent object is an act, and their mutual internal relationship—that
is, the cause of their being in opposition—is the act underlying all
acts. However, in the case of pure unity—that is, when an act is functioning—the act itself cannot be reflected upon. The eye cannot see
the eye itself. Even if the act can be analyzed, it can only be considered
to be an act when its unity is pure, or when it is unified internally.
Pure or internal unity means that the act of unity itself is creative
and that the act itself creates an infinite creative world in itself.

From whence, then, arises such a thing as the unity of an act
that is impure in the perspective of the act underlying all acts, which
is creative in itself? How does the disunity of the act arise? All relations and the elements of relations, and the act and the content of the
act must have the same quality. That which appears as the content
of the act underlying all acts, which is freely creative in its essence,
must in each case be free and must presuppose free will at the foundation of each of its elements.

At what point does the standpoint of the act underlying all
acts, which takes the unity itself of the act as its object, differ from
the standpoint of the mere unity of the act? At what point does the
object in the former standpoint differ from the object in the latter
standpoint? In the standpoint of the act underlying all acts is found
a unity over and above the disunity of the act, and a harmony over
and above disharmony. What appears in this standpoint is the unity
in disunity, the harmony in disharmony. It must be the essence of
reality, which is independent and free, and it must be the fundamental essence of every phenomenon of consciousness. Spiritual phenomena appear in the horizon where what may appear to be red
physically has not appeared as red and what may appear to be straight
has not appeared as straight and at the place where one does not
arrive at the conclusion to which he should logically arrive. The essence of spiritual phenomena consists in being a unity of contradictions. Of course, many mental phenomena, such as illusions and
delusions, can also be explained biologically. But as long as they are
explained in this way, they cease to be spiritual phenomena. Only
that remainder, which cannot be explained in biological terms, is a
phenomenon of consciousness. The fact of consciousness involves the
determination of a unity over and above the biological; it is the
rationalization of that which is irrational. The unity of a mere act,
however complex it is, differs in essence on this point from the act
underlying all acts. This is similar to the fact that, however large
finite numbers are, they differ in their standpoint from transfinite

numbers. My previous statement that knowledge stands on the basis
of the unity of a finite act, whereas feeling stands on the basis of an
infinite unity of acts, must be understood in this sense.

I have stated that a phenomenon of consciousness is the unity
in disunity and the harmony in disharmony of the act. Even teleological unity must be this kind of unity in disunity, for something
spiritual must always be recognized in the background of teleological
unity. Spiritual reality must be presupposed in order to hold that
teleological unity, such as life, is real. However, a teleological unity
has not yet become independent and free in itself, is not yet internal,
and has not yet arrived at the realm of concrete unity. That is to say,
the unity of contradiction is not yet acting as reality in itself and is
not appearance *qua* reality.* On this point 'life' is still identical in
kind to natural force. Teleological unity involves the functioning of
an organic whole. In teleological causation that which will appear
last functions from the beginning. When this whole is conceived as
accidental, it becomes mechanical; when it is nothing more than a
conceptualized unity, it becomes a natural goal; when it is immediate
fact, it becomes a phenomenon of consciousness. My description of
the essence of spiritual phenomena as meaning *qua* reality† was
another way of saying this. Meaning is the unity of the whole.

I have stated that when an act is unified internally, however
complex it is, it is creative in itself as one act. The fact that an act is
independent as one pure act in this way, seen from one aspect, means
that the act leaves the individual and enters into a transindividual
plane—that is, into the plane of consciousness in general. It goes without saying that this is true in the instance of mathematical knowledge.
But art too is transindividual in that the aesthetic act is the fusion of
subject and object and is creative. From this aspect we can also think
that the internal unity of an act implies that it enters a transindividual plane. On the other hand, the fact that the act is unified internally in this way or that it transcends the individual standpoint is
the externalization of the self, and the unity of this kind of an act
must depend on the individualization of the act. That which unifies
the transindividual standpoint is individuality and is free personality.
The more acts are purified, the more they become complete in themselves and the more acts become independent of one another, and
thus the more they become disunited in one aspect.

That which transcends this kind of universalizing tendency—
that is, the objectifying direction—and which unifies them must be

* *Translators' note*: The concrete identity of appearance and reality.
† *Translators' note*: The concrete identity of meaning and reality.

individuality, and hence subjectivity. The universal of that which is universal must become individual; our self is precisely this reality. As we purify, objectify, and universalize the contents of our experience, we at the same time attain to the very depths of our self. Our true self comes to be disclosed in this way. Just as the development of the entire self is included within the self's own self-reflective activity, the totality is unified within one actuality. Individual unity obtains in activity itself. We must act to absorb within the self the objective world that transcends the self, or stands over against the self. The unity of my self and this writing brush is the action of writing with this writing brush. Through action we can synthesize the universal, objective world. At such a time we act from the unity of infinite universal relations.

Acting or being acted upon means that the mind and things, the subjective and objective worlds, are in opposition and yet form a synthesis. It can be thought that the self has acted when we have been able to unify the objective world from the subjective center. In the contrary situation it can be thought that the self has been acted upon. What, then, is the objective world? The objective world exists as that which is established on the basis of consciousness in general. The subjective center, conversely, is the center of the most specific and contingent synthesis. It can be thought that being acted upon from without means that we are unified from a universal, objective center and that acting from within means that we unify the world from a specific, contingent center. But things follow their own laws, and we cannot even change the spatial position of things without conforming to the law of things. From the perspective of the self, as in the concept of windowless monads, we cannot change even our own will, although we possess the power of the whole universe. For the self to move things, things must be within the self, and for things to move the self, the self must be within things. The act of the will presupposes a standpoint that transcends both worlds—things and mind—and unifies them. The self is able to act by transcending the plane of consciousness in general. Hence, we can say that only phenomena of consciousness are phenomena of that which is truly able to act.

Our loves and hates, hopes and desires, appear in this kind of volitional world of the unity of the polarity of mind and things. We are able to recognize these phenomena through the possibility of such unity. As the voluntaristic psychologist states, the intellectual act, too, is a kind of will. In such a standpoint the objective world exists only as a means of self-realization. It is said that by obtaining sufficient knowledge we become active; but the self is not a universal unity that transcends all emotions, capable of neither laughter nor tears. The true self exists as a unique self in those experiences of love, jealousy, happiness, or sadness; there is no such thing as a self that is no one's self. Acting means taking the universal, objective world as a means; it is the particularizing of the universal. Desire is one form of such unity. In the form of desire, the universal is fused and unified with a certain point as the center. Hence, the unity of the universal exhibits a specific directionality.

That which stands over against our individual ego as something to be overcome is not the mere objective world, but must already be the world of the act of consciousness, for the mere objective world cannot stand in opposition to the self. That which stands in opposition to the self is the self itself. Only when a thing is an object of desire does it stand in opposition to the self. The fact that the objective world, which is established by means of the unity of consciousness in general, opposes the self as the natural world means that consciousness in general, which is a unifying act, opposes the self as an act. Even the cases of moving nature or being moved by it ultimately imply some kind of union with this internal unifying act. The fact that acts are internally unified does not mean that individual acts are unified additively. It means that they become one act that creates new meaning and that constructs an independent, objective world over and above the union of these acts. In this way, even the laws of nature come to produce a human nuance for us— interpreted, for example, as fate or destiny. It must be thought that desire lies at the foundation of every objective quality. The world of color arises by means of visual desire, and the world of things arises by means of tactile desire. For an act to become real, it must take the form of desire. Reality is the struggle of the will. As Hegel has stated, reality is contradiction, and the deeper the contradiction, the more we can think of it as true reality; for the more internal unity becomes profound and spontaneous, the more it includes contradiction within itself. The fact that the self struggles with the objective world or is overcome by it ultimately means that the self struggles with or is overcome by the contradictions that arise within itself. That which moves the self is the self; the self actualizes the self within the self. It is not that nature becomes the object of our desire as mere nature. Neither can the physical state of the self be said to be exactly the object of desire, nor is pleasure itself directly pleasure as a mere object.

The will is a process of transition from one state of the self to another; it is the continual destruction of its own unity by seeking deeper unity within itself. In this kind of infinite process lie the essence and goal of the self. The self is self-moving. The internal unity of an act is the self-seeking unity within the self, and satisfaction of desire is the attainment of the state of unity from a state of disunity. This kind of unity itself is precisely the problem that must be resolved. When we advance to internal unity, it can be thought that we advance from the subjective world to the objective world—that is, our subjective desire has been actualized in the objective world—for our objective world is nothing other than the world of the object of the internal unity of the act. However, the satisfaction of the will is the death of the will itself. The internal unity of the will is nothing more than the objectification of the self and its extinction. The inner-directed act wherein we reflected upon the self within the self is directly the outer-directed act of self-development. Hence, in the self internal unity must directly involve disunity.

Our self is this dialectical unity of infinite acts. Therefore, at the ground of the self there is an unattainable depth. The volitional horizon which is the act underlying all acts, in reference to the mere unity of noetic acts, functions as a kind of mathematical limit point. This horizon, from one aspect, is the horizon of absolutely irrational free will, which cannot be unified as one act. For this reason a world of empirical fact that can be thought of as wholly irrational to us is also established as the objective world of this standpoint. This world is not the objective world of reason, but, rather, the objective world of the will. To unify this objective world, we must take the standpoint of action, that is the standpoint of unity within disunity. Only in the standpoint of the practical self can we overcome this objective world and unify it. Moreover, unification of the entire objective world in this standpoint means the particularization of its content. Just as Leibniz states that God has created this unique actual world from infinite possible worlds by His will, so, too, the particular is the irrational, and the truly irrational is grounded in free will—indeed, it is free will itself. The will is not free because it follows the laws of reason; it is transnatural and free because it particularizes universal experiential content. I have previously stated that we transcend the horizon of the objectified individual self by transcending the specific individual horizon and reaching that of consciousness in general. On the other hand, we can never separate ourselves from the specific horizon. The universal is the reflection of the specific. The more we clarify the internal, the more we discover its external reflection. The more the particular enters into its own deep unattainable ground, the more it becomes universal. The particular clarifies its specificity

by universalizing itself. Transcendence of the horizon of the individual self means, in short, to enter more deeply into the self. The
universal does not act of itself. Rather, it is the process of particularization; it is its content.

2

A certain school of thought contends that the qualities of the
elements of feeling are reducible to the two categories of happiness
and unhappiness and that other differences are based on the quality
of the intellectual content that synthesizes them. But I am arguing
that feeling has its own content in the intentionality of feeling itself;
as expressed through art, feeling has, on the contrary, a delicate and
clear content of its own. Feeling, as expressed above, is the immediate
unity of act and act, and the content of feeling is the content of the
self, the content of life, which appears in the horizon of the act underlying all acts, or the horizon of active, dialectical unity. Only when
the content of feeling stands in the horizon of the unity of subject and
object—the horizon of the unity of action—does content appear for
the first time. Without the consciousness of activity, the content of
feeling cannot be established. At any rate, feeling is established on
the basis of impulsive consciousness. Therefore, the purer the content of feeling is, the more specific it is and the more it differs in essence from intellectual content. Just as living things cannot foresee
how they will change in the course of time, so a painter, as he faces
his canvas, cannot know how his painting will ultimately turn out.
The act of unity is a transcognitional unity. Therefore, it is an unattainable depth, in contrast to the standpoint of knowledge, and what
is contradiction in the standpoint of knowledge has positive content
in this standpoint.

It is thought that the will is irrational and that impulsive life
is blind. But, on the contrary, if we consider such a thing as mathematical truth, we enter into a transindividual standpoint from the
standpoint of the individual self—that is, we depart from the intentionality of feeling and the will and enter into that of reason. However, to think rationally means that the self enters into itself, that the
self escapes from being objectified and returns to the pure activity
of itself. The state of the pure union of act and act is an infinite unrest
and logical contradiction. Our thought develops by means of internal
contradiction. The more thought deepens, the more it falls into contradiction. After it has destroyed itself, it is born again in an even
higher or enlarged intention to create a new, positive content. Upon
reflection, we see that that which first made thought fall into con-

tradiction was actually the content of the intentionality of a higher dimension. In the case of contradiction, what sort of position does the universal take? That which causes two experiential contents to be contradictory is the concrete universal, which is the synthetic whole —the unifier itself. Contradiction arises from the objectification of the act. Contradiction arises because the act attempts to project itself into the objective world of the self. If we try to determine the color of the visual act itself that discriminates black from white, we can only fall into contradiction. For we cannot discuss color in reference to the visual act.

Moreover, reality, which is independent and creative in itself, is truly this kind of infinite contradiction. If we consider that contradiction arises in this way from the demand of the concrete universal—that is to say, from the internal development of the unifier—we can know what kind of a function the universalizing act has in reality, and we may be able to clarify the kind of relation in which analysis and synthesis stand in true reality. Just as the content of clear transformation arises at the place where being maintains itself as being and nonbeing maintains itself as nonbeing, so, too, the fact that a given content maintains itself is the demand of universal validity. It is the demand of universal cognition, of the self universalizing itself. The more each content returns to itself and becomes pure in this way, the clearer the content of the synthetic whole becomes. The more the analysis of content advances, the clearer the positive unity becomes. Unity without clear analysis is not true unity; it is nothing more than a mixture. In analysis, synthetic unity must always be presupposed, and this becomes the goal of analysis. In our analysis of the experiential content of the self, we must stand in a plane that transcends content and has negated it—that is, in the plane of the intellectual self. However, continued advance in this direction is the self's penetration deeply within itself as a process of self-development. The objective world that appears in this direction is not true reality, for the world of true reality lies in the world of teleological unity; it exists in the forms of feeling and the will. We attain the content of the clearest feeling and the will through advancing thoroughly in the intellectual direction.

It can be thought that the particular is included within the universal in the standpoint of knowledge. But the universal is included within the particular in concrete, true reality. The universal is the means of development of the particular. Universal truth is the process of development of a larger individuality that is the ground of our individuality. It is the means of cultural development. At such a time, truth is not mere truth—it is power; it is reality. By this power truth maintains itself. This is the reason that we can think that when an act advances to internal unity, it transcends the individual stand-point. The depths of our personality are infinitely distant and deep, for in the flow of personality there is no starting point. The objective world grounded in this kind of personality—that is, analogous to the unity of a transfinite number—can be thought to be the purely objec-tive world that transcends the act, in contrast to the personal content of finite number. Herein the interior of the mind and the exterior of the mind are in opposition to one another, and that which unifies them is the horizon of action or behavior. Action or behavior involves the inclusion of the universal within the specific; the self exists pre-cisely in the horizon where it particularizes the universal.

However, when we view nature as a means of self-realization, we have still not attained complete unity in the standpoint of action. In true culture the objective world must be completely absorbed within subjectivity, and causal relationship must become teleological unity. Nature must be seen wholly as an expression of spirit. It can be thought that spirit began to conquer the material world as man began to use machines. But I think that culture begins in the trans-formation of the self itself. In this sense, art is the beginning of cul-ture. In art, nature is not a means, but the goal itself. Art discovers the life of the self in the background of nature. It has been said that art begins from play, that we are first able to depart from passive life through art. Indeed, by departing from a relative position with nature, we stand in the higher dimension that is the act underlying all acts. Here the foundation for cultural spirit is laid. In our utili-tarian life the objective world is thought of as a world of matter with-out any life whatever with respect to the self and hence becomes something that must be used as a means for the self. If the objective world is truly something wholly without relation to the self, the self must develop itself independently as the self; but the objective world of the self is not without relation to the self itself in this way. The self develops its own content by discovering personal content in the objective world; when it recognizes the other as person, it recognizes itself as person. While it uses the other as matter, the self is nothing other than material desire. However much we are able to subjugate nature in this intentionality, the self in itself acquires nothing at all. It is nothing more than a meaningless repetition of an identical self. We are able to change the content of our own life by recognizing spiritual life within nature—that is, through aesthetic intuition. Moreover, the empathetic projection of feeling into the objective world in this way does not mean the superimposition of some new unity upon the objective world, but it rather means returning to the concrete whole. It is the return of the prodigal son to his father.

Aesthetic creativity in this sense is an active dialectical unity of internal and external planes. On this point it differs in essence from utilitarian action. Artistic creation is often compared to an instinctive act. But instinctual life is qualitatively the same as utilitarian life, for instinctive demands constitute the core of utilitarian life. Insofar as instinctive action is thought to be unconscious, it does resemble artistic creation. But we must note that the term *unconsciousness* has two senses. Instinctive action is nonconceptual, but aesthetic action is transconceptual. In the former the self is oppressed by nature, whereas in the latter the self is released from nature. In instinctive life the self is rooted in a great natural force, whereas in the artistic act it rests on the basis of pure love. Therefore at the foundation of artistic creation there must be a great love of life.

Because the ground of love is transconceptual, it is thought of as unconscious, but the unconsciousness of pure love is not the same as the unconsciousness of blind instinct. At the ground of love there is a depth that is not moved by the object. This ground of love must always be pure and transparent. There must be the calm of the soul of Christ, who from the tree of the cross prays on behalf of those who kill Him and who presents His left cheek to the one who strikes Him on the right. Moreover, this kind of spiritual calm truly emerges from a deep understanding of human nature. It comes from piercing through the plane of desire. If we say that the understanding of knowledge is free in the conceptual sphere, the understanding of love is free in the practical sphere. In other terms, love must be understanding of the essence of action or behavior. To arrive at this point, we must pass beyond the standpoint of reason.

An instinctive act may also be thought to function prior to the division of subject and object, but it does not include the rational standpoint within itself. Consequently, instinct cannot transcend the entire objective world and unify it. The love of a parent may be the most pure love, but at the point of its being irrational it is selfish desire. Contrary to this, the romantic love portrayed in Dostoyevsky's *The Oppressed,* where, precisely because the lover loves her, he lets her marry her own beloved, may be the purest kind of love. Pure love must be extremely rational in this way. The objective world is also truly created by intellectual love. Just as it is said that the child first imitates before understanding, so, too, before intellectual understanding there must be the direct union of act and act, and, even before logical understanding, there must be the direct union of the acts of thinking. In other terms, there must be normative consciousness. Self-consciousness of this kind of act is the feeling of love. The unity of contradiction in knowledge becomes the unity of love in action. In love, the contradiction of the desires of the self and the other are unified. The unity of love in the world of action can be compared to intuition, which is the foundation of intellectual development. The content of love is the content of the concrete unity of desire.

We can only fall into an insoluble contradiction when we attempt to unify the content of the concrete whole in an abstract standpoint. When we attempt to penetrate that desire from our own perspective, an infinitely great nature stands in opposition to us. This great nature is thought to be external to the self, but what is thought of as its infinite extension is nothing more than the transfinite nature of concrete unity. In short, it is that which makes the self the self. The dark nature before us is nothing more than a shadow of the self. As we personalize the self by love, we are able to destroy this shadow.

What we term being rational means that we destroy the natural nature of the self. The fact that desires are blind means that the self belongs to the objective world of the self, that the self is abstract. The narrower the self becomes, the more the self is determined by the objective world and the more it becomes instinctive and powerless. Everything becomes the antiself. Since the rational is destroyed in this standpoint, in another respect we transcend the self and at the same time enter deeply within the self itself. However, we cannot thoroughly destroy the objective world in the horizon of knowledge. The blind self always reflects its shadow from behind. When we penetrate to the essence of the object in itself through love, we completely destroy the objective world and can extinguish the blind self. At this time it becomes clear that the horizon of knowledge is the horizon of love of the truth.

Doubts may also arise about the question of where the demands that thus conquer the self arise from, but true reality is infinite internal contradiction. The person possesses such contradiction within himself. In rational demands the synthetic whole causes its own elements to be mutually contradictory; there also exists a further demand for synthetic unity, which manifests itself from within its own elements. The elements thereby fall into contradiction in themselves, and through a process of self-destruction they arrive at a new life of the whole. However, the light of reason cannot exhaustively illuminate the foundation of reality. We are not mere reason, but we experience sorrow and joy, as well. There is infinite joy and sadness at the ground of the self. We possess the infinite extension of time, both within and without; and the infinite time that appears without is simply a reflection of the infinite time latent in the depths of the heart. Because the internal continuity that is linked to the depths of the heart is infinitely deep, it is mysterious, but it is not opposed to the self. It possesses the light of infinite personality; it is the foundation of infinite love. It is the depth of nature that is reflected in the eye of the artist and the majesty of God felt by the saint. Through union with it, we do not lose, but create the self. If we consider that the synthetic unity that moves the totality of things is true, concrete reality, then that which truly moves reality is not a physical force, but love, which can be said to be a personal force. We unite with the flow of infinite personality through profound love; at the same time, we can embrace the objective world within the self and are able truly to include the universal within the particular. Kant has sought the essence of beauty within the act of reflective judgment. But, even if the particular is given first, when the particular is subsumed within the universal it is still merely an intellectual teleology and in no way differs from natural teleology. Only when the universal is included within the particular does it become aesthetic content.

3

I shall try to discuss the distinctions and relationships between the contents of will and feeling on the basis of the foregoing. Feeling is usually considered to be unconscious. But to say that feeling is unconscious not only differs in meaning from saying that the power of a thing is unknowable, but it also differs from saying that instinct is blind. In the intentionality of pure feeling that is the content of art we transcend the horizon of material force, which is merely objective while being abstract. Indeed, we even transcend the horizon of instinct and experience in the intentionality of purely concrete spiritual content—that is, of the act underlying all acts, which is pure activity. Our cultural life can be thought truly to begin from the aesthetic act. If we understand the will in the broad sense to mean the active nature of spiritual content, then in such a perspective experience may be said to already be grounded in the intentionality of the will. That the will in the narrow sense is distinguished from feeling lies in the point that the volitional object is clearly cognized and that it takes existence as its object.

When the artist is thoroughly immersed in the horizon of pure visual perception, he spontaneously moves the organs of his whole body and becomes one expressive movement. At this time, feeling wells up within, and the artist himself cannot foretell the direction and meaning of his own expressive act. Seen from the outside, it can be thought that instinct and the unconsciousness of physical force are the same. But, internally, we cannot help recognizing that there has been a complete change of dimension. In art we stand on the basis of the completely free self, and the external world functions no longer as the means of the self, but as its expression. It is not that its unattainable depth is the depth of nature, but, rather, the depth of the self. From this standpoint even the physical world is nothing more than the expression of an intellectual act, which is a personal act. It is not some vast nature that stands over against the self; it is a vast personality. The projection of feeling in empathy involves the attainment of this standpoint. This may be the reason that the sketching of the human body has been said to be the foundation of all painting. In the standpoint of moral behavior such personal content is conscious, or, in other words, it becomes clear conceptually. While artistic content is opposed to moral consciousness, the relation that obtains between them can be considered as that between non-being and being.

What does it mean to say that that which has not been cognized becomes conscious? Generally, the object of consciousness is considered to exist apart from the activity of consciousness, and consciousness is considered to reflect it like a mirror. However, this idea substantializes concepts. As reality there is only one act (*Tathandlung*), which includes the object within the act. From the standpoint of the object, the noetic act can be considered to be an internal relation of the noematic object; but from the standpoint of the noetic act, the noematic object is nothing more than the internal determination of the act itself. Its infinitely determining direction can be considered to be the subjective act, and its infinitely determined direction can be considered to be the objective world of objects. However, we must consider the act underlying all acts that unifies acts—that is, the will in the broad sense—as the basis of this kind of particular determination of the noetic act, for consciousness arises in the standpoint of will in the broad sense—that is, in the standpoint of the act underlying all acts. Consciousness arises from the contradiction and clash between the narrower and the wider horizons, and from the contradiction and clash between that which embraces and that which is embraced. More accurately, consciousness is precisely the unity of such dialectical contradiction. Consciousness appears at the place that particularizes the universal.

Because we entirely transcend the standpoint of intellectual subjectivity in the aesthetic act, there is nothing in the natural world that is opposed to or foreign to the aesthetic act. On this point it may also be said that the aesthetic act is also unconscious. But, of course, this unconsciousness is not identical with the unconsciousness of material force. Rather, aesthetic content is the latent content of personal activity. Just as we feel mathematics, which includes the possibility of infinite development, to be something existing within ourselves, so, too, do we feel the warmth of aesthetic content in our interior life. However, there must be something like personal self-consciousness for purpose to become conscious in the will. Personal self-consciousness is established by recognizing other persons. There is no such thing as only one person. To be a person involves relationships with others. In the intentionality context of the aesthetic act, we already have personalized nature which stands over against the self, but there is still a certain darkness at the basis of artistic imagination. It can be said that, to the extent that artistic imagination is nonconceptual, it involves the nonself and is merely objective. At this point its object has not yet completely separated from the quality of nature. Only in the standpoint of moral will do we recognize a clear person at the foundation of that which confronts the self, while at the same time the self itself becomes truly personal, and true personal content is manifested by means of it. Only in the moral will do we face the foundation of the whole of reality. In the thoroughgoing moral self we must recognize a clear person even at the foundation of nature. What was implicit in the aesthetic standpoint becomes explicit in the moral standpoint; that is, it becomes clear conceptually as well. I thus hold that art presupposes morality and that the artistic imagination presupposes moral development.

At the foundation of everything there is a single life; there is only the free self. If art that is not grounded on the serious demands of life is not simply play, then it is mere technique. Apart from the sincere demands of life, where is there anything that we can term morality? If the essence of the content of consciousness lies in the dialectical unity of contradiction, we can say that both aesthetic content and moral content are unities of contradiction. That aesthetic content becomes conscious means that the content of consciousness returns to its own foundation and that personal unity advances to its own goal. The more we see personal content at the foundation of nature, the more we must believe that it is moral. The horizon of art is thought of as transconceptual, but the conceptual standpoint can be included in the horizon of morality. In the moral plane, the free self truly attains its own standpoint, and the true meaning of life is disclosed.

The idea that art is for the sake of encouraging virtue and reproving vice is, of course, a childish view. But to think that art is antimoral would not be a true and profound understanding of art, either. In art, even at the foundation of the exaltation of the flesh and sympathizing with evil, there must be the light of the entire person. The mere description of fleshly lusts and vices does not have any aesthetic value. The aesthetic value of these things arises when they are described as one arc of the larger curve of human life, as one fragment of a greater life. This is the reason that the description of individuality is also valued in art. The value of individuality arises by being viewed as one arc of the entire person. As artistic objects both good and evil must possess a meaning, such as being a 'productive point' (*erzeugende Punkt*) in the curve of human life. Mere fleshly lust and vice cannot avoid being extremely shallow and abstract as aesthetic content. The content of art lies in the life of the soul that shines forth at the base of these things. On the other hand, even moral life is not simply the following of conceptual laws. The moral conscience, which has been compared to the vast, starry heavens, must be the disclosure of an infinite life latent within our minds. Just as mere fleshly desire does not possess any artistic value, so, too, there cannot be any moral value in adhering to traditional laws entirely devoid of life.

The content of the moral life must be spiritual content latent in the background of our body, which is the foundation of our physical life and which is its goal. It must be infinite aesthetic content—that is, the self-consciousness of content itself produced by the clash of the latent powers of the person. It must be the disclosure of the entire person and the development and completion of the whole of human nature. A moral law that distorts the disclosure of this kind of perfect humanity is not the true moral law—rather, it is sin. The same life creates art and at the same time constructs moral society, as well. Our life is a merging of an infinite number of curves. This merging of curves constructs our moral life. If we consider rationality to be the center of this kind of merging, then we can understand the reasons why rationality must be immanent in moral life. To say that reason is immanent in this way would seem to mean that moral behavior is conscious. In unconsciousness the parts stand in opposition to the whole, and there are independent parts that have not yet completely attained to unity of contradiction. If the whole obtains positive content in the unity of contradiction, then everything is conscious.

In the act of aesthetic creation, personal content appears in the world of immediate perception directly as reality, without, as it were, passing through the world of cognitive objects constructed by reason. In other words, personal content appears in the world of experiential fact without passing through the construction of the categories of thinking. As Fiedler states, the development of pure visual perception is spontaneously accompanied by expressive movement and becomes the act of artistic creation. Thus, its expression has an immovable objectivity similar to that of nature itself, in contrast to our psychological self. As something that is grounded on a unity of action that is deeper than knowledge, it has unknowable significance, in contrast to knowledge. On this point pure visual perception is similar to an instinctive act, but, if we think more deeply, even an act of perception, such as seeing or hearing, is the expression of a personal act that is dynamic in itself, which is the expression of the will in the broad sense. Even if we say that the act of aesthetic creation does not pass through the world of conceptual objects, it is not the same as such things as physical force and instinct. It is already the act of the free self, and, like the sensory content that is applied to the 'anticipation of perception', it belongs to the objective world of the free self. On this point we may say that it is already rational. Just as sensation acquires objectivity by being applied to the basic principle of the 'anticipation of perception', so, too, does the real world become a cultural phenomenon—that is, it attains freedom—by being applied to the empathetic projection of feeling, which can also be called the 'anticipation of behavior'. Just as sensation possesses intensity, reality obtains freedom through the empathetic projection of feeling. Just as the so-called world of objective reality arises by means of the union of 'real things', which are established by having the 'anticipation of perception' applied to them, so, too, is cultural society established by means of the union of 'the personal'. Just as our world of experience can be considered to be a field of forces as the objective world of the will and the immutable relationships between force and force to be the laws of nature, so does the relationship between one personal reality and another personal reality create the moral law. Just as infinite physical laws are presupposed within them when real things in the world of experience are recognized, so is an infinite moral law included within it when human reality is recognized. The moral law is nothing more than the law of the development of personal content. This law constructs cultural society. The horizon of complete personal unity—that is, the person after the analogy of transfinite number—distinguishes morality from art.

Society is the matrix in which persons relate to one another. The pure content of the person can be considered to express itself only in society. Because this moral horizon is the creative horizon of the whole person it can be considered to be real and to differ from the aesthetic act. It is not that moral behavior is real because it follows the laws of nature; it is real because it includes the laws of nature within itself. Consciousness in general is nothing more than one aspect of the universality of the will in general. It is the practical self in the depths of our intellectual self; thus, the moral world is the foundation of the physical world. Of course, we also transcend the world of cognition in the act of aesthetic creation, and we immanently include reason as a personal act. But we merely possess it as an act; we do not yet possess its whole content. Consequently, the act itself cannot be directly real, and therefore it can be thought to be unreal.

It may be thought that moral behavior takes existence as its object; yet the end of moral behavior lies not in the events of the natural world, but, rather, within itself. The reality of the external world, on the contrary, is established by our recognizing a profound internal imperative. At the very depths of the entire person—that is, when we attain the consummation of the internal imperative—we stand on the ground of reason, in which the objective world is included. Consciousness in general is the direction of the infinite unity of the entire person; therefore, the objective world of consciousness in general must be included in the more concrete horizon of the entire person. As this horizon of the entire person is purified, we more adequately embody this deeper dimension without any shadow whatsoever. The entire person becomes one personal, living act. In art the personal horizon is attained, but still there is not perfect purity of the whole personality, for art is not completely dynamic; it is a condition of suspended power.

Society is the dialectical union of persons. We may also be able to consider that our individual conscious systems are each one society, each according to its own perspective. The act of each and every moment is free, and the union of these free acts constitutes the consciousness of one individual. In this sense, we can recognize one individual unity even at the basis of social consciousness. Of course, there may be differing opinions on the view that society is the union of persons. We may even be able to say that primitive society is impersonal. However, while a child may not yet have personal consciousness, just as for an adult, personal self-consciousness constitutes the essence of individual consciousness, so, too, does the merging and unity of persons constitute the essence of society. And if this is true, we may be able to say that society is based on a moral a priori. Just as sensation, which enters into the world of cognitive objects as 'the real' (*das Reale*), is established by means of the basic principle of the 'anticipation of perception', and we thereby construct the physical world behind it, so are our individual desires already grounded on a moral a priori, and we thereby construct the cultural world in their background.

The structure of society, like the structure of the natural world, embodies the independence of unified reason. The objective world of reason itself becomes independent—that is, it moves from the sensory reality to conceptual reality. Actuality, as the specific, is not merely an index of the empirical world, but also an index of the infinite world. All worlds proceed from this point. At the foundation of the empirical world is the direct union of act and act, and the basic principle of the 'anticipation of perception' indicates this unity. But the world of personal content and the world of culture are constructed when the act underlying all acts functions in its own positive horizon. The fact that color perception attains objectivity by being applied to the basic principle of the 'anticipation of perception' means that the act of pure visual perception becomes consciously realized as one act of a person. But in this case the entire person has not yet attained to its true unity, for the parts are still in an independent state. Therefore, we must recognize an independent force in the background of experiential content. In front of us looms an infinitely dark nature. Only when we live thoroughly in the horizon of the act underlying all acts does the dark shadow of nature disappear, become the force of the self, and, directly uniting act with act, give rise to society, in which persons face each other. We may be able to say, as Tarde has, that, even at the base of physical phenomena, there are 'social facts' (*faits sociales*). Society is the place wherein personal acts become forces functioning manifestly. Just as spiritual acts include infinite potentials as pure acts, we can think that the background of personal activity, which is the unity of these acts, includes the infinite potential of the person. Such potential becomes aesthetic content.

Aesthetic content is the task that has been given to society. The content of a mere act is the world of nature that has been unified by means of reason, which is one plane of the unifying act of the entire person. The world of personal content, which takes this world as its material and unifies it, becomes the artistic world. The moral world, again, is that which has unified this world of personal content from the standpoint of the entire person. As Bergson states, the innate potentials of the person are infinitely rich, but in actuality one must abandon most of them. The reason that the greater part of one's innate potentials must remain unrealized is that they conflict with one another in the physical world—that is, in the plane of simultaneous existence, in the objective world of consciousness in general. In the aesthetic act we break through this plane and create a world of internal life, a world of life just as it is. However, within the person itself, the relationships of simultaneous existence are again established. This is the same as the relations we enter into when we recollect our own past lives within our individual consciousnesses. To attain the profound depths of the personal self, we must advance even more in this direction. This is the reason that in one aspect there must be disharmony as an element of beauty. Its development becomes the sublime.

Beauty becomes true beauty through this disharmony. Lotze states that our emotions do not always seek harmonious beauty, but do require the accompaniment of sublimity. Along with seductive harmony, they seek to be accompanied by this disharmony, which includes the danger of being burnt by fire. In this way, he says, we are able to manifest the essence of the world expressed in knowledge within artistic feeling.[1] Rational feeling expresses the requirement of infinite progress in the standpoint of the act underlying all acts. As Kant has stated, this feeling is the sublime, and sublimity, like truth itself, is severe. And Lotze writes that the feeling of sublimity arises by our recognizing in reality the absolute, which cannot be attained in thought. This kind of unattainable ultimate is established by the positive unity of infinite personal development. Kant states that at the foundation of the aesthetic value judgment is the concept of the power of the understanding, while at the base of the value judgment of the sublime there must be an Idea. Rational feeling is the functioning of this kind of Idea.

Moreover, I cannot help thinking with Theodor Vischer that the sublime is not a category different from beauty, but is, rather, one of its aspects. The sublime is the dynamic direction of beauty. Was it not because he was caught in the tradition of rationalism that Kant thought of the concept of the power of understanding at the foundation of beauty? We must also recognize something beyond the unity of the power of the understanding at the root of every aesthetic value. We cannot merely call it mathematical sublimity (*mathematischer Erhaben*), as Lotze does; we can say that everything is dynamic sub-

---

1. Hermann Lotze, *Geschichte der Aesthetik im Deutschland* (Munich: J.G. Cotta, 1913), p. 329.

limity (*dynamischer Erhaben*). Moreover, I think that every beautiful thing possesses elements of this dynamic sublimity. There must be something dynamic in the depths of the beautiful. At the base of profound beauty there is tragedy or comedy. In other words, there must be the dynamic direction of personal content. There must be the power of the Idea. Between the beautiful and the sublime there is, as it were, the relationship between discrete numbers and continuous numbers. This kind of unity of the whole personality functions, from the first, at the foundation of everything beautiful. The infinite advance of personality appears and becomes the sublime, while that which constructs the unique world of reason in the standpoint of the whole is moral action. A moral society is a work of art established in this way. That which has created aesthetic content becomes manifest, and the real world of reason itself is established. Aesthetic content can be said to be the potential of a moral act, presupposing this horizon.

4

There may still be a need for further discussion concerning my idea that the content of art and the content of morality are both personal contents, which can also be termed the direct union of act and act, and that the former is the potential state of the latter. The content of art can be considered to be nonconceptual and unreal. Every art can be considered to be inseparably related to its own kind of experiential content. There is beauty of painting that cannot be expressed by music, and vice versa. Indeed, the content of the beautiful may involve something the artist already dislikes. But the sublime is the feeling we have in facing infinite reality. The infinite nature of time itself, of space itself, or of power itself constructs an ideal reality that is independent of our subjectivity. We create the concept of the sublime in the face of these realities. The surge of the life of the vast universe, which flows at the foundation of the so-called real world and moves us from within, is the feeling of the sublime. Therefore, the feeling of the sublime is as severe as are the feelings of truth and of morality. We create the feeling of the sublime by knowing the life of that which is conceptual—that is, by intuition into the objects of thinking. There must be intellectual intuition at the base of the feeling of the sublime. The infinite nature of the creative act is the source from which the feeling of the sublime arises, and the objective nature of the real world is, in fact, also based upon it. Only a creative thing in itself can have severe objectivity for us. The feeling of this kind of creative act is the essence of beauty. Needless to say, aesthetic content is not a conceptual reality, but it would be a mistake to view it as something identical with fantasy and illusion. Aesthetic content is transintellectual, but not anti-intellectual; rather, it can be said to include the intellectual. What is given as the content of judgment is first given as this kind of intuition.

The feelings of various colors that the aesthetically sensitive Goethe tested by means of colored glass are even now considered to be classic. When he viewed a gray winter scene through yellow glass, everything seemed joyous; things were experienced as if they had been expanded. Blue glass, on the contrary, made everything seem sad. We can feel similar emotional impressions from sound. A high note seems to be joyous and stimulating, whereas a low note is somberly severe and produces a feeling of melancholy. However, if we consider that the contents of feeling that thus accompany various kinds of sensations are all common to one another and are identical, we cannot think that there is an inseparable relationship between aesthetic content and sensory material. The content of feeling expressible by music can also be expressed by painting, and such an interchange is not entirely impossible. However, if we think more deeply, as Lessing once wrote concerning the relationship between painting and sculpture, each art form can be thought to have an aesthetic content inexpressible by another art form. Pater states; "Each art, having its own peculiar and untranslatable sensuous charm, has its own special mode of reaching the imagination, its own special responsibilities to its material."

From this idea, we can also say that the fact that we can express the content of identical feelings through various arts is based upon our thinking of the content of feeling, apart from sensation, from the plane of knowledge. In the plane of art, there is an inseparable relationship between the two in a sense beyond this. We can think in various ways, even with respect to the relationship of the content of feeling and sensory material. A certain sensation is especially appropriate for the expression of a certain emotion, although another sensation might be inappropriate to it. However, this kind of relation is still merely external. The weak point of symbolic art lies herein. To say that feeling and sensation are truly inseparable, feeling must be understood as the internal spirit of sensation. The various arts must be understood as the internal development of sensory spirit. In this way the aural arts can possess artistic characteristics that cannot be expressed by the visual arts. The spirit of sensory experience means the self-generating, self-developmental quality of sensory content that is the infinite continuity at the base of sensory experience.

The personal value of this kind of act—that is, content in the stand-point of the act underlying all acts—becomes aesthetic content. The 'meaning'—that is, the aesthetic quantity that each sensation possesses as aesthetic content—is not a mere quantity as a material quantity, but an inclusive quantity—that is, intensity, in the strict sense—that elicits our response. What can be called the intensity of sensation is quantity of this kind. This quantity, on the one hand, becomes an element of the natural world, as the foundation of the basic principle of the 'anticipation of perception'. On the other hand, it also becomes an element of the artistic world, as an intensity that elicits our re-sponse. By thinking in the above way, each art can be said to possess a uniqueness that cannot be expressed by another art.

Now, what sort of a thing is moral behavior? Moral behavior conforms neither to the authority of the mere external world, nor to the commands of mere reason. The law of logical contradiction can-not give the categorical imperative to our will. At the foundation of the moral imperative must be the requirements of life. However, when the requirements of life are in contradiction in the standpoint of life itself, this is thought of as evil. The self can become a free per-son by respecting others as persons. Even with regard to nature, we are able to personalize the self by personalizing nature. The personal content still latent in sensory experience in art manifests itself in moral behavior. In the latter, personal unity can be said truly to at-tain the horizon of the independent and free self. Therefore, we must think that, just as aesthetic content seeks expression in the world of artistic expression, so, too, does moral content seek its expression in the world of cognitive objects—that is, in the world of reality. Art expresses the spirit of the world of perception, whereas morality ex-presses the spirit of the world of reality. We say that moral behavior takes existence as its goal, but it is not that it takes existence as its goal on behalf of existence, but, rather, that the real world is the expression of moral behavior. The personal content latent in the background of the experience of color and form is expressed by paint-ing and sculpture, and the personal content latent in the background of the experience of sound is expressed by music; similarly, the con-tent of the free self—pure personal content itself, which is the founda-tion of reason as the unity of infinite acts—is expressed in the real world as moral society.

Moral society is reason's work of art. If we say, with Fiedler, that our spiritual act emerges in expressive action, moral behavior is the expressive act of reason, and moral society may be compared to reason's work of art. It is thought that the difference between artistic creativity and moral behavior lies in the fact that the former is intuitive and emotive and consequently is unconscious, whereas the latter is conceptual and conscious. But both artistic creativity and moral behavior are creative acts of personal content—that is, the functioning of the free self—and consequently are one in essence. It is only that the former is abstract and partial, whereas the latter is concrete and unified. To say that something is unconscious or nonconceptual means that it is abstract and partial.

If we were to consider, as Fiedler does, that in a pure visual perceptive act the expressive act that naturally accompanies it is the creative act of the artist, a work of art still has not entered into the standpoint of consciousness in general. It is an expression of the concrete content of the act, which has not yet been reflected upon. We can think of it as an expression of our pure life, and so we cannot think of it. However, our self is not a mere visual and aural act, but an act of acts. Just as the world of objective reality is considered as the unity of various empirical contents, so, too, our entire personal content must be the spirit of infinite acts, an unending synthesis of emotional content. If we consider that in painting there is a spirit that can only be expressed by painting and that in music there is a spirit that can only be expressed by music, then our entire personality must be a synthesis of these forms of spirit. This kind of creative act of the synthetic unity of the entire personality is moral behavior, and social phenomena are its expressions. Just as aesthetic content is expressed in the world of perception and representation, so, too, is moral content expressed in the unifying act of the entire personality in the world of reality that is the objective world of reason.

Since moral content is the unifying content of the whole person—that is, the content of cultural history—aesthetic content loses its transconceptual quality by entering into the objective world of consciousness in general—that is, by being reflected upon—while, on the contrary, moral content not only does not lose its quality by being reflected upon, but makes the objective world of reflective thought the place of its expression. The objective world of knowledge is established as one aspect of the content of moral will. As Bergson states, in conflict with the real world we may have to abandon the greater portion of the rich person we innately possess. Perhaps only a small portion of our personal content can pass through the barrier of the world of reality. However, here lies the distinction between potentiality and actuality, between dream and reality. Perhaps we can say that the distinction is quantitatively small, but still there is a difference in dimension. No matter how small a solid is, it is more abundant than an infinite plane, because it is in a higher dimension.

When we move into action after having engaged in serious consideration, various imaginations and desires are first of all determined in the standpoint of the internal unity of the entire person and in relation with the external world. From one aspect, the content of our person can be thought to be determined. However, content that has been determined in this way possesses meaning content of a higher order than wholly undetermined content. Perhaps only one of many possible things becomes actual, but the former possesses the power to create the latter infinitely. Such personal content belongs to the objective world of the creative self. Moral behavior is the unity of infinite personal content, in the above sense. Of course, even an artistic act is not mere imagination, but must be determined by an expressive act. Moreover, the determination itself of this kind of behavior causes aesthetic content to possess a profounder meaning and greater objectivity in human life than mere imagination. Moral behavior is the pure aspect of such an act. It may be thought that our person becomes weak as we abandon the content of the person to biological urges. In moral behavior, to discipline biological urges means to integrate them and make them grow.

There may be some objection to my considering moral society as the expression of reason and to comparing it to a work of art. But, even if the content of art appears as a form of objective nature, its essence does not lie in objective nature. An aesthetic object is a revelation of our internal life; it is our personal creation. If we hold, with Bergson, that the eye is the channel of the visual act and that the world of perception is a reality carved merely by the eye, it may be thought that an aesthetic object is a reality carved out by the flow of a larger life that cannot flourish completely within the channel of the eye. As I have stated before, the aesthetic object is also a reality seen by the eye acting in concert with the hand. In this case the sensation of the movement of the hand expresses the spirit of internal creation. Our society of cultural phenomena is a work of creative persons, just like a work of art. It is the revelation of a profound and vast human life. From the languages, customs, mores, institutions, and laws of various nations to their myths and legends, there is nothing that is not an expression of this spirit. In this case the function of reason takes the place of the motion of the hand in the act of aesthetic expression. In sum, the spirit latent behind pure visual perception creates a work of art through the internal movement of the hand;

similarly, the forms of spirit latent behind various social experiences create cultural phenomena by uniting individually with the creative act of reason.

A work of art itself is also transformed into a cultural phenomenon by uniting with the expressive act of reason. Therefore, we can think that an aesthetic value has its value as a cultural value. There can be no aesthetic value apart from personal value, for apart from personal value there is merely technique. On the other hand, there is no meaning in moral behavior apart from saying that moral behavior is the fact of reason itself constructing the objective world of the self; it is the creative act of cultural resources (*Kulturgüter*). Abstract, formal morality is not true morality. A work of art, like a natural phenomenon, is thought of as objective and concrete, whereas a cultural phenomenon is thought of as subjective and artificial, but impulses are the given of our cultural phenomena. Natural phenomena acquire their reality by combining with sensation; similarly, cultural phenomena acquire their reality by combining with impulse. The reality of cultural phenomena is not inferior to that of natural phenomena, for history possesses a reality similar to that of nature. However, in art life is in a static state, whereas in moral behavior it is in a dynamic state. In the former, it seems as if value is complete; in the latter, value is in the process of completion. Such phenomena of social consciousness as languages, mores, and customs possess the same objectivity as nature, but their objectivity cannot avoid being incomplete. Therefore, they are regarded merely as signs or means. They are not sufficient as expressions of a larger spirit, so the whole of the human spirit cannot reflect itself in them. We can regard society in this sense as the incomplete matrix of the larger life of the spirit.

Such an idea may be thought to be an impure view of art—for example, from the perspective of art for art's sake (*l'art pour l'art*). However, it does not follow that I think that art must be subservient to morality and must be of a kind that encourages virtue and reproves vice. Pure aesthetic content is pure humanity. Even morality does not exist apart from this humanity. However, art does not reflect the unity of the entire person. Just as the hands and feet of a man possess meaning as the hands and feet of the whole bodily person, so, too, partial humanity only possesses life in its various meanings when seen from the unity of the entire person. Hence, although it may seem that my view looks lightly upon technique and ignores the special characteristic of each art, technique for technique's sake does not possess any value at all apart from mere play. In true technique content lives objectively. The fact that an artist is said to be crude in his expression must mean that his understanding of aesthetic content is incomplete. We can say that he does not understand the true content of life. The life of the world of color and form is understood only when the entire self becomes the eye, and the life of the world of sound only when the entire body becomes the ear. I do not wish to agree with such an anti-cultural view of art as Tolstoi upholds. Even if we consider that we must reject technique that is separated from the true meaning of life, mere life as nature itself is not true life. True human life must be the infinite development of the internal life.

5

Since the above discussion is extremely inadequate and lacks conciseness, I should like to add a few more comments at the end of this chapter. Both the content of the will and the content of feeling are the content of what I term the act. Both are personal contents. We can perhaps say that they are the contents of the free self. An intellectual act, of course, is also an act of consciousness, but its content is objective, and hence we cannot precisely call it personal content. We cannot know an intellectual act in the sense that we know things. We hear sound, but we cannot hear hearing. To be able to say that we reflect upon the spiritual act of the self and that the self sees or hears, there must be the content of the unity of some act. When the positive content of this unity is not clear, we seek it in physiological causes. For example, in the case in which colors seem to change by means of contrast, to that extent we can also judge them to be different colors. But from contradiction with our judgments in other instances, we consider this to be a subjective judgment, and we seek the causes of these changes physiologically. In such an instance the act becomes entirely physiological. But if we consider that we have been able to find the causes of these changes through association, this means that we have explained them from psychological causes and that we have recognized a conscious unity—that is, the self. However, the content of the self in such a case is nothing more than that of which we have been conscious. Representation functions quantitatively very much as an atom does. We may say that the self is content-less. But in reality the spiritual phenomenon of the self does not act mechanically in this way.

There are no psychologists today who do not recognize that association is controlled by feeling. However, in ordinary psychology they usually seek its cause in the elements of consciousness and further reduce it to the structure of the organism; going even further, they seek its source in the history of biological evolution. In this way the self once again becomes contentless and can be nothing but a mere name. Of course, upon further reflection, in order to recognize a teleo-logical unity beyond the structure and development of a biological being, there must first be a concept of purpose in the self. If not, no matter how exquisite an organic structure it is, it is merely an acci-dental combination of matter. Indeed, even such an idea as mechani-cal force cannot be established unless there is internal experience of the will. However, I do not wish to go into this argument here.

But, at any rate, if we do adopt such an idea as is stated above, then the reality of a phenomenon of consciousness seems to disappear; the will becomes delusion, and feeling, too, becomes a kind of sensa-tion. Both will and feeling, as phenomena of consciousness, have no specific laws whatsoever; they are consciousness only in the sense of be-ing its qualities. Moreover, mere consciousness cannot become the rea-son for recognizing a particular phenomenon of consciousness. Even a physical phenomenon arises basically from a phenomenon of con-sciousness—that is, from immediate experience. However, it becomes a physical phenomenon according to the standpoint of its explana-tion. There is first a fact that has become an object of consciousness for us, and from that we proceed to seek an explanation of it. Of course, when changes of a certain phenomenon of consciousness cannot be explained by present-day physiology, we can recognize that such a thing as a spiritual act, which differs from natural phenomena, is behind it. For example, if there are differences in results between the instances when something like attention has been added to the act of the self and when it has not been added, then we cannot help reducing it to the spiritual act of attention—that is, to the power of representa-tion itself. But here, too, if its physiological causes become clear, then the spiritual act disappears. At least, in such a case that which is termed a spiritual act has been projected into the world of cognitive objects apart from the actual self, and on this point it is no different from a physical force.

When we do not seek empirical content—that is, the unity of contradiction of intellectual content—externally, or when we are able to find it directly internally, the content of consciousness that differs from intellectual content is established. We can say that it is the true content of the self and that a phenomenon of consciousness in the strict sense does not exist apart from it. For example, let me consider the case when consciousness has changed from the perception of blue to the perception of red. If that is all, we may be able to view it ob-jectively as changes of the thing. In the case that perception of color

has changed into perception of sound, we can think that the thing has
changed physically. We may be able to think this in the sense of there
having been changes of immediate consciousness. It is proper to think
of a physiological phenomenon in explaining physical contradictions,
or, in other words, it is proper to think that the centers of aural perception have functioned by following upon the centers of visual perception. In such a case, even if there is unity of consciousness, it does
not possess any content. However, if volitional consciousness is added,
such as the thought of wanting to hear music after seeing a flower, it
may still be true. But if judgment is added, such as that red and blue
differ or that color and sound differ, then our perspective differs
greatly from the previous one, and our eye is turned inward from
without. In contrast to seeing or hearing, judgment has independent
content as the act underlying all acts.

Of course, even if the experience does not go as far as judgment, when recollections accompany the self, then we have already entered into the standpoint of reflection. Leibniz also considers memory
to be one of the characteristics that distinguish a 'bare monad' from
'spirit'. Physiologically the same brain cells may be stimulated; but,
in terms of consciousness, a self-identity can be thought to become
the basis of self-reflection. Various associations can be thought to
function on the basis of this immediate, internal self-identity. Here
for the first time an independent content of consciousness is established, such as the 'feeling of familiarity' (*Bekanntheitsgefühl*).

Next, in what sense can we think that thinking is a phenomenon of consciousness? And to what extent can we think of the
content of consciousness in respect to the act of thinking? Judgment
is a teleological act; teleological realization is the essence of judgment.
If we consider that the teleological content of judgment transcends
the sphere of causal relations and has its own internal laws whereby
it operates immediately, then we can say that thinking, as the act underlying all acts, has conscious content independent in itself. In this
way the content of judgment may be thought to be subjective, but, as
present-day epistemologists emphasize, the object of judgment is not
subjective, but objective. It is transindividual. On this point we still
cannot say that the object of judgment is personal content. The content of knowledge again becomes objective, and only such a thing as
error is based on subjective cause. If we consider that apart from a
state of consciousness as the content of a conscious act there is no
positive content, we can do nothing but seek it, as I have stated, in
physiological causes or association. Even to hold, with Wundt, that in
apperception the goal representation is clearly an object of conscious-

ness from the beginning, if such a thing as the direction of the apperceptive unity—that is, meaning—is objective truth, then it still cannot yield any positive content whatever as a pure phenomenon of consciousness. Perhaps such a thing as the 'object' of Meinong's 'hypothesis' may be considered to be the content of consciousness; but even what he terms 'objective' (*objektiv*) is also not directly the content of consciousness. Within the 'objective', untrue or unreal content can also be included, but the 'objective' is still the content of an act and not of the act underlying all acts.

In these terms, we may have to say that, in the strict sense, the content of consciousness is simply the content of feeling and of the will. However, if we go so far as to include even Meinong's 'objective' in the world of objective objects, then what remains as the content of subjective consciousness? If we consider that such things as Bolzano's 'proposition in itself' or Meinong's 'objective' relate to transcendental value, or, in other words, that a teleological act such as the act of judgment is established by a normative standpoint's being added to it, what kind of content can this kind of act of judgment itself possess as consciousness of the self? We cannot hear hearing, and we cannot make the act of judgment an object of judgment. If we speak in this radical way, then such a thing as a spiritual act must disappear entirely. However, if we are conscious of the act to any degree, then there must be some content in it. Usually we think of this kind of intellectual content in the sense that it is known by reason of reflection. But if we consider that reflection has the same meaning as judgment, then we must fall into the self-contradiction that judgment knows judgment.

Here we cannot help recognizing two mutually opposing directions of consciousness. What we usually term reflection is still an objectification of the self. Hence, it is the same as thinking of such a teleological unity as life in the external world. In this sense we cannot know the true self. The direct consciousness, or personal experience, of the true self must be something different from reflection in this sense. We must recognize such a thing as consciousness prior to this kind of judgment. For consciousness of judgment—indeed, judgment itself, too—is truly established on the basis of this consciousness. Maine de Biran considers that there are two kinds of results of habit. First are sensations that become dulled through habit. For example, we cease to be sensitive to perfume as we become accustomed to it. Conversely, there are active sensations, such as voluntary acts, that become increasingly clearer through repetition and habit. We are able to grasp and to analyze the forms and qualities of things through the voluntary movements of the hands. Our intelligible world develops in this direction. At the base of judgment, as well, there is effort. In voluntary effort the consciousness of the self is unified. He states that this self does not negate itself and cannot objectify itself. We possess immediate consciousness of the act in this kind of sense. I think that only by there being consciousness of the above kind of voluntary effort is such a thing as consciousness of the act established. We cannot hear hearing, and we cannot see seeing. However, we can know them as Maine de Biran's 'active sensations' in the standpoint of the pure union of act and act. We can know them in the unity of goals.

How do hearing and seeing differ? There is no question but that color and sound are extraordinarily different. However, the difference lies in color and sound, not in hearing and seeing. The positive content that differentiates hearing from seeing must be the infinite coloration of the self. I think that the subtle, painterly feelings that accompany color and the sensitive, musical emotions that accompany sound are the positive contents of visual and aural perceptions as acts. Putting it this way, doubts may arise as to whether an intellectual act is not also consciousness. However, if the representation itself or the proposition itself is considered to be objective, this would merely mean that they are simply objects of consciousness as contents of the intellectual act. The rest would be nothing more than simplicity or complexity, or some goal representation preceding or following. We can think of the intellectual act as a pass through which one enters into the subjective world from the objective world and as the gateway through which we pass from the universal to the particular. The positive content of pure consciousness beyond this would seem to be the content of feeling.

In these terms, a phenomenon of consciousness in the strict sense is always a content of feeling, and if we consider the intellectual content to express the universal relationship of experiential content —that is, to express objective content—then the content of feeling and the will, on the contrary, may be thought to indicate specific content. Therefore, the content of feeling or the will can be said to be a unity of contradiction, the rationalization of the irrational. The process of synthesis toward this kind of specific center, or the particularization of experiential content—that is, the individual unity—must be a unity in the standpoint of behavior. In behavior we encompass the universal within the particular. Maine de Biran's idea of the unity of the unobjectifiable self can also be thought to be a unity of expression. Unity in the beginning is not unity that has been given, but unity in destination is a final unity. The expressive understanding that is based on the empathetic projection of feeling is deeper and more fundamental than intellectual understanding. Even intellectual understanding is established on the basis of such understanding. A particular unity is a unity of internal continuity. It is the unity of one arc of the infinite curve of human life. The more this kind of understanding is repeated, the clearer it becomes. Our actuality is truly one point of this kind of curve. We normally think that the particular is included within the universal, but actually the particular must include the universal within itself. The universal, on its part, must possess the tendency to be included within the particular. For example, just as in the coordinates of a curve the curve itself is expressed by the tendency of the curve in one point, so, too, a productive point itself is expressed by means of the relationship between productive point and productive point.

If the content of feeling and the will can be expressed in the above way, then in the differences between feeling and the will the latter can be thought to be the ultimate unity in the direction of such particularization, the ultimate phase of a process of particularization. Just as Leibniz states that God has created the best world from infinite possible worlds, so can we, too, attain to ultimate particularization only on the basis of the unity of the universal will—that is, only on the basis of the absolute will. At the foundation of actual consciousness, which includes the infinite universal within the particular, we always touch the great curve of creative evolution. That which is determined at the forward edge of this great curve is the content of the will. Therefore, the will includes the plane of consciousness in general, which is the unity of every universal—that is, it contains the world of cognitive objects. The will is the real. This kind of ultimate horizon is not merely the total sum of possible content; there must also be a leap of dimension in it. There is nothing beautiful that does not have meaning in human life, but we cannot say that the beautiful is directly the good.

Chapter 4

The Objective World
of Reflective Judgment

1

At the beginning of his *Critique of Judgment*, Kant makes a distinction between determinative judgment and reflective judgment. If we follow Kant, we can in general consider judgment to include the particular within the universal. When the universal is first given and the particular is subsumed within it, judgment is determinative (*bestimmend*); on the other hand, when the particular is first given and the universal is discovered in reference to it, judgment is reflective (*reflektierend*). However, both the act of reflective judgment, which is an act of teleological unity, and the act of determinative judgment, which may be considered as a mere intellectual act, are considered by Kant to contain the particular within the universal. They differ only on the point of whether the universal is given first or discovered afterwards. But I think that we must consider whether the universal that is the foundation of unity in the act of reflective judgment is qualitatively similar to the universal that is the foundation of the act of determinative judgment. For if they are the same, then we cannot clarify the content of artistic beauty. Strictly speaking, will not the notion of teleological unity also become meaningless?

In ordinary logic it is thought that judgment includes the particular within the universal. Yet, in such a case the true basis of judgment is not merely an abstract universal concept, but a constructive principle. Something truly universal must be a synthetic universal. A principle of the act of determinative judgment, such as the principle of causality, must, of course, be a transcendental principle that constructs the world of cognitive objects. If we follow Kant, apart from such laws of the pure understanding that refer to the general possibilities of nature, there are many laws of nature that can be thought to be contingent to our understanding. In other terms, there are manifold forms of nature apart from the universal, transcendental concepts of nature. Even such specific laws of nature, insofar as they are laws, must necessarily be unified by one unifying principle. The act of reflective judgment, which thus moves toward the universal from the particular, must also possess a transcendental principle. We term this kind of principle the teleological quality of nature. However, what does the teleology of nature mean? Can a concept of nature and teleology in the strict sense be compatible with each other?

To conceive of a teleological act implies that there is a subjective act in some sense in its background, for only by the form of the act of consciousness can we think of such a thing as a teleological act. If we proceed from a strict concept of nature, then the various empirical laws based on the pure concept of nature, which are its specific differences, must be the laws of purely natural causation, and there will be no room to include something like a teleological act within any causal series. No matter how well unified a law of nature may be, there is no teleology whatever in it. There is only the particular included within the universal. Indeed, in nature the particular vanishes entirely within the universal. If we attempt to combine teleology in some sense with the concept of nature, then it will not be something that can be included within the concept of nature, but something added from without. Among natural phenomena, biological entities are phenomena in which it can be thought that teleological causality is operative. However, from the strict standpoint of the concept of nature, we cannot allow anything apart from strict causal law. We must reduce even physiological phenomena to the laws of chemistry and physics. Only in this way can we attain the goal of natural science. To hypothesize some kind of life force would be incompatible with the strict concept of nature, for when we hypothesize such a force, are we not abandoning natural-scientific explanation?

Of course, this does not mean that there are no natural forces inexplicable by the laws of physics and chemistry that are known today. Nor does this mean that all natural laws must be quantitative. But even if, as Bunge states, digestion in the stomach depends upon a force that we cannot explain chemically, he is still trying to find the causal law in purely objective terms. If we do not add the qualities of consciousness to the individual cells, we cannot reduce them to causal relationships, which have a foundation wholly different from teleological causality. Even the phenomena of biological evolution must be judged from such a causal standpoint according to whether they exhibit continuous or rapid progress in empirical fact. But even if the latter, we have necessarily adulterated the natural-scientific standpoint by reducing them to teleological causation. Strictly, we should say that these are the only kind of physical causal laws. When various curves are unified by a universal equation in analytic geometry, we may feel a kind of beauty about it. But no one would think that number itself is teleological. The teleology is nothing more than our admiration, added subjectively. Even such a basic principle as the 'smallest function', setting aside for the moment the question of whether we consider Maupertuis' thought as the foundation, does not include the least teleological quality as a fundamental law of physics.

On the basis of the above ideas, I would submit that the teleology of nature is incompatible with the strict concept of nature. The teleology of nature is simply a viewpoint added from a standpoint utterly different from that on which the strict concept of nature is based. Indeed, I think that teleology is nothing more than an aesthetic or religious view. If we consider, as Kant states, that we are able to intuit the teleology of nature through the power of intuitive understanding, then we are no longer considering nature, but a kind of work of art. Between the objective world of pure aesthetic intuition and the pure natural world, which is grounded by the categories of space, time, and causality, various objective worlds arise as we mix these two perspectives. Even teleological nature can be considered to belong to this kind of objective world.

When we consider a teleological act in the background of nature, it is no longer nature, but spiritual reality, and it belongs to the objective world, which is grounded on an even higher standpoint than nature. Even teleological content can be considered only as the content of the act underlying all acts. It cannot be termed teleological content; in the mere objective world there is neither life nor consciousness.

2

Concerning the relationship between particular and universal, there is no difference whatever in the point of whether the particular is given first and subsumed by the universal afterwards, or the universal is given first, and subsumes the particular thereby. If cognition, in the strict sense, subsumes the particular within the universal, then the content of the particular that appears in the standpoint of Kant's reflective judgment cannot be sought within the pure, objective content of consciousness. It must be sought within the content of the act underlying all acts. It is not the content of judgment, but the relationship between acts of judgment. As Kant himself states, the meaning of modality (*Modalität*) must be sought not within the objective content of cognition, but within the act of cognition. Therefore, is there any difference at all, in the standpoint of the act underlying all acts, between the particular's being first given and afterwards subsumed by the universal and the universal's being first given and subsuming the particular thereby? Can it be viewed merely as a problem of time sequence? I think there is profound significance here, beyond mere time sequence in the psychological act. Differences of standpoints must mean differences in the qualities of the unifying universals themselves. In Kant's *Critique of Pure Reason* all changes are considered to be in 'time', but 'time' itself does not change, and we cannot perceive 'time' itself. Therefore, there must be a basic entity that represents 'time in general' (*Zeit überhaupt*) in the background of the objects of perception—that is, in the background of phenomena. But the unity of reflective judgment must be a unity of pure time, for it is not unity of 'time that has flowed', but a unity of 'time that is flowing'. It must be the unity of pure activity; pure activity is pure 'time'. Pure activity, pure 'time', as Kant has stated, cannot be perceived—indeed, cannot be reflected upon. The actual entity that is seen in the background of phenomena is the reflection of 'time'; it is not time itself. In the unity of pure 'time', the particular is given first, and the universal is sought in respect to it. The true universal cannot express itself. It is expressed in the particular; in pure activity the universal is contained within the particular, and the unity of 'time' is an individual unity.

3

I think we can make three kinds of distinctions within the unity of experiential content. The first is unity in the standpoint of pure objective cognition, as in the plane of determinative judgment. The second is the unity in the standpoint of the unity of subject and object, as in the horizon of behavior. The third is the perspective of unity that exists in the horizon of the mutual opposition of these two. The second standpoint, as the horizon of pure, internal unity, which proceeds to unify from act to act, transcends the standpoint of judgment, and is the most fundamental and concrete standpoint, in relation to which even the act of judgment can be considered to be one of its contents. The world of objective objects in the first standpoint objectifies this kind of concrete reality from the plane of consciousness in general. Reflection upon the second standpoint from this first standpoint is the objective world in the third standpoint; that is, it is the objective world of reflective knowledge. In this world, the con-

crete unity in the second standpoint becomes the goal, and everything
is unified teleologically or by teleological causality. The objective
world of Kant's reflective judgment must be this kind of world.

What I term the horizon of behavior entirely transcends the
plane of conceptual knowledge and is the horizon of pure act, which
embraces this plane within itself. It transcends consciousness in general; it is the horizon of the creative, free self that includes it. Perhaps
it may even be appropriate to call it aesthetic intuition. However, it is
not, as is usually thought of the term *intuition*, a standpoint of quiet
contemplation. In my opinion, even aesthetic intuition does not exist
apart from the creative act of the artist. The standpoint of aesthetic
intuition is the horizon of the aesthetic, creative act. In other terms, it
is the horizon of behavior, in the broad sense; the transcendence of
the plane of knowledge means that it has become dynamic. Some may
wonder whether what I term the horizon of behavior, then, is not
something like an unconscious will. However, I think there are two
meanings to the term *unconscious*. One refers to such a thing as instinctive behavior in which we are wholly unconscious of the object;
but in this case unconscious will is an idea added from without and
does not differ from material force. True unconscious will acts consciously from within and cannot be made into an object of cognition.
Actually, such an unconscious will is operative even at the base of the
cognitive act. We can recognize this kind of conscious act clearly in
the aesthetic standpoint. We may be able to recognize a resemblance
between an aesthetic and an instinctive act on many points. However,
we must recognize a radical difference between the two in that in the
former the self is wholly free from the object. In art, the self becomes
free spirit. This means that it transcends the plane of consciousness
in general. In the plane of consciousness in general, the objective
world becomes a construction of the self; by transcending this plane,
the self becomes wholly free and creative.

In the above sense, in what kind of relation do unconscious
will and what is normally called the will stand? If we consider unconsciousness to be similar to instinct, we must think of it as a material
force similar to a 'tropism'. Or, at least, we must think of it as a kind
of unclear, weak will. But not only is unconsciousness, in the sense
of internal behavior that moves from act to act like aesthetic intuition, not anticonscious, but we can even think that all consciousness
is established on the basis of this kind of unconsciousness. We can
view what is called conscious will as something that has appeared as
a process of such development of consciousness. Even in ordinary psychology it is thought that whatever appears as content of the will is

first given in the form of impulse. It is thought that the will of which we have been conscious arises from a conflict of the impulsive will. But I do not think of the distinctions between will, on the one hand, and instinct and impulse, on the other, in such a way, for the latter are nothing more than projections of the former. Consequently, I do not think that consciousness simply emerges from unconsciousness and returns to unconsciousness. The transition from consciousness to unconsciousness, such as can be seen in artistic virtuosity, is not a reversion to an original unconsciousness. On the contrary, it can be thought to be an experiential process in which consciousness becomes increasingly clearer.

Maine de Biran's recognition of the two mutually opposing tendencies between passive sensation and active perception has taken account of this point. A goal becomes the object of consciousness because it takes the establishment of representational life as its background. In life in the horizon of representation, the act already departs from the mere objective world and enters the world of the act itself, in which one act gives birth to another. The fact that the act itself is active and becomes an independent reality must mean that the act itself is an infinite internal continuity. There must be a profound, unattainable, internal depth in its background. This depth is incomprehensible, but not in the sense in which the external world is incomprehensible. It is not something confronting the self; it is the self itself. The inscrutability of the external world is nothing more than the self's own shadow. There is this kind of internal continuity even in the background of things that are considered transcendental, such as mathematical knowledge. New knowledge is created from this point.

Intuitive unity, which I term active dialectical unity to express its dynamic meaning, must strictly transcend conceptual understanding. Here there is no room to allow for a teleological relationship. This is the reason Bergson also denied teleological causality to pure duration. In artistic unity there is not even the opposition between means and goal—nor, indeed, between whole and part. The whole must be the flow of one life. Of course, the transconceptual is not the anticonceptual. The horizon of behavior contains the plane of knowledge and causes it to be established within itself. Knowledge is one form of practice. However, we must recognize the horizon of this pure, intuitive unity, on the one hand, and that of conceptual unity, which is opposed to it, on the other. If we use Bergson's terms, we must recognize the horizon of pure duration in contrast to that of simultaneous existence. When from the former horizon of pure duration we have reflected upon the objective world that exists in the latter horizon of simultaneous existence, the infinite world of teleological causality is established. The experiential content in the horizon of intuitive unity, that is, the content of pure feeling, becomes the goal, in contrast to which the world of cognitive objects, grounded in the plane of consciousness in general, becomes its means. Herein everything is combined in the relationship of purpose and means. This teleological world is of an even higher order than the world of cognitive objects. Indeed, because intuition subsumes cognition within itself, intuition cannot be explained by reducing it to universal law; its nature can only be clarified in the perspective of synthetic unity. Categorical concepts must be employed instead of generic concepts. Hence I think there must be categories of reflective judgment that differ from the act of determinative judgment. The world of psychological phenomena is established by such categories.

The position I have articulated above turns from the intellectual self to the practical self in the standpoint of the absolute self, and the objective world of this standpoint still belongs to the world of cognitive objects. In my view, the synthesis of the intentionality of pure behavior and that of pure knowledge must be based on this standpoint. Eternal truth and laws must enter the world of behavior and first become its means before they have their own meaning.

What relation obtains among the above three standpoints? What position does the plane of consciousness in general take among them? Reality, which is immediate, independent, and concrete, is an infinite internal continuity of pure acts, and the absolute will, or absolute self, is this kind of unity of acts. Consciousness in general is nothing more than one plane of this absolute will, and the world of cognitive objects is one plane of the intentionality of the will. The facts that the self reflects upon itself and that the reflecting self and the self reflected upon are identical signify this infinite dialectic of pure acts, which can also be termed 'a flower that blooms anew on a tree without root'. Moreover, this kind of infinite dialectic itself constitutes the unity of the self.

For example, if we consider that the color tones of red are infinitely distinguishable from one another, there must be an infinite continuity at the foundation of red in order to establish such a discrimination. Infinite discrimination of color becomes possible through this concept. The infinite continuity of color becomes act at the limit of this process of discrimination, and if we objectify it and consider it from outside, the infinite continuity of color may even be considered to be nothing more than an abstract concept. The act of judgment can also be thought to have been added to perceptual experience. However, the essence of a phenomenon of consciousness lies in this limit point of continuity's becoming internal. Perceptual judgment is self-consciousness of the Idea itself. Perceptual judgment is not the mere sum of perception and judgment. The fact that perceptual judgment is established only when we apply the principle of the 'anticipation of perception' signifies the self-consciousness of the Idea.

If we consider the concrete experience of color in the above way, then consciousness in general is the limit point of this kind of infinite, internal series. This plane is the limit point of subjectivity, which cannot be objectified. Every color becomes its content in this standpoint, and at the same time we can consider that color transcends the horizon of color itself. Of course, our concrete experience is not mere activity; it is the infinite act underlying all acts. More precisely, if consciousness in general is the limit point of this kind of act underlying all acts, then the plane of consciousness in general must be considered to transcend the plane of mere knowledge and to be one aspect of the creative will already. The reality of the natural world is based on this plane of consciousness in general. Our natural world is not a world of mere value, but of reality. Yet while the natural world may be complete in itself, when its standpoint is further transcended, the spiritual world appears as the objective world of the act underlying all acts. It is infinitely particularized and specifically unified in this horizon. That which appears in this horizon must be history. When we further transcend the historical plane and enter into the dimension of the absolute self as the unity of subject and object, then we transcend the determination of time and space and enter into the eternal worlds of art and religion. The eternity of these worlds means, not an eternity of time, but the transcendence of time. From the horizon of the most concrete absolute will, the objective world of consciousness in general is always the means of the development of absolute dialectical will.

4

In our understanding of things there is this intuitive, in addition to intellectual, intentionality. The understanding of a child is said to begin from imitation. This kind of understanding may even be considered to be merely instinctive. But, however much our knowledge advances rationally, intuitive understanding or comprehension is always at its root. Intellectual understanding is truly established on

this basis. The more we advance rationally, the more intuitive understanding deepens spiritually. There must be intuitive understanding
also at the base of any kind of abstract understanding. The Southwest school states that our knowledge begins from normative consciousness, but self-awareness of the normative consciousness must be
a kind of intuition of the internal life. Our life may begin from dark,
instinctive impulse, but when the early morning mist of instinct
burns off, the life of the shining intellect becomes manifest. Instinct
and intelligence are not mutually contradictory, independent acts.
They are merely two sides of one act. The form of intuitive intentionality that is distinguishable from conceptual understanding can
be clarified, I think, in the intentionality of the expressive act. The
content of our feeling directly appears in expressive movements without passing through the plane of reflection in conceptual thinking.
We immediately intuit the content of the feelings of another person,
for example, through such an expressive act.

In the expressive act our spiritual functions do not pass
through the objective world of reflection; that is, they are not reflected
upon, but constitute an immediate unity. In the understanding of the
reflective act, a thing is not a mere thing, but can be understood as
the expression of spiritual content. Things immediately fuse with the
self as the creation of that which is spiritual. Objective spirit and the
self become one unity of feeling. The form of the understanding of
the above kind of expressive act obtains, I think, even in one aspect
of mathematical thinking. The realm of mathematics is still a kind
of objective world given to our subjectivity and can be viewed as a
creation of a kind of objective spirit. Mathematical understanding
involves our uniting directly with this objective spirit and creating
in unison with it. The transcendental, necessary nature of mathematical knowledge resides in this. The difference between mathematical understanding and aesthetic insight lies in the former's being an
objective world that is accessible to reason, while the latter is the
content of feeling that is inaccessible to reason. In the expressive intentionality the object is not static, but dynamic and creative, and
our spiritual acts form an immediate unity with it.

Understanding begins from intuition, and profound intuition is always at the base of understanding. From this standpoint, the
myriad things of life are all expressions of the self. But because this
horizon of intuition is infinitely deeper than the plane of thinking,
the object of the former differs from the self and becomes an infinitely
objective world that is irrational and seems to oppose the self. Yet
thinking, too, is one kind of act of the self; the content of thinking

unites with the content of experience in this intuitive horizon and thus attains the objectivity of knowledge. It seems to be a paradox, but knowledge attains its own goal by ultimately being irrational, by uniting with the horizon of intuition, which is contrary to it.

Chapter 5

The Union Point
of the True, the Good,
and the Beautiful

1

In the horizon of what I call absolute will, or absolute self, the myriad things all become expressions of spiritual content. Saint Francis of Assisi wrote in his famous "Hymn to the Sun":

> Be Thou praised, my Lord, with all Thy creatures,
>> above all, Brother Sun,
>>> who gives the day and lightens us therewith.
> And he is beautiful and radiant with great splendor,
>> of Thee, Most High, he bears similitude.
> Be Thou praised, my Lord, of Sister Moon and the stars,
>> in the heaven hast Thou formed them, clear and precious and comely.
> Be Thou praised, my Lord, of Brother Wind,
>> and of the air and the cloud and of fair and of all weather,
>> by the which Thou givest to Thy creatures sustenance.

In the sun, moon, stars, wind, and clouds there is nothing that was not a symbol of God. If we deepen this viewpoint even further, we may be able to say, with the Zen master Seng Chao, "heaven and earth are of the same root as the self, and the myriad things are of the same substance as the self." We must not seek enlightenment (*bodhi*) above, nor depart from the world of birth and death (*samsara*) below. But such a horizon is neither that of pure nonreflection nor of unconsciousness. Even the statement that "unless one become an innocent child, one cannot enter into the kingdom of heaven" does not mean that the spiritual state of the child is directly the state of the religious spirit. He who will enter into the kingdom of heaven must first penetrate to the root of the self. Even "to attain to nondistinction" is not the same as "the mist and rain of Reed Mountain and the billows of Che-Chiang," before which all thoughts are destroyed.

What does it mean to penetrate to the root of the self? What is the self in this case? The self is identical with the self that looks back upon itself as object and in which the reflecting and reflected self are one. Perhaps such a self may be thought to be mere intellectual act. But, in essence, the self must be pure behavior (*Handlung schlechthin*), pure will. As Fichte states, knowing must be acting in self-consciousness. In this horizon, the myriad things appear as expressions of the self. Without even borrowing the Faustian phrase "the sign of the great universe," we can speak in this standpoint of the 'spirit of earth' (*Erdgeist*). However, since the self's reflection of itself within itself involves an infinite continuity of acts, the realm of cognitive objects must also be incomplete, and knowledge must always be imperfect. The incompleteness of knowledge is the essence of knowledge itself. This kind of infinite continuity of acts—that is, the infinite acts of the self—becomes projected externally as a world of infinite reality with respect to the present self. But the dialectical unity itself of these two mutually opposing directions is the true self, and hence when the 'self' is self-conscious of the unity of this kind of dialectical contradiction, it can include the infinite external world within itself. In other terms, it turns from the intellectual self to the practical self. Self-consciousness* may usually be thought to be a variety of conceptual knowledge. But we cannot know the self as an object of judgment; self-consciousness cannot become the content of judgment. On the contrary, it is intuition that becomes the foundation of judgment. My saying that the self penetrates to its root means its attaining of this dimension. At this juncture, we can even transcend the plane of consciousness in general and include it internally. No matter what kind of phenomenon each phenomenon of consciousness is, we can always think that it is essentially grounded in this dimension of intuitive, dialectical immediacy.

Hence, we can think that phenomena of consciousness arise only in the horizon of expression. Even in mere sensation and perception we transform the domains appropriate to each into expression. Therefore, color, sound, and form can be regarded as transformations of our own subjectivity. This point is the same as being able to think that the world of reality is the articulation of reason. When we think of the physical body of the self, we already begin the transformation of objectivity into expression. In phenomena of consciousness we can regard the external world as the transformations of the self, as the Idealists think. But in this kind of expressive horizon, we must recog-

---

* *Translators' note*: It would appear that here and elsewhere, Nishida employs the term *jikaku* in a multi-nuanced way, the Japanese characters standing simultaneously for the Western notions of "self-consciousness," "self-awareness," etc., and the Buddhist notion of "self-awakening" (*satori*).

nize an infinite process in reference to which we always stand before an infinite task. When this direction of infinite advance has not been completely experienced in the present standpoint, a phenomenon of consciousness can be conceived of that is in contrast to the world of matter; when it has been internalized, it becomes the aesthetic standpoint. In the former case, we unite with the infinitely vast material world with the body as the center; in the latter case, infinity is embraced internally. Bergson states that consciousness is the remainder of expression over above action, and this may express the essence of a phenomenon of consciousness. But at the ground of consciousness there is a consciousness that cannot be obstructed by action. Such a thing as the intuition of the artist becomes deeper and clearer through his actions. Just as thought advances by means of representation and language, aesthetic intuition develops through action. Action itself becomes consciousness.

In the aesthetic horizon we have already transcended the planes of consciousness in general and cognition. We experience in the dimension of the free self, which includes them immanently and in which objectivity becomes the expression of personal content. The horizon of the aesthetic act is not that of mere instinct. At this point we must think that there is a complete change of dimension. What, then, does it mean further to recognize infinite opposition and to advance on the basis of the expressive horizon, which already takes objectivity to be a modality of the self? For example, what does moral consciousness mean in contrast to the aesthetic consciousness? In the aesthetic standpoint everything, even the fallen stones and flowing water, is an expression of spiritual content. But we regard the stones and water as unconscious. In contrast to this, the body can be regarded as an expression of spiritual content from the aesthetic standpoint, but at the same time directly as an organ of spiritual content, for spiritual content functions and becomes actual through the body. In the creative act of the artist, personal content itself directly becomes the action of the body, becomes self-conscious of itself, and enters into its own world. The body is the fusion point of various realms in the material world.

When we view nature in the standpoint of aesthetic intuition, the spirit that we see behind nature is directly the spirit of the self. When we view the cherry blossoms and the moon and transform them into poetry, we individualize and personalize them. Shelley's famous poem "The Skylark," which is said to have been composed in the heightened feeling he gained at hearing the cry of a skylark as he wandered among hedges in which fireflies were gathered on a summer

Item # 3942400724432 routed to XWI.

Item # 3942401658050 routed to FAL.

evening in Italy, is not the expression of the spirit of the bird, but of
Shelley himself. Moreover, such heightened feeling is precisely the
essence of Shelley himself and also the substance of a profounder
nature. True reality is not the content of the universal concept, but
the specific content of feeling and the will. Shelley himself was simply
this kind of medium of the self. Shelley's true self-consciousness entered deeply into this creation.

In what relationship do the inspiration of the poet, his action, and his consciousness stand? We can think that when aesthetic
content appears as a creative act, it moves directly from inspiration
into action without passing through the consciousness of judgment;
or, as Fiedler states, in the case of painting the artist moves directly
into expressive movement from pure visual perception. The content
of pure visual perception is not the content of mere perception, but
is personal content. Since the poet's medium of expression is language, poetry can be thought to be closer to conceptual knowledge,
but the poet's language is nothing more than his means of expression.
Even if a scientific discussion is included in a work of literature, it
is not as science, but as a means of expression. There is no difference
between words as medium, in the case of the poet, and color and
sound as medium, in the cases of the painter and musician, respec-
tively. But in the case of the poet the free personal content in the
background of conceptual knowledge is also expressed. As in the
aesthetic content of "The Skylark," the rapturous feeling for nature
is the subjective feeling of the poet for nature and hence may be
thought to be completely unreal; for it is neither an imperative with
respect to subjectivity nor conceptual truth with respect to nature.
But when the content of aesthetic imagination is a human being, we
can think, contrary to the previous instance, that aesthetic content
itself possesses a direct relationship with moral content.

Needless to say, we should distinguish aesthetic and moral
intentions. In an aesthetic intentionality, we may be able to describe
nature and man in identical terms. However, when man himself has
directly become an object of art, we cannot deny that its content is
aesthetic and at the same time possesses the possibility of being directly actualized in the self and can unite directly with the world of
reality through the self. Aesthetic content, which thus takes man as
the object, can be directly realized because knowledge itself is included within the aesthetic content. To say that intellectual elements
are included does not mean they are included as elements of feeling
in the sense in which the psychologist speaks, but as means to be included as truth. Aesthetic content having man as its object is simul-

taneously knowledge of man himself. The impressions of the poet with regard to nature are not knowledge of nature in itself; but the insights of the poet with regard to man must be profound knowledge of man himself; they must be objective at the same time that they are subjective. Since they are this union of subject and object, they are actual.

That in the aesthetic horizon we transcend and immanently include that of consciousness in general can be best clarified in examining the aesthetic content that takes man as object. Even the poet's description of nature is not merely an objective description of nature, but a reflection of the person of the poet. But we can think that in the poetic description of man the personal content becomes self-conscious. Here the person profoundly illuminates his own interiority, as it were, and is able to know himself. Behavior becomes self-conscious of itself. Personal content is established by internally including the plane of consciousness in general—that is, reason. Only in this intentionality does personal content positively know itself.

I have stated that when the artist moves from the description of nature to the description of man, the aesthetic content of his work touches the world of reality and becomes a potentiality of realization. Of course, when the poet moves from his exaltation to actual practice, he already loses his standpoint as poet. There is a profound change of dimensions here. Poetry is always separated from reality; this is the reason that lyric poetry is thought of as poetry within poetry. However, the personal content, which essentially functions in the horizon of free will, returns to itself in behavior. There is no poetry apart from the person of the poet. The content of aesthetic feeling of nature does not include knowledge; but the content of aesthetic feeling in respect to man does include knowledge itself. Of course, the former content is already personal in one sense, and the latter content, as aesthetic content, must be unreal in another sense. Yet, we cannot help thinking that a deeper truth of human life is included in great art and that because it is true it is beautiful. Needless to say, this is not psychological truth or sociological truth; it does not imply any practical significance. But in the aesthetic act where man describes himself there must be the quality of knowledge in some sense. At least, there must be objective significance. Schopenhauer states that knowledge is liberated through the self-illumination of the will, but such an intuition must be knowledge of itself in the profoundest sense.

The reason it can be thought that aesthetic content concerning man differs from that concerning nature and that in one aspect it itself is knowledge is that there is the aesthetic feeling of conceptual reality itself. We conceive of natural-scientific reality in the background of perceptual experience as the object of thinking, but such a reality cannot become a complete object of personal feeling. Therefore, a feeling about conceptual nature is nothing more than a utilitarian feeling, and the world of natural science is only complete in intellectual feeling as the creation of pure knowledge. In contrast to this, our self is the object both of thinking and of intuition. Thinking and intuition are one in the self. In the self we can have immediate aesthetic feeling, in contrast to conceptual reality. Knowledge and feeling are one in the self, which is an infinite continuity of acts, and are two planes of the same self. The pure act is knowledge on one plane and feeling on the other. Knowledge is feeling, and feeling is knowledge and activity.

True reality is an infinite internal continuity of acts. The infinite greatness and depth that we feel in reality is a projection of the depths of the self itself. In facing the boundless expanse of the blue sky, we are struck with awe at the infinity of space. But this must be nothing other than a feeling of mystery about the act of self-consciousness in projecting the self within itself. Our knowledge deepens infinitely within itself, and we see infinite objective reality in this direction. The psychologist states that consciousness begins with the impulse of movement; in like manner, the beginning of our consciousness can be thought to be infinite unrest. Knowledge develops from this kind of infinite impulsive consciousness. Yet, however much knowledge develops, we can neither transcend the accompanying impulsive consciousness nor succeed in completely intellectualizing the will of the self. Even though the consciousness of the will appears to be the result of intellectual development, this standpoint is already included in the beginning of consciousness. Consciousness of impulse also is established, is differentiated, and develops in this standpoint. When we face the infinite depth within the self in this intentionality, we see an infinite objective world in the direction of its development and an infinite spiritual act in the direction that reflects it within itself. We possess the realms of infinitely profound and free art, philosophy, and religion in the direction of the concrete self itself, the union point of these two mutually opposing directions. In contrast to the self that is reflected upon, the objective world appears as the means of the self, while in the horizon of the concrete self the objective world becomes the expression of the self. There is infinite prog-

ress in the direction of this kind of self; other infinities are merely the
reflection of this infinity.

Following Schopenhauer, I think that music can be felt as a
pure expression of the infinitely deep, internal self itself. In music
conceptual judgment completely loses its authority, and there is only
the dynamism of pure life. Lyric poetry resembles music, but lyric
poetry can still be considered to be something in which intellectual
content predominates. I think that Litzmann's statement concerning
lyric poetry, that lyric form gives expression to feeling in a form of
rhythm to a degree that accompanies content but does not blind it,
well expresses its nature. There is a clear distinction between music
and lyric poetry at the point of rhythmic form that accompanies content but does not depart from it. Turning to drama, we find that some
objective intellectual content must preserve its own authority as an
element. In a play there is a mutual opposition between character and
circumstance, and behavior becomes its center. Nature can constitute
the content of lyric poetry, but it cannot constitute the content of
drama. Needless to say, we cannot directly equate a philosophical
world view and tragedy, but it is no accident that the writers of Greek
drama resolved the deepest problems of human life through tragedy.
Music also inherently expresses personal content; but the insertion
of the slightest intellectual content must be thought to destroy the
beauty of music. Music must be purely sensory. Herein lie both the
strong and the weak points of music. Music can be thought to have a
position in the world of cultural phenomena similar to that of sensation in the world of natural-scientific reality. Consciousness in general takes sensation as its material and constructs the natural-scientific
world; and at the same time it takes personal content, like that expressed by music, as its material and constructs the world of cultural
phenomena. In this instance, consciousness in general simply expresses the infinite direction in which the act reflects upon itself.

Cohen states that sensation obtains objectivity in the world
of experience by the application of the 'principle of the anticipation
of perception'. But this has added will to reason. The addition of will
to reason does not mean that something extrinsic has been added to
reason, but that the self returns to its own concrete basis. When I
move my hand, it is neither the union of muscular or articular perception that the psychologist talks about, nor is it the union of an
indefinite number of positions from point to point. It is an infinite
continuity as one straight line unattainable by analysis. As the movement of my hand, content and continuity possess an inseparable rela-

tion and are the development of one muscular force; indeed, it is the self-consciousness of one feeling of power. Infinite internal continuity is simply the spirit of muscular perception itself. Even the 'principle of the anticipation of perception' is established in the standpoint of this kind of pure act; it is established by the self-consciousness of pure force. However, the self is not mere force, but the unity of infinite forces. We can feel the 'rhythm' of an infinite person behind the movement of our hand, and we are self-conscious of the infinitely profound flow of life. If we deepen this idea, we can think that each of our movements is also the dance of God. Thus, what is given to the self is that which is sought by the self, and if within that which has been given as sensation is included the infinite development of the cognitive self, the infinite development of the free self may be thought to be included within aesthetic content such as music.

The personal content that is included within lyric poetry and music becomes actual as it develops itself—in other words, it functions spontaneously—for personal content both transcends and immanently includes the subject. Therefore, subjectivity essentially involves the act of particularization. It is the basic principle of actualization; the more particular it becomes, the more real it becomes and the freer personal content becomes. With regard to mathematical thinking, the purer its standpoint becomes, the more its content is purified as objective truth. However, from another point of view, it can be thought that development in this direction is a departure from reality, similar to physical knowledge, which is thought to be empirical. If this kind of direction of infinite development is the direction toward consciousness in general—that is, toward transcendental subjectivity—then in the content of pure knowledge, such as mathematics, we depart from concrete reality as we advance in this direction. In personal content, on the contrary, we become more concrete and actual as we advance in this direction. The personal horizon becomes unity in an infinite developmental direction. As the self advances toward its own center, it is able to embrace all development. In other words, it can be thought that by moving toward the plane of consciousness in general it becomes objective, on the one hand, and yet subjective, on the other. But in personal content, the more it develops, the more it becomes objective in all aspects. This means that the self becomes free and creative; in other words, it becomes absolutely active. If the world of reality is established by consciousness in general, then it must be free will that is the ground of consciousness in general.

2

The more personal content enters within itself, the more it becomes dynamic—in other words, the more that which stands over against the self enters into the act of the self. Things merge within the activity of the self. The deeper we advance in this intentionality, the more we enter into activity without a subject of the activity—that is, the more we enter into the world of pure will from the world of knowledge. We already embark on this road in sensory art. But to proceed further in this direction, we must dissolve even the objective, real world, the objective world of thinking, within the act of the self. The self is not only the lawgiver of nature, as Kant states, but also the creator of the world of objective reality.

How can the self create a world of objective reality? At this point we must pass to the intentionality context of morality from that of art; we must enter into the horizon of free will. Of course, in the natural world we cannot create even one atom or particle. But the natural world is not the world of true reality. At the base of the natural world is the world of history, and we are creative in this world. The moral self possesses its own content that is profounder than the natural world. If the moral self does not possess its own world, then we are forced to say that freedom of the will is merely freedom of choice. However, such an idea depends on thinking of nature as the only world of reality. The world of cognitive objects stands on the basis of normative consciousness, but normative consciousness is one aspect of moral consciousness. Without the self-consciousness of the free self, there can be no normative consciousness. When we say that a certain judgment is true or false, we have left the plane of mere objective knowledge and have already entered into the plane of the will, the teleological world. We can even interpret Lipps's 'demand of the object' as this kind of consciousness. When what is considered to be its object is impersonal, we see the world of knowledge outside; but when the object itself is personal, we can think that the demand of the object and the act of the self are one. At such a time things dissolve into the self and become infinite strata of acts within, for even the world of things is only an object of thinking that is one plane of personal acts. Just as a photographer moves back a bit to include a broader scene within his lens, so, too, are we able to include the world of things within the acts of the self by entering infinitely within the self. The plane of consciousness in general becomes included within the self and becomes normative consciousness; there must be an ethical imperative at the foundation of the logical imperative. At the base of the norms that fix the relationships among objects there must be a norm that unifies act and act. The moral law exists at the foundation of the law of contradiction; the latter is a projection of the former. An object must follow the norms of logic, while our submission to duty is submission to the law of contradiction between act and act. As Fichte states at the beginning of *Science of Knowledge,* there must be consciousness of self-identity, such as 'I am I' (*Ich bin Ich*), as an immediate fact at the foundation of the law of logical self-identity. The positive content of consciousness of self-identity is infinite self-respect and infinite self-love. The feeling of infinite self-respect arises when we face the foundation of our infinitely deep self. There is infinite self-love when there is the pure movement of entering within oneself. When we attempt to overcome contradiction and deepen the truth on the basis of the logical, normative consciousness, the sentiment of profound self-respect for our own self is involved. There can be no serious search for truth apart from this sentiment.

Considering Kant's statements "act as if the norm of your action becomes a universal law" and "treat the persons of yourself and others as ends in themselves," in what kind of behavior can one use his person as a goal in itself so that his behavior can become a universal law? The action of taking the only rice bowl from your table and your only garment to give to a person who is suffering from hunger and cold may involve regarding the person of another as an end in itself, and such behavior may also be able to become a universal law. However, to satisfy the material desires of another person does not mean to satisfy his spiritual needs. To succor his biological life is not directly to save the life of his soul. For the moral law to pass into reality from mere thought, it must possess some content. Of course, as Kant states, when the will attains some content, it cannot be said to be the absolutely good will. Even when the will desires the truth and seeks the beautiful, it cannot unconditionally be called the good will. However, when Kant states that if we want to know whether a false promise violates a duty, we should consider whether it can become a universal law, what makes us think that the false promise cannot become a universal law? We can even think this from the viewpoint of utilitarianism. But, needless to say, in Kant's standpoint we should not adulterate the moral sphere by the least utilitarian considerations. We must think this way from the idea of pure respect for law for its own sake.

If so, how can we purely honor law for its own sake, apart from every utilitarian motive? How can we act from the idea of honoring law for its own sake? Kant states that the reason is that only

human beings understand law and are rational beings who can conform to it. However, law must have some content, for there cannot be
law entirely without content. What kind of content do the laws that
we honor and act by have? Kant states that there must not be any
content to law; he states that we must act purely from the idea of
honoring law. However, to honor law must mean to honor its content. Law without any content cannot even be conceived of. Of course,
a mere understanding of law may remain apart from the content of
law, but understanding of law entirely separate from content must
be the same as an abstract universal concept, such as that of visual
and aural perception apart from color or sound.

Because a norm that deviates from its position by means of a
false promise destroys the norm itself, what does the fact that it cannot become a universal law mean? In his explanation, Kant states
that if we consider making an empty statement to be law, then, of
course, the original promise disappears, for it is useless to say anything concerning one's future behavior to another person who does
not believe in one's pretexts and who, even if he does believe them,
immediately deceives. However, does the fact that a false promise
destroys itself in this way mean that a promise cannot attain its goal
as a promise, or does it mean that the concept itself of a promise falls
into logical contradiction? If we say that the reason is that the promise
cannot be the goal of the promise itself, then there must be something
that is the goal of the promise. Moreover, if we follow Kant's position,
we cannot allow any content at all in moral law. Is no law possible,
then, unless it contains logical contradiction within its concept itself?
That a false promise is a promise that is not a promise may mean that
the concept itself is a logical contradiction, but such a merely logical
law cannot become the norm of our behavior. Kant's statement, too,
of course, does not merely mean that it is in contradiction as a concept. He thinks of it in the sense that it includes the condition of a
universal law. But it goes without saying that if people deceive each
other, such a thing as a promise cannot be established. But if the
criterion of whether a false promise can become a universal law does
not lie in the goal itself of the promise, then it is merely a law of
logical contradiction.

We can respect the law because it is the law and act morally
from the idea of pure respect for the law without any utilitarian motives because pure obedience to law is a perfection of human reason
and a goal of rational man. In this sense, the moral law possesses positive significance. The reason it is thought that the perfection of human life is heteronomous with respect to the strict moral standpoint

is that we have projected the demands of human life into the world of cognitive objects. The reason that Kant says that pure moral will must be formal and contentless is that he limited our content of consciousness to intellectual content. However, we cannot see the fact of seeing in the standpoint of cognition, but by "seeing seeing" we possess the infinite, objective world of art. We cannot hear the fact of hearing, but by "hearing hearing" we possess the infinite world of music. By being able to "will the will" the infinite worlds of history and of culture open up before us. In this way we can think that Kant's categorical imperative, which has been thought of as contentless, possesses infinitely rich content. Thus, the fact that keeping a promise possesses moral value does not merely mean that it becomes universal law, but that justice constitutes one factual aspect that constructs cultural phenomena as a great requirement of life.

Kant's statement that one must act so that one's own norm will become a universal law and that one must treat one's own and another's person as ends, must mean that we must not merely objectify the content of the pure act. The history of the free person opens up not by respecting the content of law, but by respecting law itself. The laws of ethics do not affirm their specific content, but, rather, negate them. With respect to the free development of the person, there is no such thing as a universal law similar to natural law. Even in the case of keeping a promise, if one is restrained by its content, it will hinder the free development of the person. Even our logical demands must be based on ethical requirements in the above sense. We can say that intellectual development is one aspect of the free development of the person and that the consciousness of logical value is one aspect of the consciousness of ethical value. Of course, truth is not directly the moral good, and there may even be instances in which being faithful to truth becomes incompatible with moral duty. However, there is no such thing as merely abstract good, apart from the synthetic unity of the infinite demands of human life. The reason Kant thought of the good in formal terms is that he did not recognize the transcendental nature of experiential content. It only seems as if intellectual conscience and moral conscience are incompatible when one adheres to a partial standpoint. Various truths may be established on various a priori, but concrete truth must exist in the teleological unity of these truths. We are able to discover this meaning even at the place where Kant thought that mathematical knowledge becomes objective knowledge by acquiring sensory content.

We are able to think of various instances of the relation between knowledge and morality. Always to advance faithfully toward

truth requires a faithful character in one regard. The sincere search
for truth must be based on the sentiment of profound self-respect.
The pursuit of the resolution of the contradictions of thought lies in
our direct search for the unity of the person. Moreover, when knowledge possesses practical content, knowledge and morality have not
only this kind of indirect relationship, but a direct relationship, as
well. But if we think of what may be called the content of morality
without making a distinction between knowledge and morality in the
above way, then what sort of a thing is true duty in regard to the idea
that the good is considered to be duty for duty's sake?

The highest duty for us must be the actualization of that
which has value in itself. We may be able to think that the pursuit of
truth is one such duty. Thus, without even regarding knowledge itself
as the good, we may be able to think that the advance of intellectual
content naturally influences our views of life and changes the meaning of human life itself. Within knowledge there are also elements
that have significance only as means in human life. But the deeper
even scientific knowledge becomes, the more it comes to have direct
significance in human life itself. Reconstruction of the basic concepts
of scientific knowledge must influence human life itself. Philosophy
is knowledge in such a sense. Even in the instance I first mentioned,
we can think superficially that the content of knowledge and morality
do not seem to have any relation. We can even hold that with regard
to any kind of content of knowledge, if we are faithful in its pursuit,
we shall not lose our integrity of character. But, even if another person thinks that the values of both knowledge and its pursuit are unrelated, they must not be unrelated in this way within the person
concerned. If that person himself pursues the truth while thinking
that knowledge is without significance, it will directly destroy that
person's moral character. In order to demand an ethical value, such
as a person's behavior's being sincere, that person must view the
knowledge he is seeking as something that has value. To be able to
separate moral from intellectual value is the attitude of the bystander
and not of the person concerned. In the horizon of behavior the good
of the goal must be the good of the behavior, for content and form
are inseparable. As far as another person is concerned, I think that
it cannot be held that there are two standards in morality, even in
the case when in form it is seen as good but in content it is seen as
nongood.

In knowledge we may still be able to separate form and content or even think that, although the content is erroneous, the form
of the logic as such is not destroyed thereby. But in the form of good

will we demand that the form itself become the good of content. The form of logic does not necessarily imply truth of content, but the form of morality demands the goodness of content, for it is the form of teleological unity. The logical process can advance a given hypothesis as a hypothesis; but the good will cannot allow its motive to stand on a hypothesis. The moral good will is the behavior of the self seeking union with the absolute good. Of course, no one can possibly know the absolute good, but pursuit of this union on the basis of faith in an absolute good is the raison d'être of the good will. That such formal good as good will can be thought to have value in itself must be true in this sense. The content of the good will is not the means to another, but, rather, must have value in itself; it must be the content of pure value consciousness. The purity of such consciousness is the reason that the person can be thought to be an end in himself.

In this perspective, knowledge for the sake of knowledge must also be regarded as one content of the good will. Perhaps even devotion to a valueless thing can be thought of as moral, but devotion for its own sake is not true devotion. Devotion on behalf of the highest objective is what makes devotion truly devotion. The pragmatists, who think of knowledge merely as a means and holds that it is difficult to know the content of life, or if not that, seem to think that knowledge is without relation to the person, would seem to be bound by the theory of correspondence. Knowledge is one process of the internal development of personal content, and there is nothing that can be termed true knowledge apart from the internal development of the person. Of course, the good of content is not directly the good of the will, and good will must possess some quality apart from the good of content. However, the person is not merely the sum of various contents. Between the good will and the truth there must be an internal relationship beyond merely selecting the fact that good will takes truth as that which has value. The content of concrete truth can be thought to be directly personal content.

Kant states that mathematical knowledge is not knowledge; it only becomes true knowledge by uniting with perception. The Marburg school also holds the knowledge becomes objective by returning to its concrete foundation. But the most concrete foundation for us is precisely that personal content that is the immediate content of the will. Knowledge must ultimately attain the standpoint of behavior. We can say that the highest truth is the highest good. There is profound meaning in Plato's thought that the Idea of the Good was above all the other Ideas in dignity and power. Needless to say, knowledge is true in various intentionalities. For example, algebra is true in the standpoint of algebra, and geometry in the standpoint of geometry; the truth of algebra is what it is, regardless of its applicability to geometry. However, advance in a single abstract standpoint apart from the entire system of knowledge would merely end in meaningless play. The fact that one kind of knowledge can be purified in its own standpoint may be superficially thought to be a departure from the unity of the whole. But as the essence of that knowledge is clarified, the unity of the entire system of knowledge is also clarified. In this way, the autonomous unification of knowledge means the return to its concrete foundation, and its objectification. It is, as it were, to follow the moral good of knowledge itself. For example, analytic geometry did not simply arise for the sake of convenience in algebra, but, rather, from the demand for a deeper concrete unity at the foundation of both. For this kind of union to have meaning as the development of concrete knowledge, algebra must be purified in the standpoint of algebra, and geometry in the standpoint of geometry.

We must thus recognize various intentionalities in knowledge, but truth is established on the basis of the idea of an infinitely unattainable internal unity. Only because of the ideal of truth are we able to affirm the value of knowledge; knowledge separated from the system of knowledge must be valueless as knowledge. Mathematicians often make the comment that geometry is nothing more than invariant groups, but to establish groups there must be an intuition at their foundation. Of course, such intuition is not intuition in the sense of seeing by the eye. Since the goal of knowledge itself is to become objective, if we consider that objectivity means to attain synthetic unity, then for geometry to have meaning as truth it must be a requirement of the goal of knowledge and a manifestation of the ideal of knowledge.

From the standpoint of pure number such a construction may be thought to be merely artificial. However, such a question as what kind of subgroups exist within groups must await the guidance of intuition. The principle of particularization does not arise simply from abstract universality. Such union must await the manifestation of concrete unity. It must depend upon the development of the universal that is dynamic in itself. I wonder whether it is not true that here lies the reason "geometry as a science" possesses its own a priori, for people who think that geometry is merely artificial do not recognize this kind of internal intuition. If we consider dynamics to be based on the concepts of time, space, and quantity, apart from the concept of force, as Hertz attempted to do in construction dynamics, then the a priori of dynamics is lost and dynamics becomes superficially nothing more than the application of mathematics. But the concept of force is not the mere union of the concepts of time, space, and quantity. We cannot think that in the establishment of dynamic relations force emerges from the concept of number itself. Herein, too, there must still be a transcendental creation.

I think that the concept of force cannot be established without the internal experience of pure will. Perhaps we can analyze the relations of force and reduce them to mathematical ones; but force is not merely the artificial union of mathematical relations. In distinguishing whether a synthetic unity of a certain relationship is transcendental or artificial, it can be clarified by knowing whether or not an objective world is constructed by it. I think that in investigating whether or not a certain body of knowledge is merely an application, it will be clarified by ascertaining whether its unity is heteronomous or autonomous. When the unity itself is productive, we cannot view it as mere application. Purpose and the act fuse and construct an objective world, infinite in itself. In the above sense, I think that geometry and dynamics each possesses its own a priori, and neither is merely an applied science.

At the foundation of knowledge there is the ideal of the good, there is teleological unity. The fact that knowledge becomes objective means that knowledge advances toward that foundation. The moral significance of the behavior of many scholars in the past who committed themselves to pure learning must be in this sense.

In the correspondence theory, the goal of knowledge may be the attainment of the complete view of that which one is attempting to know. But if we consider the epistemological problem from the idea that "what is given is that which has been sought," then the goal of knowledge lies in the constructive fact of knowing itself. Moreover, since this kind of subjective activity itself is the objective object and is cultural reality, true moral behavior cannot exist apart from the construction of such reality. No matter how abstract knowledge is, it must have personal significance when it has been reflected upon in the deep foundation of knowledge—that is, when from the standpoint of the a priori underlying all a priori the a priori itself has been reflected upon. There is profound self-conscious experience at the foundation of knowledge. We cannot even know number without the experience of self-consciousness. True infinity does not advance toward the outside, but enters deeply within.

The task of philosophy lies in clarifying personal meaning at the foundation of knowledge in this sense; it is the reflection upon a priori from the standpoint of the a priori underlying all a priori.

The independent domain of philosophy and the significance of the
unity of knowledge lie in this. Philosophy is established on the 'Idea
of the Good'. Philosophy is reflection on reason itself and is the self-
consciousness of reason itself. Just as art emerges by discovering personal content at the foundation of perception and sensation, so, too,
does philosophy emerge by discovering personal content at the foundation of objective knowledge. When knowledge becomes philosophy,
it can touch the person itself internally. Indeed, it constitutes one
element of the person. Just as musical feeling becomes the beauty of
content itself in lyric poetry, so, too, does knowledge itself become
the good by becoming philosophy. Herein form and content fuse. We
have no person apart from reason. The self-consciousness of reason
itself must always stir the person. In true moral behavior there is
nothing more noble than the reform of the person himself. The so-
cialist who shouts in the street may give food and clothing to people,
but he cannot reform the human heart from within. Knowledge
emerges from actual practice. But, as with every other cultural re-
source, the more knowledge is purified, the more it cannot help
changing man himself. Astronomy, which arose from the necessity of
tilling the soil and navigating the seas, finally caused Kepler to be
called a god.

Are truth and good, then, directly identical? Are there no
cases where knowledge and morality conflict with each other? While
I expect much opposition, I firmly assert the identity of the two, since
I believe in teleological unity at the base of knowledge and since I
believe in the Idea of the Good. The idea that the two are mutually
opposed is based upon leaning toward one abstract side of either of
them. Such an abstraction involves the separation of knowledge from
its goal and signifies that morality goes against its own goal and destroys its essence. Truth and good must fuse in knowledge of man
himself. Mere natural scientific knowledge is not directly related to
morality. The direct imposition of law on man through natural-
scientific knowledge by taking academic research as the only goal and
thereby neglecting duty and sacrificing other things can be thought
to be the divorce of learning and morality. However, the former is
based on the incompleteness of knowledge; and in the latter it is not
that content clashes, but, rather, suppresses other demands of human
life. In other words, evil arises when that which leans one-sidedly to
one given demand destroys the larger unity of the person itself.

When we forget the duties of society and abandon love of
mankind or when we are idly absorbed in learning and art, then,
even if each of these has value in itself, our behavior cannot escape

moral censure. In such a case, why must we suffer moral censure? If
it is merely on behalf of the many material requirements of man, the
pursuit of value in itself may be praiseworthy as the work of man.
That social service and charity have a moral value even greater than
learning and art must mean that these actions themselves have value.
However, at this point we must again fall into the contradiction that
I mentioned previously. To work for the sake of man is nothing more
than to aspire to make man's life more secure and to elevate it. But
we cannot seek the elevation of man outside of such things as learning and art.

What does it mean to say that moral behavior has value beyond these cultural values? That which is not value as the means of
another but which has value in itself must have its own objective
world and be creative. Something without content must be the means
of another. Something independent must contain relations within
itself and be infinitely productive and must be value *qua* reality. The
superiority of one value over another must mean that both former
and latter stand on the basis of teleological unity and that the former,
as the concrete totality, embraces the latter. The superiority of the
moral good over other cultural values as the supreme value does not
lie in the fact of duty for duty's sake or love for love's sake; it must
have an independent, objective world that synthesizes and unifies the
world of other values. It must be something such as the extremely
poetic Homeric valley that Plato discusses in *Philebus*. The content
of concrete unity that opens the door to every human desire, even to
sensual lust, fame, and wealth, and that cannot be analyzed into any
desires behind it must be discovered. To be rational in sensory experience does not mean to neglect the authority and prestige of the senses,
but, rather, to find an objective world on the basis of the synthetic
unity of these experiences. Similarly, rationality in moral behavior
does not mean negating various desires, as the ascetic maintains, but,
rather, it lies in penetrating deeply to the root of desire and discovering there a free, objective world.

Therefore, morality is not separate from historical content.
If we consider nature to be the only reality, the significance of moral
behavior appears. I think that the reason Kant had to postulate the
immortality of the soul and the existence of God was that he thought
of morality also in completely formal terms. Each of our actions, as
in the poem "The Lady of Shalott," has the significance of a rigorous
imperative only as something that is woven on the loom of history,
the concrete foundation of nature, by the shuttle of 'time'. From the
standpoint of Kant, such an idea may be thought to run counter to

the autonomy of morality, as in the 'theory of perfection'. However, the perfection of a thing, in contrast to the perfection of man, may be heteronomous and the content of the goal of our self; but the content of the will in itself is not heteronomous. Formal morality, on the contrary, is merely subjective. Our individual person is not the sum of knowledge, feeling, and the will. Rather, as these things are expressions of the whole person, the culture of a given period must be the expression of objective spirit. Truth, goodness, and beauty have their foundation here. The more mature culture becomes, the clearer this unity becomes.

Heinrich Stein states that the temples of Greece are the forms that grew from the root of the lofty human life that was given by both the natural environment and the way of life in Greece. We do not exist merely for the sake of existing, but together with our neighbor we recognize personal value in one another and respect and love one another as the builders of culture. The moral imperative also emerges from this viewpoint. Of course, I have great respect for the patriotic activity of Fichte, but I do not necessarily condemn the fact that Hegel was quietly writing his *Phenomenologie* as the artillery of Napoleon's army sounded in the streets of Jena. The decision as to what kind of behavior is truly good must await the judgment of history. If the truth or falsehood of physical knowledge can be tested, as Planck states, by means of the unity of the world of physical symbols, then the good or evil of behavior and the objectivity of morality must be tested in the world of historical reality, which is the objective world of the will; the objectivity of morality is established thereby. Therefore, the first meaning of morality does not lie in acting superficially in accordance with dead customs, but, rather, in a deep consideration of cultural spirit. The good will takes understanding that is modest and equitable toward cultural spirit as its condition.

As I have discussed, teleological unity is at the foundation of knowledge, and knowledge must attain to personal content by returning to its concrete foundation. If we consider that the self-consciousness of knowledge itself in this kind of personal standpoint is philosophy, then in philosophy knowledge must be the union of art and morality. In art, even the description of nature is not merely the description of external things. Its essence is personal content. Just as art that takes man as its object is beautiful and true, so the work of the pure theoretical scientist is also not description of nature from the outside, but a personal, constructive act. When such knowledge becomes self-conscious in itself, it must come to have the elements of feeling in the will as philosophy. Knowledge must touch behavior at its ultimate point. Such a direction is not something to which knowledge is heteronomous; it is the direction toward its own goal—that is, knowledge particularizes its own content and arrives at the particular from the universal. Knowledge attains its own objectivity thereby. Knowledge, as it becomes particular, attains immovable objectivity; the foundation of the feeling of factuality lies herein.

We may say that there is nothing to gain from the unity of truth and life. Whether algebra is synthesized with geometry or not has no relation whatsoever to the truth of algebra; and we may also be able to speak this way even in the relationship between dynamics and experimental fact. However, just as Kant states that thought without content is empty, I think that our thought must unite with intuition in order to become objective truth. Mere abstract truth is only a dream of transcendental subjectivity. Truth is that which every man must recognize, but it does not need to be universal. The fact that knowledge can attain universal validity means that it enters deeply within itself and hence unites with the transcendental will. Concrete truth must, rather, be sought in the direction of particularizing unity. Every kind of knowledge can attain true objectivity only in the unity of life in the deepest sense. Just as art demands philosophy, so, too, does philosophy demand art. The concrete spirit possesses its knowledge in philosophy and at the same time possesses feeling in art and will in morality. I think that by entering into the profound unity of life and expressing it, philosophy attains something similar to what dynamics attains by uniting with empirical fact. This certain thing itself seeks its expression as art and its realization as morality. It is not that knowledge finds its exemplification by being concretized; but it can accomplish new development only in the direction of concretization. Without intuition there can be no development of knowledge. If we consider that morality, which is the unity of our behavior, is the concrete unity of culture and the form of particularization, then art and philosophy, as well, unify and are unified and come to possess infinitely new content, in this standpoint. Only the morally pure character—or, at least, only when one is morally pure —can be creative in philosophy and art and can truly grasp the new content of life. Even "duty for duty's sake" and "act as if the norm of your behavior was to become a universal law" must be meaning that seeks to be pure in such a horizon of behavior.

3

I have stated that something like music can be considered to be purely sensory; but, even in the arts, there are such things as lyric poetry in which the content of thinking maintains itself while continuing to be aesthetic; and that the problem of human life itself can become the content of art, especially in the theater. But adulteration by the content of thinking in its pure state seems to destroy the arts of music and painting. As Max Klinger states, the ideal of the painter is the development of form appropriate to the position of the body, relationships with space, and the arrangement of colors, and it does not matter whether the subject is the mythical Endymion or the mortal aesthetician Pater. Even in lyric poetry one must not confuse the beauty of poetry with the truth or artificiality of content. However, sensation is not as anti-intellectual as is usually thought; it is not simply the irrationally given. If it were what the psychologist terms sensation, no art whatsoever could emerge from it. We can say that, just as sensation becomes the material of knowledge by being applied to the principle of the anticipation of perception, it first becomes the material of art by being further applied to the profounder principle of the anticipation of the will. To become the object of the free self in this way must mean to return to an even deeper and more concrete foundation of the sensation of sound, color, and form. It must mean to penetrate to the foundation of the self.

At the same time that we can think this way concerning the content of art that is intuitive, we must recognize personal content, also, at the foundation of conceptual knowledge. As I have stated, philosophy is the self-consciousness of knowledge, and we can say that in philosophy conceptual knowledge becomes aesthetic. Of course, intellectual content does not possess any authority in sensory art, and objectivity of knowledge is not the point. Conversely, philosophy that has neglected the objectivity of intellectual content cannot be said to be true philosophy. In lyric poetry more than in music and in drama more than in lyric poetry, intellectual content itself becomes aesthetic, but the truth can be called the beautiful in art when it takes man himself as object. I think that we also touch philosophical truth in the consummation of this kind of aesthetic truth. Of course, there may be many objections to thinking of truth and beauty as similar in this way. However, there is nothing that is both false and beautiful. In things that emerge from an impure goal and in things that are merely technically adept, we cannot recognize aesthetic value, no matter how brilliantly contrived they are. In something truly beautiful we must come in contact with some immovably objective value at its basis. It goes without saying that art does not reproduce factual truth. Art, in essence, does not aim at reproduction of conceptual, factual truth. It is not artificial in that it no longer has such goals, for artificiality that confesses to being artificial is not artificial. On the contrary, even in myths and children's stories there are many profound, human feelings. From these we can discover more of the eternal truths of human life than from history.

Of course, what is felt as true in this sense is neither felt as factual truth, nor as causal law, which we must follow. However, we can only sense a certain objective thing in it such as we feel in truth. In art, expression itself is truth. Technique itself must be truth. Aesthetic content and intellectual content approach each other as the material that is the means of expression becomes more representational than sensory and as it becomes conceptual. Even Kant's consciousness in general is not a mere synthetic consciousness, but a creative act. The essence of the transcendental self must be the transcendental will of which Fichte speaks; there must be behavior prior to knowledge. As Hildebrand states, in his famous Problem of Form, pure visual perception is the unity of visual factors and tactile factors. In an ordinary person the relation between these elements lacks clarity; truly to unite them successfully is the task of the artist. The sculptor takes the tactile elements as material and unifies them visually. The painter, on the contrary, adds tactile elements to visual elements as the basis. The space that the artist and sculptor take as object is not identical with the space of conceptual thought. Fiedler states that in the standpoint of pure visual perception an infinite prospect opens up; similarly, this kind of space must be the infinite behavior such as Fichte's 'act'. If the fact that the act becomes free and creative apart from the bonds of the object means that we are personally free, then we may be able to say that this kind of behavior is also one kind of moral behavior. Hildebrand further states that, even though the kind of factors the artist selects from among the infinite material that nature gives him depends upon the individuality of the artist, the artist must always follow the laws that obtain between visual and tactile elements. Still, the artist's goal is not merely such objective relationships but, rather, lies in the form of things. This form of things is not merely the universal form of things, but one that has individuality—that is, it must be an individual reality. This individuality is the individuality of things and at the same time the individuality of the artist. Our regarding a work of art as the expression of the artist's individuality must have this meaning. The fact that various associations come to be added to color and form must be in this standpoint. It is not exactly that we *remember* the times of the past by smelling the scent of a rose, but that we *smell* the memory of the old days within the scent of the rose. This is the reason that it can be thought that the content of art has an inseparable relationship with sensory content.

The truth of the painter and the sculptor must be infinitely individual truth in the world of pure visual perception. Moreover, in the establishment of this kind of factual truth we must think of such a thing as the plane of pure visual perception in general, which supplements the plane of consciousness in general. A work of art, as a reality based on this latter standpoint, always constructs a world by being unified into one system. The history of art must express the development of this world. Some may say that it is inappropriate to call that which does not include the concept of 'time' a world of fact, but 'time' is merely the form of the internal development of the concrete universal. 'Time', the foundation of the world of fact, may also be thought to be the universal of such form. When we feel beauty in a work of art, it is not merely that we have a pleasurable feeling with regard to it, but that we feel objective life in it. We discover truth in the world of pure visual perception. In this sense beauty is precisely truth. It is the same as discovering historical truth in the plane of consciousness in general.

If we say that the nonconceptual constitutes truth, various objections may arise. But truth is not that which is established merely by conceptual relations. Rather, at the foundation of conceptual truth there must always be a creative intuition. We can think that the various meanings of truth can be established by the quality of this creative intuition. Of course, in history we cannot say that because something is beautiful it is true; nor can the true be said directly to be beautiful. However, when we feel cosmic life in the background of historical truth, we can have a kind of aesthetic feeling with regard to it. This is religious emotion. It can be thought that the relationship of historical truth to religious content is very similar to the relationship that Hildebrand speaks of between the relations among both visual and tactile factors and aesthetic content. That one must not distort historical fact by religious emotion is similar to the viewpoint that the artist or sculptor must not distort the form of things by feeling. We must view truth just as it is. All falsehood destroys the beautiful and defiles the sacred. Just as truth means to look at the form of things as they are without preconception, religious feeling means to view historical fact just as it is.

True religious feeling must be an absolutely humble attitude. It must be an attitude in which one has wholly effaced the self; not only does one abandon the intellectual self, but the emotional and volitional selves, as well. Sacred religious feeling appears when one has abandoned one's entire person. When we know truth, we must abandon the self and conform to truth itself. To view a thing aesthetically must mean to submerge the self within the thing in itself. In abandoning the self, one conforms to objectivity itself. But since learning cannot unite the emotions and the will, it is thereby subjective; since art cannot unite knowledge, it is subjective. Religious feeling emerges when one has become objective in either sense. Often aesthetic feeling and religious feeling are viewed as the same, but the object of religion must be reality. A sense of reality must be included within religious feeling. Religion is not mere appreciation and pleasure; it must include a profound adoration of truth and sincere practice. Religion is often thought to be antirational. Just as it can be said that "in the true Dharma there is nothing strange," an antirational religion would be nothing more than superstition. Even the depreciation of the search for truth, which is often found in men of religion, can already be said to be going against the feeling of religious humility.

As the psychologist often states that the representation of the sun does not shine, the fact that it can be thought that there is an unbridgeable gap between sensation and representation and between sensation and concepts, is one aspect of truth, but not the whole truth. There may be a world of difference between space as an object of art and space as an object of geometry, but I think that there is some essential relationship between the two. The above idea arises from the premise that the acts of sensation, representation, and thinking are fundamentally different. If we think, like Brentano, that the qualities of acts are based on the qualities of their immanent objects, then when we view or remember red and when we see or think of space, there must be some internal relationship between the acts themselves. In natural phenomena, perhaps, continuity in such a sense may not have significance in actual fact. However, in spiritual phenomena, which are meaning *qua* reality, the meaning of real continuity is in the continuity of meaning expressed by the same words. In such a case, language as the direct expression of thinking possesses significance beyond the psychical act.

Usually it is thought that our spiritual phenomena, which appear and disappear in time, are unified by the spatial unity of the body, but I think that the unity of various acts that are psychologically distinguishable can be unified by an expressive unity that transcends them. The objectivity of meaning or reality means that they transcend the changes of various acts. When we sense, represent, remember, and think about red, it must be objectively unified. We may be able to say that the representation and the concept of red differ. However, if we adhere to such an idea strictly, we must think that objective reality changes according to the act, which shifts from moment to moment, even though it is in the same sensation. In this way there would ultimately be no way for such an object to be established. An objective object may be thought to change according to the act, but at the same time red must retain its self-identity as red. When an object that does not change according to the act is thought of as an object of a given act, it is thought of as 'simply objective' from the standpoint of another act. That which we usually think of as objective is the objective world of mere thinking, while, on the contrary, the world of objective objects that continue through the changes of acts becomes the world of expression as the objective world of the act underlying all acts. Therefore, in this standpoint we discover the conceptual within the sensory and the sensory within the conceptual, and meaning and reality unite. If we can say that we see a certain thing, recollect it, and think of it, then we have to recognize the objective world of the act underlying all acts, the objective world of the expressive act therein. From language to art, all structures are established in this intentionality. Art attains the ideal, which is the essence of sensation, in this direction. Even the fact that sensation is applied to the principle of the 'anticipation of perception' must be in this standpoint.

To enter into the essence of the world of sensation does not mean to enter into a world different from that of thought. When the musician attains freedom in sound, he enters into the world of musical thought. His experience is not of mere sound, for it includes infinite memory, and he enters into a world that includes infinite thought. It is said that the musical spirit became independent of poetry in Mozart and Beethoven. But Beethoven's music that sings of the battle with destiny could not have achieved such heights without being rich in profound philosophical thought and heroic spirit. Of course, even such a term as *musical thought* may invite opposition from some people. However, profound accomplishment in art does not mean to become unconscious. He who truly knows sensation is not one who has been captured by sensation, but one who has been able to free himself from it. He is one who is able to use sensation freely. He must be one who stands in the standpoint of the free self. He must be a person who stands in the horizon in which he feels, remembers, and thinks of a certain thing. By entering into this horizon, sensation can include infinite memory and thought. Max Liebermann states that a good painting is only a painting that has been well conceived. No matter how correct the form and how beautiful the colors, if it lacks something internal, it is nothing more than a piece of painted canvas. He further states that art can live only by means of imagination. Imagination must fill the artist to his very fingertips.

Of course, the essence that is at the foundation of the various arts must not be regarded as being directly identical with thought. Rembrandt replied to a pupil's question about "how to paint well" that the pupil should "first take up his brush," for the thought of the artist never departs from his brush. The artist thinks through his technique. Each artistic thought has its own unique characteristic that cannot be expressed by another, and at the same time each has its limitation therein. For example, in language the freer the means of expression becomes, the more deeply and superbly it can express the world of thought. Just as in Bergson's philosophy there is one stream of biological life that assumes various forms, so does our spiritual life take various forms. Each area of life possesses its own value, and at the same time—just as it can be said that the bones in the necks of the giraffe and of the whale are equal in number—they equally exemplify the flow of one life-force. Althought poetry as thought is freer than architecture and music, this does not mean that it is superior as art; we cannot help recognizing that there are naturally differing significances and positions of the elements of cultural life, which is the concrete unity of the entire spiritual life. As long as the person is not a mere union of various acts, as long as our lives are not so many unrelated changes, then it must be thought that they have a center and a direction.

The self is that which sees, hears, recollects, thinks, desires, and moves things. The object, in respect to the self, is seen, is heard, is recollected, and at the same time must become the object of thinking and of behavior. That which unifies various objective worlds in this way is precisely the most concrete unity given to us. What we see and hear is not true reality; true reality must be the object of thinking. Indeed, even a mere object of thinking is not reality, for true reality must be that which is one with experiential content. The objective world of cognition is still not concrete reality, which is immediately given. As long as it is universal and abstract, it is a world that can be conceived of in various ways. Immovable and unique concrete reality is established by means of the actual will. Moreover, that will is not merely a transcendent will; it must be a specific will that has content. What is immovable for us is the actual will, for the actual will is precisely the self. The object of the actual will—indeed, the actual will itself—has access to all objective worlds and moreover is continuous—that is, it is a concrete reality that unifies various objective worlds.

In the actual will subject and object are one, and the self functions in the horizon of behavior. This is precisely the horizon of absolute will. To enter into true reality that is the object of this kind of actual will is aesthetic activity. To enter into this reality, the whole body must become one living power, one activity. True actuality is not a point that has been determined by the forms of space and time; on the contrary, it is something that projects consciousness in general internally. True reality contains the advance of the infinite ideal within experience itself. Particular unity, individual unity, sees unity in an infinite direction. The artist does not think idly without taking up his brush. Only when he takes up his brush and faces the canvas does it become clear how he should paint, and an infinite direction opens up before him.

I think that by proceeding along this road we attain to the moral world. The moral world is not something which can take abstract universal law as its point of departure; rather, like art, its points of departure are actual facts. It enters deeply into the totality of reality that is seen, heard, thought, desired. Morality is not separate from art, learning, and the various desires. It enters infinitely deeply into their foundation. Moral social phenomena appear on this kind of pathway. We may be able to satisfy the demands of the actual self through the actual self directly. But from the standpoint of the self, which is a unity of past, present, and future, we must have different demands. Just as in cognition we enter into the object of recollection from the object of feeling, and from the object of recollection into the object of thought, so do moral, social phenomena come to appear even in the direction of impulse when we proceed in the direction of such reality. Reality entirely independent in itself is a unity, as well as infinite differentiation and development; it possesses infinite contradictions within itself—indeed, contradiction itself becomes the unity. The direction of unity in concrete reality is aesthetic subjectivity. The direction of its differentiation and development is the moral imperative. Thus both aesthetic intuition and the moral will take reality as their points of departure. But the moral will in such a direction is opposed to aesthetic intuition at the point of being an infinite endeavor to reach its ultimate point. Unity at the ultimate point of morality must no longer be art, but religion. Religion transcends and includes knowledge; it transcends and includes morality, as well. Therefore, religion in one aspect resembles art, but, like morality, it is thoroughly rigorous and practical.

Chapter 6

Society and the Individual

1

Some persons hold that actual society is itself the direct manifestation of ethical value; others seek the basis of ethical values wholly in the subjective demands of the individual. Now, the relationship between society and the individual is an important question of ethics, but society does not produce ethical values simply because it is a group of many individuals; nor is the psychological individual directly the basis of ethical values. The concepts of society and the individual are merely distinctions of a psychological reality that is reflected onto the world of intellectual objects. The truly meaningful and fundamental opposition in ethics is not that expressed in the distinction between two existing things, but between nature and freedom. If we carry this line of thought to its logical conclusion, we can say that it lies in the opposition between act and object. The individual who has autonomy over and above society is not the psychological individual, but must be the free person latent in the depths of the so-called individual. The reformer, too, can have moral value, as one who discloses such personal content. Thus, the bearer of direct moral value is not the self united with the body; it must be self-conscious free behavior at each and every moment. This free self vanishes without a trace from moment to moment in time, yet it must be the self that transcends time and is eternally present. In this horizon of freedom, the distinction between the individual and society is comparable to the difference in size of circles in the same plane.

On the one hand, the self may be thought to be part of nature, which is the world of cognitive objects; on the other hand, it is directly one with what I call absolute free will. As Boehme said, "Wherever you stand and go, there is heaven." Psychology contends that consciousness begins from impulse. But we must recognize that even sensation, which is merely given, has a certain transcendent thing behind it as concrete sensation. Even in the background of the consciousness of the simple motion of one's own hand there is a transcendent thing that cannot be completely analyzed. Infinity contained within finitude must be the essence of consciousness itself.

We can think that when this kind of transcendent thing becomes manifest—that is, when it becomes self-conscious—it becomes the act of thinking. Thinking can thus be thought to be the legislator of nature. However, in the act of thinking the self is still constrained by the object. We can only enter into the world of the creative, free self and into the world of moral duty by transcending the objective world of thinking. Just as it can be thought that the content of thinking is included in the background of sensory experience and sensory experience is grounded on the content of thinking, personal content can be thought to be included in the background of the objective world of thinking and the volitional self to be included at the foundation of the intellectual self. We may say that our world of experience is based on the unity of the pure ego, but the self that constructs the world of reality must possess a tendency of realization in some direction; it must possess some goal, and thus a unique world of reality is constructed. It is said that time as a schema constructs the real world, but 'time' must be a flow in some direction. If not, it is no different from space. If we consider that 'time' is the form of the act of imagination, then the act of imagination that takes the schema of 'time' as its form is not some passive act of imagination but must be active. Indeed, we can think that the act of the active imagination, as the constructive act of reality, rather includes the act of judgment of so-called abstract thinking; the former thus becomes an even more concrete standpoint than the latter. The will is the highest standpoint that takes this kind of active imagination as its material and unifies it. The will unifies and gives a unique direction to infinite, active imagination.

Even in psychology, in the case of a volitional decision we first imagine various instances actively, and then the will selects and decides upon one of them. The act of active imagination may thus be said to be one part of the will. We must recognize the free self that transcends and includes the intellectual self at the foundation of the pure self, which thus cognizes the world of reality by means of its own unity. The standpoint of this transcendental will is already included in the background of sensory experience also, and hence consciousness may be thought to be always rooted in the horizon of free will. This is also the reason that it may be thought that knowledge acquires true objectivity by combining with sensory experience and that factual knowledge possesses authority over and above mere thinking. That an actual fact has absolute authority as something irrational does not depend upon its contingency as given material; it depends upon its being a determination of the absolute free self itself, for it is an expression of the depths of the self itself. It has an absolute character not because it is irrational, but because it is transrational.

Actuality is the focal point in which absolute will reflects itself. It is the road along which history advances. Therefore, something actually given can be thought to be immovable, and at the same time the self can be felt as free only in actuality. In actuality we cannot say that a red thing is blue or that a hot thing is cold. However, in actuality we can find the self within that which is red or hot. It is the self that desires that a red thing be blue and that a hot thing be cold, but also the self that views a red thing as red and feels a hot thing as hot. Consciousness of the contradictions of the self simultaneously implies the potentiality of its unity. This, in turn, implies the infinite freedom of the self in actuality.

A self viewed as born in a certain place on a certain day of a certain year, possessing certain features and characteristics and having a certain kind of life history and dying in a certain way, is a self as an object of thought. This objective self does not differ from the self of others on the point of its being an object of knowledge. However, the place at which the self is distinguished from other selves is none other than the internal synthesis of the individual unity in the background of this kind of temporal phenomenon of the self that is functioning in actuality. What does internal synthesis mean in this case? It must mean that the knower is the known and that the actor is that which is acted upon and that knowing is acting and vice versa. In the horizon of the true self, there is the identity of the objective object and subjective act.

Needless to say, a self that transcends space and time is nothing more than an abstract concept. But, while the self is part of the world of time and space, in another dimension it must be thought to participate in the world of eternal Ideas, which transcend space and time. The particularity of the self is one that immanently includes the universal. It is transcendent in the sense that the self includes all kinds of objective worlds within itself and enters infinitely deeply into itself. The concrete self includes the plane of consciousness in general within itself. This may be a logical contradiction, but this kind of contradiction is the condition for the existence of our consciousness and is the essence of the self. Life does not exist in the uni-

versal separated from the particular or the particular separated from
the universal. There is true life in the horizon where the particular
and the universal intersect.

When the universal is included within the particular, there
must be that which develops naturally—that is, it must become conscious. We can thus think that the more it becomes internally contradictory, the clearer consciousness becomes. Our self-consciousness
emerges only in the horizon of self-realization of the transcendent
will. Therefore, it is thoroughly particular and present. Our self does
not arise in the objective world of consciousness in general. Consciousness in general is nothing more than a process of self-development. Just as Heraclitus stated that in dreams each man returns to his
own world, so, too, we are not born in the world of things, but are
first born in the world of dreams. The objective world shared in common by everyone cannot avoid being an unreal world comprised of
abstract subjectivity. We always think of the world of reality with
our own actual will as the center.

2

Usually morality is considered to exist in the relation between the 'I' and the 'Thou', but I submit that it also obtains between
the 'I' and the 'I'. Just as the 'I' has responsibility and duties toward
others, so does one's 'I' in the present have responsibility and duties
to itself. As we have responsibilities toward our ancestors and descen-
dants, the present self must also have moral responsibilities toward
its own past and future selves. We only become moral beings as we
transcend the objective world of cognition and become free in ourselves—that is, by internally subsuming the plane of consciousness in
general and becoming infinitely creative. The world of the moral will,
needless to say, is the horizon of the relationship between free persons.
The free person can become free of itself only by recognizing the free
person of another. This kind of I-Thou relationship already has its
basis within personal self-consciousness. In our self-consciousness,
each act, as a continuity of pure acts, is acting *qua* knowing; similarly,
the personal relationship of the infinite free will must be at the basis
of consciousness of the free will—that is, the free self—which recognizes the self in the actual present to be free. There is thus a moral
society at the foundation of personal consciousness.

Thinking does not appear in the plane of mere perceptual
consciousness. Instinctive animal life may be regarded as a continuity
of mere perceptual consciousness, but a case in which a certain act is
not developed is not the same as that in which it is not essentially

included. Just as every kind of perceptual consciousness can be considered to be impulsive, we cannot help thinking that it also includes something ideal. The identity of meaning and reality is the condition for the establishment of consciousness. Self-consciousness in this sense is thinking. However, thinking is not of itself acting. There must be something that moves it at the foundation of thinking, or, in other words, there must be the will. The will moves thinking, so to speak. A phenomenon of consciousness can have a deeper reality than a natural thing by being self-generative—that is, by having the will as its foundation. For a spiritual phenomenon to have reality in itself as a spiritual phenomenon, even if it is in the form of impulsive consciousness, there must be at its ground a certain personal thing that cannot be analyzed into natural scientific causality. Our consciousness must begin and end within itself. The independence and freedom of consciousness exist in it. In this sense, the center of consciousness is present, free consciousness. It is not the self that is born on a certain day of a certain year and dies on a certain day of a certain year. Consciousness includes the universal within itself to the extent that it becomes particular.

There may be many objections against considering that each momentary consciousness is the act of a free person or that there is a kind of social organization at the foundation of individual consciousness, and, further, that from this standpoint there is no absolute distinction between the relation within individual consciousness and the relation between the individual and society. However, what kind of idea makes us think of the consciousness of the self and the consciousness of another as being entirely different in quality? Needless to say, the common-sense distinction between the self and others cannot be sought merely in spatial distinctions of the body. Merely in the plane of meaning itself, we can be thought to be able to be immediately united with the thought and feeling of others, and, at the same time, as seen in the phenomenon of a double self, we can have more than two selves in one body. If we seek the distinction between consciousness of self and others in purely psychological terms, we must find it in the internal feeling of self-identity. However, if, as the essence of the feeling of self-identity is considered by ordinary psychology, there is something like an organic sensation that accompanies volitional behavior, then, however much the self-identity is thought to be unchanging, it still is nothing more than mere degree of similarity between self and others. Essentially, we cannot find a true self-identity anywhere.

Therefore, true self-identity in any sense cannot be sought in the phenomenal world. We can only find the essence of true self-identity on the basis of the moral imperative "because you must do it, you can do it." This kind of conviction is merely a postulate from the standpoint of knowledge; it only becomes self-evident in free consciousness that is immediate to us. Knowledge can also be validated in this personal standpoint. The term *postulate* may connote something artificial, but the postulate "I am" is always the foundation of objective knowledge. It must be thought that in this horizon we transcend the distinction between space and time and simultaneously the distinction between self and other that is reflected in the world of cognitive objects. Individual consciousness can be thought to be asymmetrically continuous and unable to return again to the previous instant. But independent consciousnesses can be thought to be coexistent in social consciousness. However, if we argue the matter merely from the content of objectified consciousness, we can also think that there are two contents of consciousness; we can also view them as two consciousnesses on the same level.

It is a difficult problem to know how to define what a state of consciousness is. If we conceive of consciousness as the linking of mental compounds, then we can conceive of two consciousnesses in the individual consciousness; however, from the idea that each phenomenon of consciousness is a synthetic unity, in no case can we allow the coexistence of two states of consciousness. In sum, consciousness is established by the concept of actuality (*Aktualitätsbegriff*), which is the identity of many and one. That consciousness is always one is a logical, formal demand based on the category of the establishment of consciousness and is not an empirical fact understandable in terms of natural science. As an empirical fact, it is merely an analogy. Consequently, empirically speaking, we only see one common content that embraces the manifold of conscious content reflected upon and objectified, and its totality. From such a standpoint, is it not true that, apart from saying that the difference between individual and social consciousness is that the two entities differ materially, we can recognize merely a difference of degree of unity?

We usually think that when a certain individual is conscious, a spiritual unity is functioning in the individual's background, but that when two people are talking together there is not this kind of unity. We think that the individual and social consciousness differ completely in quality. But, as empirical objects, there is no such unity, even in the background of individual consciousness. If, then, we ask whether our self, which cannot become an object of cognition, but which is the foundation of the establishment of consciousness, is such a thing as Kant's 'pure ego', and if we consider that it is indeed such a thing, then we are forced to recognize merely a universal self, and the distinction among individual selves must disappear completely. Only with the realization of the self that is a transnatural unity, that is a 'transcendental causality' (*transcendentale Kausalität*), can we recognize the individual self, for the concept of the individual self is based primarily on the conviction of free will. Apart from this we cannot logically find the foundation of the uniqueness of the self. Therefore, as in Leibniz's monads, both self and others are unique 'windowless' realities. In confronting one another, there must be a world of meaning *qua* power that takes the imperative as its essence. Only by there being a world of historical reality formed by individual monadic unities can the unique reality of each self be truly conceived. If not, there are only analogical spiritual phenomena and transcendent universal values.

Individuality is thus a unity of an infinite ought, which cannot be objectified. The world of this kind of individuality is established in the horizon of the moral a priori, which is the ought underlying all oughts. It is not that moral demands arise because there is individual reality, but, rather, that because there are moral demands the world of individual reality can develop.

In these terms, the distinction between others and the self as independent, personal realities does not lie in the consciousness that the self and others are in opposition simultaneously or that the successive states of consciousness of the self are linked temporally, but in the scope of the potentiality of actualization of a certain ideal content. The center of this kind of freedom always lies in present free will. Not only do we not possess freedom with regard to our past self, such as we do in respect to the selves of others, but we do not even have freedom with regard to our future self. Freedom with regard to the future self lies only in the decisions of the present. On the contrary, we can think that by moral persuasion we can internally influence others. How, then, must we think of the relationship between the self and others in such a world? In the moral world, as in Kant's 'kingdom of ends', the more each person becomes an independent, free reality, the more he lives in harmony with others. The fact that each person becomes a unique and independent reality means that each person enters into union with others.

I think that this moral a priori constitutive of moral society already lies at the foundation of individual consciousness. We usually think that there is consciousness without self-awareness. For example, impulsive consciousness and perception can be thought of as kinds of unselfconscious consciousness. However, impulsive consciousness is not yet individual consciousness. It is nothing more than the material that constructs individual consciousness. As such consciousness differs in its point of unity, it can become the material of anybody's consciousness. As can be seen in the phenomenon of dual personality, one experiential content can be unified in two personal centers. The fact that we can think that impulsive consciousness, which is not accompanied by self-consciousness, is already individual and belongs to a certain individual and not to another, is not that we think according to the content of consciousness itself, but, rather, according to some individual unity thought to be in its background. This would be to reduce the unity of mind to the unity of things. Even if it were a teleological unity, such as instinct, it would still be nothing more than a unity superimposed from without. On this point, there would be no difference from conceiving of there being some material force in its background in order to unify the content of experience and at the same time of a unity given from without by means of another self-conscious entity. When the content of experience finds internal unity within itself—that is, through being self-consciousness—it can become an independent, unique, individual consciousness and can give unity to the self through itself. Only in this case can it be said that a certain individual consciousness cannot belong to another individual.

Consciousness in self-consciousness is usually thought to be something added to perceptive consciousness. But I think that the meaning of the whole must change when the content of consciousness becomes self-consciousness. From this kind of idea we may contend that we attain to an even deeper self-consciousness in aesthetic intuition than we do in mere conceptual self-consciousness. It is an error to think that aesthetic intuition is unselfconscious or nonconscious in a sense similar to perceptive consciousness. In aesthetic intuition we transcend the plane of conceptual self-consciousness, include it internally, and truly attain to self-consciousness of the free self. Just as content of consciousness in aesthetic expression arises as the content of this free self, it attains to a unique individuality.

Strictly speaking, there is no consciousness that does not internally possess subjectivity in some sense. Not even impulsive consciousness is content merely objectified. As long as there is a phenomenon of consciousness, the plane of consciousness in general can be said to be internal and to possess a tendency to individualization; on this point it differs radically in quality from natural phenomena. However, even if impulsive consciousness immanently contains its own subjectivity, it merely possesses a kind of universal subjectivity. The development toward many individual persons is only contained implicitly and still is nothing more than the content of abstract, universal subjectivity. Within the consciousness of an animal, which acts by instinct, there functions only a kind of racial self, which cannot yet be called an individual self. We cannot yet say that the animal has a soul, since it still cannot avoid being an abstractly universal consciousness.

That we can think of animal consciousness as immediately unique is nothing more than an idea that has been added from without, as I have stated. Only when we attain to conceptual self-consciousness does the content of consciousness belong exclusively to a certain individual and manifest the fundamental meaning of the establishment of consciousness that directly and immanently contains consciousness in general. It is usually thought that self-consciousness develops from the standpoint of impulsive consciousness—in other words, that the particular arises from the universal. But, just as Bergson states that the material world represents something that has been subtracted from the spiritual world, so, too, can the phenomenon of impulsive consciousness be said to be something that has been subtracted from a phenomenon of individual consciousness that is truly independent. Such a phenomenon of consciousness can only be said to exist in a sense similar to the objective world of universal subjectivity, such as the physical world.

The idea that this is my consciousness and no one else's—the idea of individual consciousness such that both the other and the self are windowless monads with respect to one another—arises in the moral horizon wherein our selves are united precisely because they are mutually independent and free. If consciousness unaccompanied by self-consciousness is not consciousness in the strict sense, we may be able to say that there is a moral society at the foundation of consciousness. The relation between the 'Thou' and the 'I' obtains even within our individual acts. Our individual acts cannot in the least be objectified—that is, they do not pass through the objective world of knowledge. The more that such acts are directly and freely united, the clearer consciousness becomes; and the more they are internally contradictory, the clearer it becomes. True self-consciousness, in which the act directly knows itself through the acting, as in Fichte's concept of *Tathandlung*, is a potentiality in the moral horizon. The internal unity of mutually independent and free acts is the essence of self-consciousness. The internal union of free acts in the depths of individual self-consciousness constructs the objective world of the independent free self within and the moral social world without. The latter is nothing more than the extension of the former.

Even if unselfconscious, impulsive consciousness is spatially divided, it must still be regarded as the consciousness of the racial self. So long as one does not adopt a merely material standpoint, racial consciousness must be based on the unity of the content of consciousness itself. When animals that had no eyes evolved and developed eyes, their unique racial self saw things through those eyes. Even in the present day, when we are not self-consciously conscious and merely see another thing, it is not the individual self, but the racial self that is seeing. The distinctions between various visual perceptions that differ according to individuals are merely kinds of phenomena of the vast universal flow of visual perception. However, advancing beyond the standpoint of this kind of racial self, individual acts of perception also come to possess personal content through individual selves' becoming objects themselves—that is, by advancing to the moral standpoint. Individual visual images become individual, and herein arises aesthetic creativity.

For spiritual content to actualize itself, it must pass from the universal to the particular; the more particular it becomes, the more it becomes concrete reality. The concrete universal must contain the universal within the particular. In the aspect of its being universal consciousness, it is one with other consciousnesses; it is racial and impulsive. However, in being spiritual, truly concrete, it is the unique flow that Bergson states can never return to an earlier moment; the universal is nothing more than its reflective aspect. With respect to physical phenomena, the more universal they become, the more real they become; with respect to spiritual phenomena, the more particular they become, the more real they become. Usually we consider the universal to become particular from the standpoint of thinking, but the particular does not appear from the abstract universal. True concrete reality must be something that contains the universal within the particular, something that moves of itself. It must be something such as Cohen's 'productive point'.

At the end of his book *Die sozialen Gesetze*, Tarde discusses the origins of social phenomena. To sum up his view, he holds that all things arise from and return to the infinitesimal particular, which he calls the alpha and the omega, and that we are also part of the myriad things of the universe, and therefore we, too, arise from this infinitesimal and by death return to it. If we follow Tarde, we may say that social phenomena emerge through imitation and that, not only social phenomena, but even natural phenomena essentially exist only in particular experiences. The natural world is established when we enter into the plane of consciousness in general from that of the communal will that is the foundation of imitation. We can still call the plane of imitation personal, contrary to which the plane of consciousness in general, as Planck has stated, is completely liberated from anthropomorphism and to that extent is completely devoid of creativity.

We usually think that individual and communal consciousness differ in their realities because we view them from without. Spiritual phenomena arise from and return to the particular, which is their alpha and omega. Spiritual phenomena are not distinguishable from without through the forms of time and space. They must be distinguished only according to whether they are abstract or concrete, creative or created, free or necessary. The reason individual consciousness, compared to communal consciousness, which is a kind of simultaneous existence, possesses true reality as a continuous unity is that it is creative. What is creative must be continuous. Whether consciousness is individual or communal, it functions in a dimension that transcends time and space; it acts as a focal point unifying time and space, as it were. Bergson states that space and time are nothing more than the two aspects of the relaxation and tension of pure duration. Because communal consciousness is the aspect of relaxation, it can be thought of as a kind of simultaneous existence.

From the standpoint of pure consciousness, the usual distinction between self and other in the natural-scientific sense is not the essential one. When our consciousness becomes self-consciousness by reflecting itself within itself at its foundation and thus reproducing itself within itself, the self and the other must both oppose each other and be united in the social consciousness, which presupposes infinite acts that are similarly independent and free in another respect. In this sense, we can say that the individual and society are dialectically constituted. From the standpoint of natural-scientific analysis, it is difficult to say that even our present consciousness is simple. From the standpoint of history, we may be able to say that even social consciousness is one continuous conscious reality wherein one act directly gives birth to another, in the sense of being one irreducible, dialectical process. Just as individual contents of consciousness meet and conflict with each other in the focus of present consciousness and thus produce new personal content, so, too, contents of social consciousness meet and conflict with each other in the consciousness of different individuals and thus develop new content of social consciousness. And, just as in an individual certain thoughts and feelings occupy a central position as the content of the self and perform creative functions, in society, also, certain individuals assume creative roles as the monadic centers of social thought. Such people are what we term geniuses. And, just as there are patterns of representations in the individual consciousness, so are there patterns of the consciousness of groups of individuals. In individual consciousness, for example, in judgment the more two representations oppose one another, the more they are united internally. Similarly, in social consciousness, mutual self-conscious independence among individuals rather signifies their profound internal unity. As in the case of individual consciousness, the mutually independent self-consciousness of each individual in society indicates a profound self-conscious unity of social consciousness. Moreover, this kind of self-conscious development of spirit becomes the world of objective spirit and the world of cultural development.

In pure, self-conscious consciousness the objective world emerges within the self by virtue of consciousness in general's being internally included. In this horizon, the objectified self and the other are the same and are freely interchangeable. At the point where a present act actualizes objective value—that is, where the free self functions—there is no distinction between the self and the other. As a man loves and respects another in the plane of pure morality, so does he love and respect his own self. From the religious standpoint, at any rate, it cannot be said that to sacrifice oneself for another meaninglessly is morality. Simply to act on behalf of the other or on behalf of society is not morality. Neither the other nor society possesses any moral value as a mere existent. The fact that social reality possesses moral authority over us must be as expression of objective value.

Social spirit also, like individual spirit, is self-conscious spirit as the identity of fact and act. It possesses value as the expression of a larger person. A mere majority does not have any authority whatsoever in the moral realm. When a certain individual exhibits great personal value, it is not that sacrificing the majority cannot be allowed, for we must recognize considerable reasonableness in Nietzsche's 'aristocratic morality'. However, when the concrete universal that is the internal unity of time and space manifests itself, the direction of its immediate development is individual, and the direction of returning to its foundation is the union of self and other. The latter is the direction of respect and love. Of course, in self-consciousness, which is reflection *qua* development, the return to a profounder subjectivity must be the direct development of a larger self. In the plane of knowledge, what comes to appear to us immediately may be an individual consciousness, but as free will we always act in the horizon of the union of self and others. This horizon—the horizon of the absolute self—is not a unity conceivable in the standpoint of knowledge, but must be a unity that presupposes infinite individualization. This is the reason that infinite individualization reveals this unity, as in art.

3

Speaking from the standpoint of present free will, the self, in the sense of being an act itself that cannot be reflected in the objective world, transcends the psychological distinction between self and others and is the same as the self of any other man. The feeling of justice is born from it. The self, however, that is entirely distinterested in the objective world, that is entirely without relation to objects, cannot avoid being an abstract self. The true self must be the acting self. For the self to act, it must have direction and individuality. There is no individuality in the self that merely sees. The acting self must be an individual, and its individuality must have meaning in being an acting self. Acting must mean that the self creates the objective world of the self.

If we consider that freedom meant to become disinterested in the self or another apart from the objective world, then our self would be lost within a universal intellectual self, the individual self would be a delusion, and only the eye of the one God would shine in the universe. From the standpoint of pantheism, the world of the individual does not appear. To understand the world of the individual, we must take as our point of departure the world that Kant terms the 'kingdom of ends'. We must see the experiential world entirely as the expression of moral society. However, neither individuality nor the distinctions of the contents of the self appear from formal ends themselves. In concrete individuality, content itself must become directly the moral ought; within its content it must include infinite oughts. Individuality does not become free apart from content. It enters deeply into content and goes on to transcend it internally. The true moral world is one in which the individual enters profoundly into himself and comes to appear in the dimension that has completely broken through the communal world. Seen from this kind of dimension, our worlds of experience can for the first time be characterized as individual subjects that are not interchangeable with one another. When we have purely entered into and have seen life in this horizon, events and things can be considered to be mutually and personally

one as expressions of personal content. The world of moral law is another example of this.

4

As discussed, in the usual idea of society as a mere group of
individuals, the psychological individual belongs to the world of
cognitive objects and only becomes material for the development of
the free person and hence cannot become its norm; the psychological
individual possesses existential value, but not moral value. The expression of the free person lies only in the present, free consciousness
from one moment to the next. From this perspective, both society and
individual are the same, and both social content and individual content are created in present, free consciousness. As individual consciousness can be called a society as the union of various expressions,
so is there no individual, in the strict sense, in the world of cognitive
objects. The idea of individuality is based on the consciousness of the
free person—that is, on moral consciousness.

Perhaps the idea of the individual may be thought to appear
from mere intellectual self-consciousness—that is, from the unity of
consciousness. But pure unity of consciousness is consciousness in
general, and from it individual distinctions do not appear. How,
then, can the distinctions of individual consciousness that are contents in the experiential world emerge from moral self-consciousness?
The free and concrete self is neither a mere formal nor a mere intellectual self-consciousness. It is the infinite act underlying all acts. If
we wish to see, we look; if we wish to hear, we listen; if we wish to sit,
we sit; if we wish to go, we go. Herein lies our true freedom.

True freedom of behavior is the rationalization of the irrational. From this standpoint, reason is nothing more than its means,
and consciousness in general is nothing more than the process of the
development of the will. The intellectual self, in which the reflecting
self and the reflected self are one, is still not the individual self. The
individual self that is truly unique and independent must be self-
determining. In the background of self-reflection there must be the
direct union of act and act prior to reflection on the self. There
must be the union of act and act. There is self-consciousness prior to
this kind of self-consciousness in the form of thinking; the latter
comes to appear as one of its aspects.

Only when there is freedom of behavior is there the true self.
Freedom of behavior implies contingency beyond thinking and presupposes a profound depth inaccessible to reflection. When we
transcend this standpoint and have been able to include it within the

self, we are truly free. Therefore, free will is deeper and broader than the unity of thinking, which at times it even destroys. Our self is not necessarily a conscious duration. However, why, even when we forget ourselves, do we have the conviction afterwards that we were acting? The self is a pure continuity of acts that cannot be reflected upon; it must be an infinite self-determination of acts. The unconscious unity of consciousness, such as in aesthetic creativity, can be established in such a standpoint. Terms that express self-consciousness as the unity of that which is reflected upon and that which reflects are merely conceptual expressions of such a continuity of pure acts. It is not that self-love arises after consciousness of the self; rather, there is self-love first, and then self-consciousness arises. Consciousness of the ethical ought must be at the foundation of consciousness of the logical ought.

When we have attained to the horizon of the internal continuity of pure acts, there is neither thing nor mind; there is only a unique life. The distinction between mind and things, interior and exterior, can be expressed by this horizon. This horizon contains every objective world and thus is the plane of consciousness in general as well. It is valid consciousness in the sense of causing logical and ethical planes to be established; as the plane of consciousness in general, it is the consciousness of validity; and, as the immediate unity of acts that are internally self-conscious and independent, in its positive function it is pure love. Pure love is unique; in it there is neither love of the self nor of the other. If we attain to the very root of the self, it is simultaneously love of the self and love of the other. Love of the self and of the other are simply two aspects of the one act. The above intentionality of pure love is the plane of consciousness in general with respect to knowledge and is the plane of the moral ought with respect to behavior. As Hegel states, just as we attain to concrete truth by means of the internal contradictions of individual thoughts, we also enter into the relationships of moral society and attain to the world of pure love by fulfilling our individual individuality; in pure love we 'live by dying'.

The idea of unique individuals that are not interchangeable with one another must take its point of departure from the above horizon of pure love—that is, from the intentionality of transcendent love. In the objective world of this intentionality—that is, in moral society—individuals are independent persons and at the same time are mutually one. When we think of one person, we immediately objectify it. Therefore, we think of it as an actual entity, and we think of many persons merely as elements in reference to it. But personal unity must be said to be infinite dialectical differentiation. The unity of the person is one in which individual acts are infinitely free, and thus the objective world becomes unified and one. The person of God is not a one as a substance; it must be infinite personal differentiation, a personal dialectical unity. Even individual consciousness is a moral society in this sense, and the unity of psychological consciousness is one reflection of this unity.

The self that is the foundation of our consciousness is active and individual; it is not merely cognitive, but volitional. Since personal unity is not the same as substantive unity and since dialectical differentiation is involved in unity, the consciousness of every moment must be independent and free in order for our individual consciousness to be a personal unity. Individual consciousness is thus established as the union of free ends in themselves. We can conceive of something like a mere intellectual self-consciousness, but the mere intellectual self would be such a thing as Kant's 'pure ego', a mere universal ego; a universal ego is not the true self, for the self must be individual, and we can thus attain true self-consciousness only in moral self-consciousness. There may be a phenomenon of consciousness even when there is no moral self-consciousness, but, as I have said, a phenomenon of consciousness that is not self-conscious stands on the basis of universal subjectivity and thus can even be understood as a natural phenomenon. Although this kind of phenomenon can develop into an individual self-consciousness, we cannot directly consider it to be individual consciousness. That we usually think of it as an individual consciousness indicates that we think of it in terms of a kind of organic sensation. If we truly seek the distinction between individual consciousness and social consciousness, I think that it is to be found only at the point of intersection of the creativity of the moral individual and natural causality. The content of moral society, in the sense of being a mere ought, cannot be said to be directly one with nature. But in the individual consciousness the moral ought and natural causality directly intersect.

Chapter 7

Consciousness of the Act

There is no visual act apart from form and color and no aural act apart from sound, but neither are there color and form apart from the visual act nor sound apart from the aural act. Act and object are interrelated. The dynamic content of self-generative and self-developmental experience is the content of the act, and what is constructed by it is its objective world. If we interpret Kant's a priori in dynamic terms, then the a priori is precisely the act, and the world that it constructs is the objective world that we cognize by means of it.

However, while no one will deny that we are conscious of color, form, and sound, there may be room to raise objections concerning our consciousness of the acts themselves. It is often said that we cannot see seeing or hear hearing. However, the term *act* cannot avoid being ambiguous. We usually say that we see things with the eye and hear sound with the ear, but, to be precise, it is neither the eye that sees things nor the ear that hears sound, nor yet the brain that sees or hears. Present-day psychologists attempt to reject such terms as *visual* and *aural acts* as being substantializations of concepts. When we think of some entity or force in the background of the continuous change of a phenomenon and view it as real, then, needless to say, this would be to take a concept as reality. However, when a phenomenon changes, what is it that is conscious of this change itself? If we consider that the color red has changed into blue, what is it that is conscious of red changing into blue? Consciousness of the change does not emerge, even if we have red and blue occurring in sequence. Not only does the consciousness of change not emerge from a mere sequence of colors, but the representations themselves of red or blue are not directly sensations. For something to become sensation, consciousness must be added to the representation itself. The psychologist states that, apart from concrete sensations such as red or blue, there is no such thing as consciousness and that concrete sensation is one process; he thinks of quality, intensity, and degree of clarity as the attributes of sensation. However, the mere sum of these attributes cannot be sensation. These attributes must be the attributes of one process of sensation.

What, then, is this process that can thus be called a continuous unity? If it is merely a concept defined just for the sake of the unity of the phenomenon, then we cannot distinguish between a spiritual and a material phenomenon, for this distinction requires that the unity itself be internal. Internal unity must not be a concept added from without, as in the case of a material phenomenon, but it must be internal to the phenomenon itself—in other words, function internally within it. The phenomenon must include development within itself, and it must move of itself. In a spiritual phenomenon the act is not a concept merely added from without. It may be thought that the view that sensation is an internal act and internally includes the act is merely an explanation added afterwards, but when I speak of the act within sensory experience, I do not mean that it is included self-consciously. I mean that the whole is one continuity. A spiritual phenomenon cannot be conceived of as a synthesis of discrete elements. To think of a synthesis of elements is to negate a spiritual phenomenon and to make it into a material thing. In a spiritual phenomenon, an intuition of internal continuity—an intuition of the whole—must be the basis. Moreover, this means that the relation—that is, the unity itself—is phenomenal and that the unity includes differentiation and development within itself.

We cannot see seeing and cannot hear hearing. What does the dynamic content of self-generative, self-developmental experience mean, and in what sense can we know it? No one can deny the fact that we have such experiences as awareness of movement or consciousness of change. How are such modes of consciousness possible? In the case that a thing moves from one point to another, we know its former and latter positions and may think that we have been able to infer movement thereby. Of course, there are many instances in which we know the movement of things in such a manner. The case of seeing something that is actually moving before our eyes can be thought to be the paradigm of such consciousness. We can perceive discrete elements but cannot perceive continuity, which seems to be only conceptual. From such a way of thinking, the dynamic content of self-generative, self-developmental experience is the product of thought, and it is not the immediate content of consciousness. However, when we think of a mathematical system in terms of its internal necessity, we cannot deny the fact that there is a unity of meaning that transcends time, between prior and later contents of consciousness. This unity is not a unity added from without by thinking, but the unity of thinking itself. In this case the unity itself must be said to be an immediate content of consciousness.

Of course, even in this case, we may say that there is a strict distinction between act and object and that the object becomes the content of consciousness by transcending the act. But, taken to its logical conclusion, how can these two be united if, on the one hand, we think of an eternally unchanging object that transcends time and, on the other, of an act determined within time and moving from moment to moment? On the contrary, when we are conscious of the fact that the self is thinking—that is, when we have the personal experience of thinking—we must say that we are conscious of the union of act and object—conscious of something moving of itself. Within this consciousness of the moving thing, the consciousness of continuity must be included. Act and object must be strictly distinguished, but that which distinguishes them must be an act of thinking. This act of thinking must include act and object and be freely interchangeable with them. If not, then to which of them does such an act of thinking belong? Can it be called a mere act? And how can an act entirely distinguished from the object transcend itself and distinguish itself and its object?

An act distinguished from its object is no longer a true act, but merely another kind of object. A phenomenon of consciousness, as Brentano states, must include the object internally. Indeed, it is not yet a phenomenon of consciousness because it includes the object internally. When I see a thing, there is only the thing; only when it has been thought that the thing I see points to an object outside the mind as the representation of the thing, does the phenomenon of consciousness become clear. Consciousness of the act—the standpoint of reflection—must be present in a phenomenon of consciousness. Of course, in this regard it may be said that when a phenomenon of consciousness has become an object of consciousness, it ceases to be a phenomenon of consciousness, and there is even an unreflective, unself-conscious phenomenon of consciousness. But such a thing can still not be called a phenomenon of consciousness. It can only be called an immediate experience, or pure experience. When such an immediate experience has been reflected upon, the distinction between act and object emerges.

What does it mean to say that such experience has been reflected upon? If we think that something wholly different from this experience is added from without, we cannot understand how things wholly different from one another are able to unite. Such an idea is nothing more than the result of deduction from some dogmatic theory that substantializes the opposition between subjectivity and objectivity. As immediate, direct experience, when the experience of blue has been added to the experience of red, the consciousness of the difference between them arises. Of course, the consciousness of difference is not yet the consciousness of judgment. But, when such consciousness of difference becomes independent and free from its content, it appears as the consciousness of judgment, and, accordingly, the consciousness of the self that discriminates, judges, and unifies various experiences comes to be born. When we have reflected from the standpoint of the consciousness of this kind of self, we think that both the previous sensation of red and blue and the consciousness of their differences were conscious states of the self. To think this way must mean to think that the reflection that appears later was present internally. Consciousness, even in the state of unreflective and merely sensory consciousness, is not merely a synthesis of the representation itself and the force that moves it. It must be a quality *qua* reality. We can say that the red or blue that have appeared therein are not mere red or blue, but include infinite transitions. In other terms, we can say that each is a continuity. Nothing whatever emerges from consciousness of mere red and blue. However, from the infinite transition that is included in their background, there is produced not only other sensations, but consciousness of difference. Will does not arise from perception, but, rather, perception arises from will.

In the case in which consciousness of the self has arisen, recollection and recognition of the sensations of the past as the consciousness of the self depend on this kind of continuity. In other words, they depend on the transtemporal unity that is included in the background of consciousness. Sensory consciousness is established only as this kind of unity that is present in the background, while consciousness of the self arises as the development of this kind of unity. Consciousness of self-identity is the self-consciousness of this kind of unity. We may say that there is consciousness of the self only when reflective self-consciousness is created, but it is not that the self emerges when we know the self, just as it is not that things emerge when we know things. Only in consciousness of the self are the knower and the known one. The fact that the knower and the known are one in this way does not mean that it begins in self-consciousness, for it is already this way in sensory experience. Even in sensory experience the sensory self and the sensory object must concretely be one. The reason that when we know a thing we think of the self and thing as different is that we think of the self merely as a conceptual self. However, the conceptual self is a judging subjectivity that accompanies the judging consciousness and is not sensory subjectivity. That which knows color and sound is not a judging subjectivity, but a sensory subjectivity. The true individual self must be the unity of such subjectivity. The universal self, such as Kant's 'pure ego', is no one's self; the self that is no one's self is not a self. The self of which we are conscious in self-identity is the very act in which the self reflects upon itself. It is the *Tathandlung* of the identity of act and object. We cannot help recognizing this kind of *Tathandlung*, even in sensory experience. Recognition of past experience as the experience of the self also becomes possible in such a standpoint of unity.

Self-consciousness is nothing more than the content of the will, the basic act underlying all acts. It can be thought that in perception the universal is implicit and unconscious, whereas in thinking it is conscious, but even perceptive experience is not a union of simple elements. Also in thinking, a universal of a higher dimension must be thought to be operative in the background of thinking. The universal that is acting in the background of thought cannot be objectified by thought, even though that which is acting in the background of perception is objectified in the standpoint of thinking. This kind of universal is the transintellectual will. This is the reason that we must think that the act of thinking has been added to the object of thought. That which transcends universal reason and unifies it must be the will. From this standpoint, perception and thinking are the same. If we can say we are conscious of the self in the act of thinking, we can say we are also conscious of it in the act of perception. The artist is self-conscious of himself in perception apart from thinking. This must be similar to being conscious of self-identity by transcending time and taking even past experiences as experiences of the self.

Thus, there must be something moving and an internal continuity at the foundation of consciousness. On this point there is a distinction between spiritual and physical phenomena. If not, a spiritual phenomenon could not be distinguished from a natural phenomenon. Any psychology must be based on the standpoint in which consciousness is conscious of itself. Such a thing as reflex action must be regarded as a mere physiological phenomenon. Even a case of self-movement that transcends obstacles, such as that of the frog whose brain has been removed except for the thalamus and optic nerve, cannot be regarded as a conscious phenomenon. There is a conscious phenomenon only when there is the fact that 'I am conscious of it' (*mir bewusst*). Of course, there is not this kind of consciousness simply in the case of perception. It only appears in the will. However, the statement 'I am conscious of it' signifies an internal continuity. An internal continuity must be the self-development of the universal. The differences among the grades of consciousness are merely differences of this kind of universal. The rationalism of ordinary psychology regards the internal unity, which actually is unclear in perception and association, as clear in thought. But in perception there is the life of perception; in association there is the life of association. And, just as the content of art can be considered to be inexpressible by thinking, so is there meaning content in perception that cannot be exhausted by thinking. Perception has its own clarity. Indeed, as we often see in art, the adulteration by thinking can be regarded as destroying the clarity of perception. Of course, the content of thought contained within perception—that is, intellectual content—may be considered to become clear in thought, but this is not the essence of the content of perception. Perception as the content of the self of perception has an intentionality that cannot be described by anything else.

When I say "I am conscious of it," what is this 'I'? The essence of the 'I', as William James puts it, is not something repeatable like a brand. The self-identity of 'I am I' is the foundation of all knowledge; when experience is unified from this standpoint, every experience becomes a phenomenon of consciousness by virtue of being an internal continuity. The fundamental fact of the consciousness of the statement 'I am' must be prior even to the 'pure ego' as the legislator of nature. Before Kant's 'I think' there must be Fichte's 'I act'. Thinking also is one kind of activity of the ego. The ego is not an act, but must be an infinite continuity of acts. The 'I am' signifies an infinite continuity of acts. Seen from this standpoint, everything is unified as something moving. We say that there is consciousness of something moving, but here that which moves of itself is consciousness. And this can be demonstrated in our own self-consciousness.

How can the above idea be reconciled with the idea that we do not see seeing or hear hearing? Let me first attempt to investigate the idea that the act cannot know itself. We say that we see color or hear sound, but there is no color or sound apart from the acts of visual and aural perception. So, what do these acts mean? The psychologist thinks of organic sensation or emotion accompanying the activity of reflection as a sign of self-identity, but, being on the same level with these kinds of sensations, they cannot unify the others. They can only stand in the position of unifier in the sense of being representative of an even higher dimension. Just as the sun attracts the planets as the center in the physical world, even among things on the same level one can be said to stand in the position of unifier with regard to the others. However, if one of them on the same level stands in the unifying position, then, depending upon the case, others, too, can occupy that position. Even in the solar system, some planet could occupy the central position if it acquired the power. However, in a phenomenon of consciousness does the consciousness of a pure object as red or blue stand on the same level as consciousness of the self, and can consciousness of the object be considered as the unity of the phenomenon of consciousness?

Of course, when we see color and hear sound, there may not be such a thing as consciousness of the self. But this is the fact that the self is not cognized as object; it does not mean that the self is not active. It is not that the self unifies others as one of the phenomena of consciousness; it becomes the condition for the establishment of the phenomena of consciousness. The self is similar to a work of art in which some specific place becomes its center, but the meaning of the totality appears in all of its parts; in other words, each part is the whole. Even in unity there may be various meanings, but the unity of the self is a creative unity. If the self, while being creative, stood outside of the objective world, it would be the same in respect to all its parts, and doubts might arise as to how a certain part could represent the self as the center. But the self is the infinite act underlying all acts, and in a phenomenon of consciousness all of the parts are unified with one another as one act. The hierarchy in phenomena of consciousness must be a reflection of the hierarchy of the acts of the self. It is said that we see color and hear sound, while we cannot see seeing or hear hearing; but when we see color or hear sound, color in itself or sound in itself is each an individual act. On this point, the representations of color and sound differ from the sensations of color and sound. That we cannot be conscious of the act itself of the sensations of color or sound must have the same meaning as the fact that consciousness cannot be conscious of itself.

However, in the experience of the will and of self-consciousness, is it not true that we clearly possess consciousness of the act itself? To negate this fact is to negate oneself. The direction of the act of which we are able to be conscious in sensory experience is the direction of this kind of self and the intentionality of the will, and the fact that we cannot see seeing or hear hearing must have the same meaning as that we cannot know the depths of our own self or objectify the will. However, if we know the self in self-consciousness and know the will in the will, we may be able to say, in the same sense as above, that we are able to know visual and aural acts. Are we not able to say that, so long as we are able to see even sensory experience in the form of self-conscious experience, the act knows the act itself? But what does it mean to say that the self knows the self in self-conscious experience? We cannot know our self as object, for the self that has been objectified is no longer the self. Even so, something merely functioning in the background of experience is no different from a physical force. In self-consciousness, acting must be knowing, and vice versa. What, then, does knowing mean?

From the standpoint of Kant's epistemology, knowing does not mean the reproduction of external objects, but the unification of a manifold of experiential content. In the language of the present-day Southwestern school, it is the unity of value and act, and a cognitive act is established when a transcendent object becomes one with an act as content. In such a case, what is the act? If it is a fact that has been constructed by the categories of time, space, and causality, it is already a cognitive object and not the cognitive act. Of course, we may be able to distinguish between the act of knowing and the fact of having known. Even though the latter becomes a cognitive object, the former cannot. Consequently, we may also be able to say that it belongs to a state prior to cognition.

However, how are we able to explain the fact of our self-consciousness from such a standpoint? We cannot understand knowing without the experience of self-consciousness. Apart from consciousness of the unity of subjectivity and objectivity, there is nothing but the movement of things. If we consider that knowledge of facts is constructed by the forms of time, space, and causality, which can be thought of as the 'categories of the given', then even self-consciousness is simply knowledge of fact that has been applied to these categories. Whence arises Kant's 'I think' and the fact that the 'I think' must accompany all my representation (*das 'Ich denke' muss alle meine Vorstellungen begleiten können*)?

If we consider that epistemology itself is already a form of knowledge, then upon what kind of categories must we consider that epistemology that discusses the establishment of cognition depends? We may be able to say that such a thing as Kant's consciousness in general is also a limit concept. However, a limit must refer to the transcendence of standpoints. Consciousness in general cannot belong to the objective world of consciousness in general. If we say that consciousness in general is the ultimate of subjectivity, then we must already allow for subjectivity in a limitless sense. In being able to distinguish between subjectivity and objectivity there is the fact that consciousness is conscious of consciousness itself; and the fact that consciousness is conscious of itself must mean that it is different from consciousness being conscious of things. If not, there would be no way for the distinction between subjectivity and objectivity to be made. From the outset, subjectivity is a limit concept with regard to the objective world. However, it does not become a limit by thinking of it as an infinite distance. If we consider that consciousness in general is the ultimate of subjectivity that takes all empirical content as object, then such subjectivity must always function within an actual consciousness. The free self, which causes the consciousness of present actuality to be established, must include the standpoint of consciousness in general. Phenomena of consciousness, established by consciousness being conscious of itself, have not been completely objectified in the plane of consciousness in general, which is the limit of subjectivity. We must think that they are established by fundamentally different categories. The fact that personal experience prior to cognition is not knowledge is bound up with the point of departure that distinguishes between object and act.

How do we judge experience that we cannot know as being something that we cannot know? What kind of a category is the category of knowing categories? From what kind of an a priori do we discuss a priori? Herein we can only think of such a thing as a 'category of categories' and an 'a priori of a priori'. Kant states that we cannot perceive 'time'. Needless to say, 'time' cannot become an object of perception. But when Kant discussed 'time' as a schema, what was he conscious of? Without such experience as the infinite continuity of acts, can we understand 'time'? There is neither truth that demonstrates truth itself nor knowledge that knows knowledge itself. Because this is an endless circular argument, we must reject it. It is said that "*Da mithin dieser Cirkel unvermeidlich ist, so muss man ihn reinlich begehen,*" but knowledge that knows itself is not the same as ordinary knowledge. In ordinary knowledge contradiction cannot be allowed as contradiction. But, as Hegel states, in the standpoint of knowledge of knowledge, there is truth because there is contradiction. The one cannot be the many at the same time; to say that the one is directly the many is a contradiction. However, the one is precisely the many in self-consciousness in which the self knows itself. Just as Fichte takes act (*Tathandlung*) as the absolute first principle of knowledge, all knowing is established on the basis of knowledge that knows itself. To say that knowledge knows itself is neither a contradiction nor an impossibility; philosophical knowledge is actually established in this standpoint. However, this knowledge is established on categories that differ from those of ordinary knowledge. Plotinus, in explaining the understanding of silence, writes: "That which in me contemplates, produces a work of contemplation, like geometricians who while contemplating describe figures, for it is not in describing figures, but in contemplation, that I let drop from within me the lines that outline the forms of bodies." Or, as in Goethe's "Mother's Country," seeing is creating, and creating is seeing.

This may be thought to be a mere postulate from the standpoint of ordinary knowledge. Kant states that a postulate is not knowledge and does not give any content to knowledge. However, a postulate is not merely artificial; it has an objective nature by virtue of the categories on which it is established. These categories must be sought in the transcendental will, which is the unity of knowledge and practice as the act underlying all acts. For the above reasons, at the ground of knowledge there is a knowledge that differs from knowledge that generally knows objects; there is knowledge that knows knowledge itself. Knowledge of the act of consciousness is established by it. Seeing is not color; hearing is not sound. We cannot see seeing or hear hearing in the sense that we see color and hear sound. However, as in Plotinus' statement "in contemplation . . . I let drop from within me the lines that outline the forms of bodies," color and form are produced by seeing seeing as a continuity of pure acts. There must be this kind of consciousness of consciousness at the foundation of seeing color and hearing sound.

It is usually thought that there is no consciousness of the act in the perceptual act. However, experiential content is not established by judgment, for judgment concerns experiential content. As is usually thought, there must first be consciousness of the act for us to reflect upon the act and take it as the object of judgment. The act must be something that differs from movement or from change of a thing that is a mere object. In other words, its transition must be infinitely continuous, internal, and self-conscious. Even in the act of judgment, the act of judgment itself does not immediately become the object of judgment, for that which takes the act of judgment as object must be a judgment of a judgment. This judgment of judgment causes judgment to be established and at the same time cannot become the object of judgment. We are only conscious of it in 'the will to truth' (*der Wille zur Wahrheit*). Even in our self-consciousness there must be something that assumes this place; in other words, there must be something like a 'will to perception' (*der Wille zur Wahrnehmung*). This will is in fact present when we are conscious in self-consciousness. Even in thinking, it is not that the act of thinking is conscious of our self as object, but that the will is self-conscious of the will. When we say, "this flower is red," if we consider that there is first consciousness of red and we are conscious of it as the content of judgment, then that which is intended as the 'I' when we say. "*I* have seen this flower," must be considered to be that which is cognized in a sense similar to red's being cognized as perception. Perception is consciousness of mere quality, within which consciousness of the act must be contained. If the reason is that the act is not reflected upon, we must say the same even in the case of red. The idea that only the object is cognized in perception must be the result of rationalism.

At the beginning I stated that the dynamic content of experience is consciousness of the act, but what does this dynamic aspect of experience mean? In the case when we see a certain thing move from one point to another, we may be able to divide the distance between them into infinite points and to consider the thing as passing through them. However, no matter how great the number of points, a continuous line cannot be produced from the union of discrete points. The idea of an infinite series must be introduced to establish continuity. An infinite series is established in the horizon of the a priori of all a priori. This horizon first becomes clear in self-consciousness. But when the content of the continuity that arises in this horizon is not sufficient with respect to the horizon itself, some kind of physical force is considered to exist in the background of experience. Bergson states that when we have moved our hand from one point to another we have an immediate and pure sensation, and that even though the hand can stop anywhere along the line between the two points the sensation in itself must be considered to be something entirely separate. The fact that Bergson says that in this case sensation is direct and simple does not mean *simple* in the sense in which the psychologist uses the term. Rather, it means something infinitely complex in terms of quality. That which cannot be divided must be infinitely divisible; if not, we cannot establish the meaning of *movement*. Movement is a series of points that cannot be attained by division. Those points must be a transition in a specific direction.

In ordinary psychology, perception of movement is thought to be established from the union of the feeling of pressure, muscular sensation, and articular sensation. But, needless to say, perception of motion cannot be produced from the mere union of these sensations. Rather, these sensations are constructed by an intuition of motion. An intuition of motion must be simple in the sense that a monad is simple. Rather than speaking of an intuition of motion, I should like to think that intuition is the motion—indeed, an action or behavior. Consciousness of motion is not produced from consciousness of the given, for, strictly speaking, not even consciousness can be produced merely from the given. Consciousness of motion is consciousness of our behavior. It is self-consciousness in the profound sense. Usually, if we use such terms as *self-consciousness* or *behavior*, it is thought that they first appear on the basis of conscious reflection—that is, of judgment. But, as I have stated, self-consciousness or behavior involves the fact that what comes later functions from the beginning and the fact of "moving, therefore not moving." Self-consciousness is merely the conceptual consciousness of this kind of act.

Our objective world is the infinite union of worlds that have been given in various intentionality contexts. But a world that moves from the union of such worlds cannot arise; that is, the world of consciousness does not appear. The world of actuality does not emerge from a mere union of possible worlds. Our conscious world of actuality, as the unity of such an objective world, is a world of infinite continuity irreducible to such an objective world; it is the world of the act underlying all acts. In this horizon the object must be precisely that which moves. There it must be object *qua* act. The fact that we usually think of 'motion' as an object and attempt to include even our conscious act within it is an inversion of cause and effect. For motion, on the contrary, is cognized as the object of the act underlying all acts. Of course, this does not mean that first there is consciousness of self-consciousness and that afterwards the consciousness of motion is possible. Just as Kant states that we cannot experience 'time' itself, which constructs our world of experience, so, too, we cannot cognize the act underlying all acts, in the usual sense of cognition. Even in the case of consciousness of judgment we cannot cognize it as an object. And yet, we can say that phenomena of consciousness are established only by this standpoint.

When we try to think deeply concerning the consciousness of the self, we do not cognize the self as an object of judgment; rather, we know it, in critical consciousness, as the direct, free unity of one act with another. However, we are still caught in objective ideas, even in critical consciousness. Consciousness of the truly free self accompanies free will, which negates the true, the good, and the beautiful. Rather than saying that consciousness accompanies such will, this will is precisely true consciousness. Our act of consciousness is not mere activity, but it must evaluate activity—indeed, it does not merely evaluate activity, but it acts through such evaluation. This is the reason that in chapter six I stated that there is a moral relationship at the ground of the phenomenon of consciousness. The reason we think that there are phenomena of consciousness separable from free will is that we simply objectify these phenomena of consciousness. However, that which is objectified has already been transformed into a material thing, while consciousness consists only in present free will.

This being so, doubts may again arise as to how consciousness is conscious of itself. We usually think that things are cognized by contrast with one another. When we have seen only a certain color, what sort of a color it is has not become an object of consciousness. However, in this instance, not to be an object of consciousness means not to be an object of judgment, and not that it is not an object of consciousness as sensation. Therefore, if we say what the consciousness of this sensation is, it is hardly simple, as is usually thought. A mere sensation does not differ from expression itself. Consciousness of a color as a concrete sensation must possess a transition to infinite other colors. A material element is determined within the totality of space, and it has potentiality to move in infinite directions; but it cannot contain infinite directions within itself, nor does it act of itself. In a spiritual phenomenon, however, even if it is a sensation, we must consider that it contains infinite changes internally. For example, even in the case of space, consciousness of concrete space can be thought to contain infinite space internally. When we see a certain color and say that it is red or blue, it can logically be considered a simple quality, but this time the concrete object that is the subject of judgment is hardly simple. However, in what sense is it not simple? Its object can also be thought to have infinite qualities other than color, but, even if seen simply from the point of color, there is not merely red or blue in the color of a concrete thing, but something extremely complex. The fact that a color of a thing is thus infinitely complex means that subjectively our sensation is infinitely complex, not that there is color in sensation. The sensation of red is not red, and we cannot talk about color in reference to the sensation of color.

What, then, is sensation of color, and what is an act of visual perception? Prior to sensation or perception we say that a certain thing has various qualities—for example, that it is red, blue, heavy, or light. But let us consider what this means. Lotze states that existence is activity, and that which is generally considered to be a quality can be considered to be an act. If we think this way, a thing becomes a unity of acts. Infinite complexity in quality means infinite complexity of acts. In these terms, what does it mean to say that a thing is red or blue? Just as we cannot say that visual perception is red or blue, we cannot say that the act itself is red or blue. In the case of a red or blue thing, even if its 'existence' is an activity, red or blue are already functions, and it is not that the act is red or blue. It is only that the qualitative means something that is directly acting. As a certain quality it differs from such a thing as representation itself and thus must be something that always maintains itself. Of course, even if there is representation itself or meaning itself, it is unchanging in respect to the act of judgment of any man. However, the categories of space and time must be applied, to be able to say that a certain thing having certain qualities 'exists' as a reality; at least, it must be something unchanging in time. When an object is considered to be unchanging in reference to an act of judgment, the act as an event in time can be thought to be added from without in an entirely accidental manner to the object itself. That it has certain qualities and that, even if it acts in a certain way, it is something that has had certain qualities mean that that thing itself is unchanging with respect to activity from without. To say that it is unchanging in this way means that one change is independent of other changes.

However, when we look at and know a color, what is it that maintains itself as a certain color? Needless to say, that which maintains itself in consciousness is not something like physical force in the external world. Therefore, on what force does a perception of a certain color depend in order to maintain itself as perception of a certain color? Can it be based on the discriminatory power of consciousness? But, as the psychologist states, consciousness is merely consciousness, and if it does not have any content, a given color cannot be said to maintain that given color itself or to distinguish itself from others by the power of consciousness. We must think that two colors are directly distinguished from one another.

However, there must be a universal that unifies the two, for two colors to be autonomous and to distinguish themselves directly from one another in themselves. If it is a universal concept, it can be regarded as something without any power at all. But there must at least be distinguishable aspects in order for the two things to be distinguishable. Material entities are distinguished from one another in space, but what is such a thing as Herbart's concept of 'intelligible space', which distinguishes red from blue? This kind of space must have a universal quality with respect to the two. It is similar to a material entity's being considered to have extension. Just as physical space has various qualities, so must 'intelligible space' be considered to have certain qualities. We can think that color in general is a quality of intelligible space. Physicists at first considered space to be the field in which forces operate; and then, based on Maxwell's idea of electromagnetism, space became thought of as the field of forces. Whatever is universal is active and in motion. When we attempt to determine this kind of universal as the grammatical subject of judgment, its content must always be inexhaustible in its ground.

When we make the judgment "Alpha is Beta," in the case that its grammatical subject was merely qualitative, does it become a judgment of identity (*Identitätsurteil*), or does it become a judgment of subsumption (*Subsumptionsurteil*)? On the other hand, when that grammatical subject is an individual such as Leibniz speaks of—that is, when it is 'real'—its subject is inexhaustible as a subjective entity. But, as Hegel has argued, the objectivity of judgment must be based on the syllogism. In the syllogism the unifier that is its subject is active and comes to possess positive content—that is, the universal becomes active. A thing unable to be determined previously in the predicate of a judgment is determined in the syllogism. As Lotze has stated, we can think that there is a transition from 'disjunctive judgment' (*disjunktives Urteil*) to the syllogism. The universal of the syllogism is the subject that cannot be determined by judgment. The universal of the syllogism is that which includes negation within itself. The universal that is the subject of the syllogism is a universal of universals. If the subject of judgment was a qualitative thing, the subject of the syllogism is a universal concept of an even higher order. If it is real, it must be a whole that unifies these universals.

Bosanquet states that in judgment the grammatical subject is reality. But in the syllogism this kind of complete reality becomes self-conscious and manifest. In this way, when we seek the foundation of judgment, we must encounter something like the dynamic content of consciousness that already differs from mere objects—that is, the content of the act. As Hegel states, we must encounter not the abstract universal concept, but the concrete universal—that which is creative. With regard to a certain mathematical explanation, if we proceed strictly to seek its foundation, we must ultimately reach the a priori of mathematics. When we see a certain color and say it is red or blue, the color that is the content of perception is not red or blue in the sense of being a mere object of judgment. If we ask how the judgment that it is red or blue arises, the system of color itself must become the foundation of the judgment. Its intentionality is fixed, and the determinative judgment of color is established within the system of color itself. Just as Kant states that we must allow an intuition at the foundation of the judgment of mathematics as a synthetic judgment, so, of course, does intuition become the basis of the judgment of color. In these two cases, what is called intuition is not so-called intuition that has been given, but a synthetic act. Indeed, it must be a kind of creative act. Therefore, we can think of intuition as concrete and infinitely complex. The system that becomes the foundation of judgment and gives objectivity to judgment is grounded on it. Even the reality that Bosanquet regards as the grammatical subject of judgment is nothing other than this kind of system. Just as we seek the basis of judgment in the syllogism and enter infinitely deeply into the continuity of internal unity, so, too, in visual perception do we enter infinitely deeply into the internal continuity of color. In the former, this process is a logical act, and in the latter it is a visual act. The content of the act, then, as the object of judgment, is an infinite transition that includes negation and that cannot be attained. I think that even the motion of material entity is nothing more than one instance of such an act.

Of course, there may be objections to thinking that seeing and deduction are the same. However, I would submit that even deduction is a kind of seeing. Thinking not only represents something else but also possesses specific content in itself. The world of visual perception represents the world of tactile perception, and vice versa. But the world of visual perception is broader than the world of tactile perception, and the former can be thought of as encompassing the latter. Intelligible space, in which thinking functions, is even broader than the space of visual and tactile perception. However, there is basically something identical. In the worlds of visual and tactile perception there is not such a thing as a unique, intuitive space. The fact that one space includes another or is included in another means that one can pass into another. Even though the space of visual perception is broader than the space of tactile perception, they are the same space. But the space of thinking is of an even higher order.

I should like to add one more point about the syllogism. Hegel divides the syllogism into qualitative syllogism (*qualitativer Schluss*), reflective syllogism (*Reflexions-Schluss*), and syllogism of necessity (*Schluss der Notwendigkeit*). In the syllogism of necessity, we can only recognize the self-realization of that which is objective. The syllogism of necessity is able to be established by the internal development of the concrete universal. There must be that which moves of itself at the foundation of deduction. Self-movement means that the universal differentiates itself into the particular from within. The difference between motion and deduction depends upon the depth of the concrete universal. The fact that things move means that the basic essence of the self moves. Therefore, the more profound our consciousness becomes, the more rational it becomes. To become rational must be to attain that which moves deeply and greatly. Deduction is the process of the development of a greater reality. We must recognize something moving at the ultimate ground of the syllogism. Consciousness of the act is established in that ground.

Chapter 8

The Subjectivity
of Behavior

There are various kinds of meanings of subjectivity. With regard to color and form there is the visual act, and with regard to sound there is the aural act. In the world of abstract meaning and truth, which differ from these kinds of intuitive acts, there is the act of thinking. But, again, there are the acts of feeling and the will, which differ from all these intellectual acts. Usually when we use the term *objective world*, it is limited to the world of intellectual objects. But there is also an objective world of feeling and the will at the foundation of the world of intellectual objects. If these acts are the acts of the self, we can say that the self has various selves or that one self is the subject of its acts. But, of course, the idea that the self is the subject of its acts is simply dogmatic. The true self, facing a certain objective world, is its own perspective and at the same time its creator—that is, it is a creative perspective. When the material world is regarded as independent, one who perceives it can be thought to exist outside of it; but in the world of present consciousness, to perceive is precisely to create.

      The self does not emerge at any single point. The self is the alpha and omega points of the creative process. But, because the self is also the eternal present, every point is the self, and thus the self must be an infinite development and dynamic unity. Since we can thus say that no point is the self and yet every point is the self, the self may be thought to be a static unity. But, although in a static unity it may be said that no point is the self, it cannot be said that every point is the self, for here the self lies outside every given point. Just as we cannot point to a leaf of a tree and say that it is the tree, we cannot point to one function of the self and say that it is the self. One function of the self in the present is only one function; needless to say, it is not the totality of the self. But it does not follow that the totality is simply implicit within the self. That which is implicit can be thought at some point to become actualized, but the 'self' can never conclude its development. The self cannot see its own end, even in the infinite future; that which could see it would not be the self. The self is present at every point. The self can be regarded neither as the grammatical subject nor as the predicate of judgment. As Hegel thinks, if we consider that judgment attains its objectivity by being grounded in the syllogism and that the system that is realized through the syllogism becomes its grammatical subject, then we can think that the true self is the subject of judgment in this sense. Just as the grounding in the syllogism can proceed infinitely, so, too, is there something infinitely profound in the depths of the self.

We attain to the standpoint of dynamic unity only in the infinite continuity of the syllogism. In this standpoint there is opposition between that which is grounded and that which provides the foundation. The process of infinite grounding is the subjective act. Subjectivity is the dimension of this grounding. When we are conscious of a certain color as red or blue, we ground it from the subjectivity of color. Consciousness of color is not outside this grounding, for the grounding is creative in one aspect. Our knowledge is not grounded by static unity; the objective foundation of knowledge always lies in dynamic unity. Various subjective acts pertain to various objective worlds, and they are unified in the one self in the form of infinite dynamic unity.

Usually the syllogism and the will are considered to be completely distinct, but I think that they are two sides of the same coin, as it were. We may be able to say that the will is the positive aspect and the syllogism is the negative aspect. That which is the basis of the syllogism is objective, as Hegel says. That which opens up before the self through objective necessity as the foundation of knowledge must be the objective world, constructed by what Kant calls the unity of the pure ego. We find the infinite foundation of our knowledge in this world. "The real is the rational, and the rational is the real." Moreover, such an objective world is the product of the self and its very depths. When we will, knowledge is already acting as we decide upon a goal; and, as we move from end to means, that which decides which means must be pure objective knowledge. If we go against the laws of nature, we cannot move even one grain of sand on the seashore. Our will takes small, subjective desires as its point of departure and attempts to conform the vast, objective world to them. Here our desires must clash with the objective world of pure knowledge. However, the objective world of pure knowledge, as Kant states, is nothing more than the world of the construction of the pure ego latent in the depths of the mind. If we regard even pure intellectual desire, which seeks knowledge for the sake of knowledge, as a kind of will, then that with which the self comes in contact cannot avoid being the self also. That which opens up before the self as the objective foundation of knowledge must also be the self.

In the horizon of the pure intellectual self, the objective foundation inaccessible to knowledge is, on the contrary, the very depths of the self. Knowing is willing, from this standpoint. Knowledge is always incomplete, and the process of thoroughly seeking its grounding in the form of the syllogism is simply such a demand of the will. From this standpoint we can recognize unique truth that no one can deny. The cognitive subjectivity of each person is grounded in this horizon; the cognitive act is such a process of the development of the will. Even if the will functions on the basis of blind impulse, the process of its actualization must be rational. This is also why the psychologist thinks of the will as a continuity of representations. However, the goal itself cannot be objectified in the world of cognitive objects. But even in the pure intellectual act the goal itself of knowledge latent in the depths of cognitive subjectivity cannot be objectified. As the voluntaristic psychologist states, all mental acts are volitional; it can even be thought that mind and will differ only in the content of their goals.

But in this view doubts may arise as to the source of the distinction between mind and will, on the basis of the fact that in the will objectivity conforms to subjectivity, while in knowledge subjectivity conforms to objectivity. I think that the process whereby we actualize subjective goals objectively means that the universal determines itself as something "unique." Objective reality must always be unique. That which is common to everyone and can be repeated any number of times is not reality. That which has been projected as a cognitive object always belongs to the world of the possible. That which has truly unique reality is only the cognitive act of the present. The will possesses a reality that is unique in itself and cannot be universalized. The will seeks its actualization within itself. The fact that the will develops as the will means that it becomes a "unique reality," and willing involves the objective actualization of its own goals. The objective world is supported by the will. The goal of cognition, needless to say, lies in truth; but to know the truth is to arrive at objective reality.

Of course, cognition is not a union with reality such as is

portrayed in the correspondence theory. As the Kantians think, we must consider that it is constructed by an a priori—indeed, we must think, rather, that it is the dynamic self-development and differentiation of a dynamic universal. As Kant thought that thinking becomes objective knowledge by uniting with perception, it becomes objective when thought and pure perception unite in the standpoint of the a priori of all a priori—that is, when knowledge is specified in the horizon of transcendental will. I believe that it is possible to ground knowledge objectively in the form of the syllogism only in the horizon of the transcendental will. We may perhaps think that, as knowledge becomes synthetic in moving from logic to mathematics and from mathematics to physics, it becomes more objective and particularized. But, in the case in which teleology, like physiology, enters into natural-scientific knowledge, even though we can think that knowledge has been further particularized, it might not be said that it has become objective; it may, rather, be thought of even as subjective.

Why is it thought that as we involve the will, which is the intentionality of particularization, we on the contrary destroy the objectivity of knowledge? Here we must consider the essence of the will. Our will is not subjective in essence. When, as in impulse, we can be thought to be moved by nature, our desires imply that we have a basis in objective nature. In addition, impulse becomes true consciousness only when actual practice is added to the will. It becomes an object of the will only by being potential. If reality is spiritual, then teleological explanation can even be considered to be the true explanation of reality. If the objective world is constructed by subjectivity and the given is that which has been sought, then we may say that the truly given was given as the objective world of the will, and the true objective world is the objective world of the will. The intrusion of teleology into science, which focuses exclusively upon mechanistic, causal relationships, may be rejected as a confusion of standpoints. But teleology involves a dimension of a higher order than mechanism. We may also say that it is an even more concrete truth and, in this sense, that it is more objective. A mere universal is not concrete. We can think of a mechanical, causal relationship as an abstraction from the process of teleological causality.

Of course, truth cannot exist apart from the plane of consciousness in general. Strictly speaking, truth is a construction in the plane of consciousness in general. However, that which is given through consciousness in general is only the form of knowledge, without content. As knowledge acquires content and becomes concrete, it gains in particularity but does not lose its universal validity, for the horizon of the will, which unifies perception and thinking, transcends consciousness in general and includes them within itself.

For example, the world of number is constructed by the a priori of mathematics. A certain mathematical truth must have a unique nature as an immovable truth in the mathematical world. This means that it has universal validity with respect to many subjects. When the self takes the standpoint of mathematical thinking, a given mathematical truth becomes a unique event and at the same time has universal validity. A historical truth is similarly unique and has universal validity in the horizon of the concrete self. However, the a priori of mathematics is not the whole of the self, and therefore the self can further differentiate and develop. Mathematical truth only becomes universal truth with respect to the individual self that thus differentiates itself. When we ground knowledge in the form of the syllogism, if it is mathematical knowledge it must be based on a mathematical a priori. At this time the mathematical a priori becomes the infinite foundation of mathematics as a concrete universal. The unique nature of truth is established by it.

In the case of physics, its a priori must be even more concrete. The more an a priori becomes concrete in the standpoint of the act underlying all acts, the more knowledge becomes concrete. Of course, because the a priori of physics is even more concrete than that of mathematics, mathematics does not have its foundation in physics. However, if to know means to pass from the abstract to the concrete, then physical knowledge must accord with the goal of knowledge even more than mathematical knowledge does. It must be based on that goal in order to decide truth, even within an a priori. That which gives the unique nature of truth is this teleological unity.

The will is not merely subjective, for our will is the center of the world we see, and the world we see is supported by our will. For an animal there is merely a world of hunger and thirst, and the satisfaction of its hunger and thirst is the only objective reality. Knowledge is a means that has no value at all in itself; the philosophy of animals can only be utilitarian. The reason we must recognize reality in knowledge is that the transcendental will constitutes the foundation of our self. There is a moral imperative at the foundation of the intellectual imperative. There cannot be the good without truth, and the good of itself demands truth. Our will always proceeds from and returns to actuality, and the unique nature of the will lies in this. The unique nature of truth is nothing other than this. Knowing begins from and ends in the will. When we have the will to know, that which is to be known is included. The process of infinitely seeking the objective foundation externally in the syllogism means to infinitely return within the self. The goal toward which my world advances lies within myself. That which unifies and determines an infinite system of knowledge lies in the very depths of myself. Truth must be such a process of the development of the will—that is, it must be the pure act of the self itself.

Our seeking the foundation of knowledge in the form of the syllogism from the demand of truth thus reveals the will as the concrete act. Reason can be thought to be one plane of the transcendental will. At the beginning of the "Transcendental Dialectics," Kant states that the principle of reason lies in finding an absolute foundation in order to complete the unity of conditional knowledge based on the power of the understanding (*zu dem bedingten Erkenntnisse des Verstandes das Unbedingte zu finden, womit die Einheit desselben vollendet wird*). But that which gives an absolute foundation to knowledge must be the creative will. Seen from the plane of knowledge, the content of the will itself can be thought to be an infinite end, which cannot be attained. However, just as the self can positively know such an infinite series in self-consciousness, in which it reflects upon itself, so can we be conscious of the act itself, which cannot be objectified in the immediate consciousness in which we will and act. The objectivity of knowledge is thus established on the basis of this kind of consciousness of the will; consciousness of behavior—that is, cognitive subjectivity—is grounded on the subjectivity of behavior.

I, who have risen this morning and sit in front of this desk, recognize it as the same desk as yesterday's. The psychologist readily states that this is based on memory. But how is memory possible? Since a past representation, as a past representation, has vanished, how can it be compared with a present representation, and how can its resemblance to it be judged? To reduce it to the act of the brain cells would merely prove something direct by means of something indirect and hence would merely compound the difficulty. In order to unite immediately yesterday's consciousness with today's, as I previously stated, we must consider that it is based on some unity of consciousness that transcends time. It only becomes possible in the horizon of a self that transcends time. Time can instead be thought to be the form of such unity. However, if we take the standpoint of the mere unity of consciousness, we cannot take even one step beyond consciousness of the self. Yesterday's desk is the content of the consciousness of yesterday's 'I', and today's desk is the content of the consciousness of today's 'I'. Even though these two things can be unified in the standpoint of the self that transcends time, this means nothing more than that they are identical and unchanging as contents of consciousness. We cannot proceed beyond idealism merely from the standpoint of the unity of consciousness.

However, I believe not only that this desk has an identity as a content of consciousness and consider it to have an unchanging nature, but that this desk continued to exist even when I slept last night. I also believe that the clock on the table continued running even while I was sleeping. What is it that compels me to believe in this way? That which gives objectivity to such knowledge is not merely an intellectual unity, such as consciousness in general; it must be the unity of the will. The will is the unity of consciousness and unconsciousness. We contain both the past and the future in the horizon of behavior and unify things and mind thereby. Just as we do not feel a desire to possess the stars in the heavens, desire does not arise without some consciousness of possibility. Perhaps the desires arise spontaneously from the opposition of the feelings of happiness and unhappiness. But that we recollect the happiness of the past in the unhappiness of the present and that a distinction of feelings arises within the mind differ in essence from willing or behaving. I cannot help thinking that there is a difference of a priori here. If we speak in familiar terms, we may perhaps say that the sensation of motion must be added, but, more profoundly, we must think that the a priori of the transcendental will that is both subjective and objective comes to be added. Just as thinking does not emerge from sensation, so, too, the will does not emerge from mere feeling. On the contrary, the will is even more fundamental than feeling or knowing. From this point of view the thesis of utilitarianism that both perception and concepts have practical meaning contains an aspect of truth.

Space would seem to indicate the scope of our potentiality of motion. The fact that I say that this desk exists even when I am not conscious of it simply means that there is the possibility that if I tried to touch it I would be able to touch it. This fact of potentiality also means simultaneous existence and the world of material entities. The world of material entities outside the mind is not established in a mere intellectual standpoint but, rather, in the standpoint of the will. That which makes me know that this desk is yesterday's desk is based on the intuition of my consciousness. There is no pure apperception apart from pure will, and even the fact that I recognize this desk as this desk is based upon the will. Pure apperception, which constructs the world of experience, must not be mere universal, logical consciousness. It must lie within present experience and construct it. It must be in the form of the will in order to unite the content and form of experience in actuality. Experiential content and logic are usually thought to be without relation to one another, and experiential content is thought to be irrational and contingent. For example, even though a quick vibration is a red and a slow one is a blue color, this is not a contradiction. The fact that we believe experiential knowledge to be incontrovertible truth is based on the factual feeling of actuality. That which constructs factual knowledge is the a priori of the will, which is the act underlying all acts.

Of course, various doubts may arise when I state, as I have above, that in the horizon of the will, which is the unity of actuality and potentiality, the existence of things is recognized outside of consciousness and that natural-scientific knowledge is also established thereby. How can we know things outside of consciousness? Has our consciousness been conscious even while we are sleeping? These questions seem incomprehensible. But when we will, we are conscious that we are willing. When we know a thing, knower and known must be thought to be different; but when we know the self, the knowing itself must always transcend 'time'. Some may even say that such consciousness is simply a hypothesis. But all knowledge is established on the basis of this consciousness. If we say that this is a hypothesis, then the law of self-identity cannot avoid being a hypothesis, as well. It is difficult to say that there has been consciousness even while we have been sleeping. However, the material world apart from the phenomena of consciousness is nothing more than a world of potentiality and abstraction. Our will unites directly with itself. The will is not merely an event constructed by the form of time. We always are within the process of the completion of our will.

I think that this is similar to artistic creation. Behavior is not a mere event in time but must be the completion of meaning. In one of its aspects there is a world of meaning that is separate from time; the material world also lies herein. In artistic creation the world of such meaning can be thought of as the world of artistic ideals. But in behavior, meaning is the personal content of that person; in world history it is the personal content of God. Just as Augustine states that there was no 'time' prior to God's creation and that 'time' is also created by God, there is no 'time' which constrains the will; and just as 'time' loses its meaning with respect to artistic creation, the will is free with respect to 'time.' Therefore, in the standpoint of knowledge, we cannot know what direction our world will advance in, and we can only be guided from the profound depths of the will. Since we usually think of the material world, which is the world of potentiality, as objective reality and of the spiritual world as subjective illusion, or fantasy, transcendence of the category of 'time' is thought to be incomprehensible. But when we consider the world of matter as the world of potentiality and abstraction, the entire world can also be regarded as an artistic creation. Hence, I think that we can understand the unity of yesterday's and today's consciousnesses and the direct union of will and will as the standpoint of the 'eternal now'.

If there is anything truly mysterious in human life, there is nothing more mysterious than the behavior of the self in the present. When we need to go, we go; and when we need to sit, we sit. In this horizon of free behavior, the self unites the worlds of thing and mind while being at home in both worlds. Because while being actual the self includes the infinite past and future vertically and infinite space horizontally, we can firmly believe the existence of an infinite world outside of consciousness in the very consciousness of actuality. Even the foundation of knowledge, which opens up before the self through objective necessity, is nothing more than the world of the union of subject and object grounded in this horizon. We must also seek the world of Kant's 'thing in itself' herein. Moreover, at the same time that this world of behavior internally includes the world of knowledge, it possesses its own positive world. This world arises by behavior's taking itself as its own goal. In other terms, it is the concrete world, which appears when behavior returns to itself. Only because the worlds of art and morality are grounded in this kind of horizon of pure behavior can we think of them as manifest worlds of the creative self. Therefore, only by sincere behavior can the artist in aesthetic creation and the moralist in practice discover a new world of art or advance to a new world of morality.

Chapter 9

The Will
and the Syllogism

Many present-day logicians hold that judgment does not just unite the subject and predicate concepts by a copulative verb but, rather, establishes a synthetic unity through division in the form of judgment. If judgment is already this kind of process, then what is it that yields the conclusion by uniting the greater and lesser premises in the syllogism? Here we must see that there is an even larger synthetic unity. The syllogism is the self-development of this kind of synthetic unity. Since our reason in the form of the syllogism is endlessly forming conclusions, this kind of synthetic unity is something infinitely vast and profound.

In the case of mathematical knowledge this infinitely deep foundation can be considered to lie in the self. Contrary to this, it can be considered to lie outside in the case of empirical knowledge. However, in terms of Kant's epistemology, since the objective world is a construction of subjectivity, the infinitely vast and profound reality we discover outside can instead be considered to be the very depths of the self. For, since the self is the infinite act underlying all acts, when we see the objective world of the entire self in the standpoint of a partial act, it can be considered to be the infinitely vast and profound real world, but when the self attains to the truly concrete, that which had been previously conceived as the endless objective world can instead be seen as the very depths of the self. When the object is complete in the act, the foundation of infinite truth is believed to lie within the self, and we are considered to have transcendental truth; but, on the contrary, when the object is not complete in respect to the act, that object is considered to be irrational, and we are thought to know it only through experience.

How can the irrational enter into the scope of our knowledge as content of experience, and how can our experiential knowledge be established? I think that it is possible only in the horizon of transcendental will, which is the unity of infinite acts, and that it is possible only in the immediate unity of pure acts themselves that have not yet been reflected upon—that is, in the standpoint of the free self. Reason is the reflective intentionality of the transcendental self, and the will is its creative intentionality. Both the irrational and the antiself in the intentionality of reason can enter into the scope of the self in the intentionality of the will and can thus be rationalized in the broad sense. To speak of rationalization may be inappropriate, but it can at least be internalized. We can clearly demonstrate how the self internalizes or rationalizes the irrational in the intentionality of the will in the cases of aesthetic creation and moral behavior. Irrational existence enters into the scope of the self through behavior. If we consider that we know and unite with truth through thinking, we can also intuit the thing-in-itself and merge with it through behavior. Just as the scholar discovers a new truth through thinking, so do the sculptor and the painter discover new facets of reality by taking up chisel or brush. The so-called world of experience must be an intermediate, objective world in the standpoint between pure reason and pure will. Its place is, as it were, between a world of pure reason, such as that of mathematics, and a world of pure intuition, such as that of art. Immediate intuition must be an act itself, and intuition means the pure activity of the unity of subject and object. When we say that the categories of thinking become objective knowledge by uniting with perception through the schema of 'time', we have already moved to the standpoint of the will from the standpoint of thinking.

Hence, I think that incontrovertible knowledge of events is only established in the intentionality of the will—that is, of behavior. There is no reason that this book before me must necessarily be red. The reason I must think in this way is that I must thus believe in the standpoint of my acting self. The reason is that I feel thus in visual perception. To feel thus in visual perception means to see thus. To see thus means that I merge with the pure, visual act that functions in the form of visual perception. Factual knowledge must first be established by the self acting. Therefore, the self must be acting at the foundation of the statement that this book is red. Empirical knowledge is established on the basis of the firm proof of this kind of will. The most fundamental union of thinking and experience must be found in the very depths of the free self. A thing is nothing more than a projection of the unity of this kind of free self. The will reflects upon itself and reproduces itself within itself as the object of itself.

Various qualities of things correspond to various acts of the self. Of course, in the horizon of this free self we can advance in the creative direction in which one behavior directly produces another and enters into the profound worlds of art and morality. Similarly, in the standpoint of reflection of the transcendental will—that is, of consciousness in general—even though we construct the world of empirical knowledge, we can also construct the world of historical knowledge and maintain the positive standpoint of the will itself. However, the world of nature appears when the will advances to the standpoint of self-reflection and when it is thought that it has even lost the standpoint of the self. Since 'time', which constructs reality, is a projection of the will, when 'time' has lost its course, it becomes 'space'.

In deductive logic we reason from the universal to the particular, and in inductive logic we reason from the particular to the universal. Natural-scientific truth, based on induction, is that form of reasoning in which the universal is established by the particular. But how can the universal be established by the particular? The particular is regarded as a manifestation of the universal, and universal truth is established by analyzing it and clarifying the relationships between its elements. This is also the reason that the law of difference can be thought to be the most functional inductive law, rather than the laws of analogy or consistency. To consider the specific as an expression of the universal is an aesthetic attitude in the broad sense, and what we term the will is the process of idealization of actuality.

What does it mean to say that we idealize actuality through the will? In the volitional act its end is included in the beginning; the whole is included within the parts. Thereby, actuality becomes unique. The will is the act of particularization of the universal. In the world of mathematics, the universal is not included within the particular; in short, there is a rational universal at its foundation. In the world of physics, contrary to this, one atom maintains itself in relation to the entire world as a self-identical reality. An actual atom must include relations with the entire world; it must include the history of past and future. How is the idea of this kind of material force established? A certain qualitative thing is viewed as moving in the present. That which has unified space and time is material force— indeed, the mere union of space and time is nothing more than a mechanistic object. The qualitative must enter into material force. It is particularized by the qualitative. Moreover, this kind of union is possible only in the standpoint of the act underlying all acts, which, transcending reason and sensation, unifies both of them. In other terms, it is possible only in the standpoint of free will. All necessary things are established as contents of free will; when free will has reflected upon its own content, it becomes necessary force. Nature is simply the object that emerges when free will reflects upon itself. This reflection of the act must be an activity. Just as a mathematical object appears in mathematical thinking as that which has been determined by it, so, too, nature appears to free will as that which has been determined thereby as its content. When a certain empirical content changes in the present, if we think of this merely as an event within our conscious unity, as the psychologist usually does, then the idea of material force cannot arise. To establish the idea of material force, we must proceed to a unity outside of consciousness and stand on the basis of transconscious unity. This proceeding outside of the scope of the unity of consciousness is possible only in the will.

Perhaps it will be thought that it is impossible for us to go outside of consciousness. The reason for such an idea is that we think of the self only as an intellectual unity. However, the self so conceived is not the true self. The true self is the unity of the interior and exterior of consciousness, the unity of potentiality and actuality. Even the idea of a conscious act distinguished from the objective world is established thereby. We are able to view the transconscious world only in the standpoint of this kind of transintellectual world—that is, of active subjectivity. The transconscious world only appears as the object of behavior. This is the reason that I believe that this desk that I now see is the same as yesterday's desk and that this desk was existent even while I slept last night. Fiedler thinks that in the standpoint of pure visual perception an infinitely aesthetic objective world of art opens up; similarly, in the horizon of the will an infinite world of ideals opens up.

Intellectually there is no way of proving whether this desk is the same as yesterday's desk. The horizon of the will transcends that of knowledge. Our objective knowledge is truly established by the will. If one rejects this as mystery, then all physical knowledge must be considered to be mystery. Knowledge unifies the particular from the standpoint of the universal, and the will unifies the abstractly universal in the standpoint of the particular. In empirical knowledge the particular must be the foundation. The universal is the means of explanation of the particular. However, the particular that is the basis of physical knowledge possesses no positive content apart from the fact that it merely acts. In other terms, since it is nothing more than the infinite projection of merely formal will, it may rather be thought that the universal is the center. On the contrary, when the will possesses its own positive content, the universal becomes the means of its actualization. As in aesthetic creation, that which is unique in the present becomes the center.

The syllogism presupposes an infinite creative act in its background. The merely formal syllogism cannot provide any objective knowledge. We may even say that it only establishes an infinite series of classes such as we see in classification. Turning to mathematical thinking, there clearly must be a kind of intuition at its foundation. Intuition must be a creative act. The uniting of one universal with another in a mathematical deduction is this kind of infinitely profound creative act. Deduction is the process of its development. However, mathematical thinking can still be thought to be established on the basis of a universal as a totality. Therefore, it can be thought that the creative act lies in the self. In such an instance, the self means the reflective aspect of the self. However, objective knowledge possessing universal validity in itself does not arise through mere reflection. Even in mathematics this is so, but it is particularly clear in physics. In physics the reflective self must conform to the intuitive self. Volitional subjectivity in the broad sense becomes the creator of truth. The world of force that unites mathematics and empirical content is the particular unity of the universal. Herein the foundation of truth shifts from the universal to the specific; it shifts from deduction to induction. It may be thought incomprehensible to say that the universal is grounded by the particular. But in the form of the will the universal is included within the particular. However, because the infinitely creative will is a depth unattainable by reflective thinking, the rational and irrational oppose each other, and an unbridgeable abyss is created between them. However, in the even purer standpoint of the will itself, such opposition comes to have positive content, and contradiction itself comes to have meaning. Personal content must be such content. In this the above infinitely vast and profound exterior is the very depth of the self; the a priori returns to itself, and the particular returns again to the universal.

All truth returns to that which is unique. That which is unique is established when the object returns to the act itself and arises when the act has reflected upon itself. It is not truly unique merely as an object, for the uniqueness of the object is established by the uniqueness of the act. Only that which creates the object can be unique. The uniqueness of the act can only be recognized in the standpoint of the act underlying all acts.

Needless to say, the truth is the universally valid, but the merely universally valid is not the entire truth. Truth must be teleological. This is the reason Kant considers that mathematics becomes objective knowledge by uniting with perception. It must be the concrete will that thus determines the goal of truth. Hegel states that the unique is the universal (*das Einzelne ist das Allgemeine*); he considers that the universal concept becomes unique and attains to concrete truth by developing itself and returning to itself. But I think that this has the same meaning as Kant's statement that objective knowledge is constituted by being united with perception. When the universal concept develops and returns to itself, it is not merely a universal returning to a prior universal; it appears in the standpoint of a more concrete universal. A small circle is united with a larger circle that subsumes it, and an abstract universal moves toward a concrete universal in the standpoint of the act underlying all acts—that is, it accords with its own teleology. The goal of the abstract lies in the concrete, and knowledge unites with the will by advancing in this direction. We must say that only the will is truly unique.

Knowledge is constructed by the subjective act, and that which infinitely grounds knowledge outside must be an infinitely creative, internal act. When its contents are determined in the standpoint of a certain act, we can recognize universally valid truth as long as that act is transindividual. But only when its knowledge is further reflected upon in the horizon of the concrete act underlying all acts— that is, of the will—and only when it is unified teleologically, does knowledge become truly objective and unique. The will is considered to be subjective, but a merely subjective will cannot actualize anything. The will must always accord with objectivity—indeed, our experience of the will is established only in the sense that the objective world that is given belongs within the scope of the act of the self. When we say that the given is that which has been sought, we already are in the horizon of the will. Even the impulsive will has the same form. The will is an unlimited unity of intellectual a priori. The clearer its positive content becomes, the more the will can be considered to be free.

That which combines and unites various a priori must be the horizon of the will. Therefore, philosophy, which is the ultimate unity of knowledge, can be considered to be knowledge established in the category of volitional unity. Philosophy arises only in the intentionality of the transcendental will. On this point philosophy differs from knowledge attained in the other disciplines. If there is someone who says that what is established in the category of the will is not knowledge, then I wish to ask that person whether he has consciousness of self-consciousness. Philosophy must be the self-consciousness of the transcendental will. It is knowledge uniting past, present, and future. It begins in and returns to the infinitely dynamic, active subjectivity of the present, which is the fusion point of the true, the good, and the beautiful.

Chapter 10

The Beautiful and the Good

1

We usually consider that the objective world of knowledge is the only world and that we live and act only within this world. However, from such a standpoint, even our will and our behavior must become mere objects of knowledge, like other objects of knowledge. There would then be no way for such conscious experiences as my will or my behavior to arise. For consciousness of will or of behavior to be established, acting must know itself—that is, acting must be knowing. In essence, knowing is also a kind of will and behavior. We do not merely live in an objective world of knowledge; rather, we are always living in an objective world of behavior.

The beautiful is not merely the feeling of pleasure, for if it were, we could not require universal validity in the beautiful. The beautiful must be an expression of the content of a profound life that transcends knowledge. In the horizon of immediate behavior everything is filled with personal life. That which expresses this content directly is the creative act of the artist. This is the reason that the creative act of the artist is considered to be an expressive movement. The content of life in the objective world of behavior can be understood and expressed only in behavior.

Neither can the moral good be explained in terms of the mere objective world of knowledge. If we try to explain it thus, we either fall into utilitarianism, or, if not that, we see it as a kind of delusion. True moral behavior must be a creative act that constructs our free and personal world on the basis of those deep requirements of life that transcend knowledge. The authority of the moral imperative "You must act in such a way" with respect to the consideration of personal advantage and disadvantage comes to be established in this way.

Since both the good and the beautiful are contents that first appear when we are self-conscious of the free self that transcends nature and that is deeply latent within the self, they can be considered to belong to the objective world of the same standpoint. As the content of pure life there is nothing beautiful that is not good and nothing good that is not beautiful. How, then, are the good and the beautiful distinguished, and what relationship do they have?

2

Independent, concrete experience always constitutes a system of self-consciousness. A system of self-consciousness—for example, in personal self-awareness—must mean that the knower and the known are one and hence that one act directly gives birth to another; it must mean that knowing is acting and acting is knowing. Even seeing or hearing have the form of this kind of self-conscious structure as independent, concrete experiences in themselves. There may be objections to considering such perceptual experiences to be self-conscious. However, in the usual consideration of self-consciousness we are merely focusing upon its reflective direction and forgetting its creative direction. A self that is a static unity as a mere object of reflection is the same as a thing, while the true self must be a creative act. The ideal is creative in the creative act of the artist. For example, the ideal of color and form is creative in painting, and the ideal of sound is creative in music. Visual and aural acts are the processes of development of these ideals. As Fiedler states, the creative act of the artist can be thought to be the development of pure visual perception. I think that the creative act of the artist can be said to be the self-consciousness of these ideals as the process of the internal development of the ideals of color, form, and sound.

If I use the term *self-consciousness*, it may be thought that the self can be conscious of itself as an object of judgment; but our active self, needless to say, cannot be the object of judgment. The act of thinking is a process of self-development. Self-consciousness of the ideal in the world of intellectual content is moral behavior. However, because thinking is the standpoint of the unity of all acts as the reflective direction of the will, which is the act underlying all acts, self-consciousness in this horizon becomes the source of all self-awareness, as the self-consciousness of self-consciousness. And all self-consciousness can be considered to be established in this horizon.

We usually think of self-consciousness as an intellectual self-reflection wherein the reflecting self and the reflected self are one; but the self is not merely such an intellectual unity, for that the self reflects upon itself means that the self acts within itself and advances a step beyond the intellectual plane. This process itself constructs the inextinguishable history of the self—that is, it becomes an objective fact. In this sense we can say that the self is a dynamic unity in which one act directly gives birth to another and is its creative act. This is the reason that I can say that the essence of the self is to be discovered in the horizon of the will and behavior. When we know a thing, we can say that there is a thing known by the self. However, when the self knows itself, we cannot say there is a self that does not know, for that which does not know is not a self. But, then, should we think there is a self only when there has been an event of knowledge? However, that which knows the self must be the self itself. Without a self we cannot say that we know the self. We must clearly recognize a kind of knowledge prior to judgment in self-consciousness. In self-consciousness acting is knowing. In the empirical world, we cannot know the actor itself; but in self-consciousness we do know the actor and the power itself. If we think of an inscrutable "self" in the background of experience in the same sense as we think of the "causes" of things, that would put the self on the same level as things and would not be the true self. From this kind of background self there is no way for consciousness in self-consciousness to arise.

The self in its creative intentionalities functions at the point of identity of knowledge and behavior. The creative act of the artist involves, for example, the intersection of practice and knowledge. We may say that there is an eye at the tip of the artist's brush or the sculptor's chisel. In this intentionality the artist treads in a world unattainable through knowledge. Even world history extending from the past of the past to the future of the future, expresses the creative direction of the transindividual self; it is nothing more than the creative act of the transcendental will. While I was sleeping, the clock on my desk was measuring time, and this desk continues to be the same desk as yesterday's desk. But the fact that they have continued one more day in time can be expressed only in the standpoint of transcendental will. The objective world is an infinite reality, which cannot be exhaustively known in thinking; yet at the same time it is constructed by thinking. The constructive direction of thinking is the transcendental will, and thinking is merely its reflective direction, for the will and thinking are two aspects of one act.

When the artist takes up yesterday's project and continues to work on it, an artistic ideal transcending time is operative. The time that has elapsed must be completely lost. When we continue yesterday's life into the present, the self of yesterday is directly continued into today's self, and yesterday's world is directly continued into the present; this self is yesterday's self, and the room is yesterday's room. We do not have anything at all to prove this, for our knowledge begins from this postulate. We can only say that yesterday's experiences or today's experiences are not delusory phenomena floating on the surface of consciousness, and that they are realities in which we and they function together and can only be affirmed in the horizon of behavioral subjectivity. In this horizon, reality exists by transcending consciousness, and thus yesterday's self is today's self and yesterday's room is today's room. That we think of this world as an endless process extending without beginning and end means that one act gives birth to another as the world of personal content. Biological cognition and historical cognition are established on this basis. Space and time are merely categories of the negative intentionality of the transcendental will.

In the intentionality of cultural development, which is the *positive* direction of the transcendental will, we transcend space and time just as the artist transcends space and time in the horizon of his own aesthetic ideal. When we view reality as the object of behavior, we can say that we are able to move it. At the foundation of actuality the content of transcendental will is active. Being thus the content of the transcendental will in which one act gives birth to another, actuality can never avoid being incomplete.

3

The term *aesthetic subjectivity* is usually thought to mean the fusion of subject and object, and the beautiful is thought to be the fusion of the ideal and the actual. But in such a case, subject and object mean nothing more than the intellectual subject and the object opposing it, and even the ideal is an intellectual ideal. In this way, aesthetic intuition can also be thought to be a mere static unity and the beautiful to be a kind of satisfaction of desire. However, when I use the term *aesthetic content*, I mean that objective content that appears in the intentionality of pure, behavioral subjectivity. I refer to that experiential content of the pure will that is the act underlying all acts. Just as it can be that 'the given is that which has been sought' and that by the principle of the 'anticipation of perception' sensation becomes experiential content, so, too, the given in the horizon of pure will must be the individual expression of the will, in the sense of being that which has been constructed by the principle of 'anticipation of the will'. It must be an individual, pure act as the object of pure will, transcending the intellectual plane as an object of behavior.

The intuition of the artist is a vision of things in such a horizon. It is not vision only of the eye, but of the eye and hand as one experience. In this way we must also interpret a creative act in the plastic arts as an expressive movement accompanying the development of pure visual perception. Various meanings and dimensions obtain even in regard to the opposition and fusion of subjectivity and objectivity. Every opposition between subjectivity and objectivity appears in the form of disunity of act and object, while the union of subject and object is the becoming of a pure act as object *qua* act and act *qua* object. The fact of becoming a pure act in this way means to return to the concrete foundation and means standing in the dimension of an even higher order.

Creativity is usually understood to imply that the act that creates and the thing created are different. However, a true creative act must create its own content from within itself. I think the experience that can clarify the true form of this kind of creative act is our self-consciousness, or self-awareness. Thus, I think that in the relation between the reflected and the reflecting self, we can clarify the true relationship between the created and the creative. Even that pure thinking produces its own content must be in the sense of this kind of relationship. We say that sensation becomes experiential content by the application of the 'principle of the anticipation of perception', but the given must be that which was created. We see our own face in things, so to speak. There is no way for experiential content to be given to mere thinking, nor any way for it to be sought thereby. The experiential world must be sought and created by the will, which is the act underlying all acts. Behind pure apperception will must be functioning. It can be thought that our will is satisfied by things, but, for a thing to become an object of desire, it must be constructed by the will. The will is satisfied by its own creations, and the self rests by seeing itself. Therefore, that which we believe we see intuitively is the self's own reflection; it is the self seeing itself. When God created man in his own image, God objectified himself, creating a world of himself. If we view the creative act from that which has been created in this way, the self reflected upon opposes the reflecting self and is always imperfect and incomplete. But, while the creative is included within the created, it is an unattainable limit. The self cannot objectify itself. The active self must be an unattainable limit.

From the above kind of idea, I hold that the content of aesthetic intuition is created by pure will and is the truly concrete and immediately given, and further that moral behavior is another creative act of the development of the pure will. The relationship between the two must be explained as that between the reflecting and the reflected self, or that between the creative and the created, in the horizon of the creative will. Just as in Vischer's statement that the beautiful is life reflected within itself (*als Leben in sich gespiegelt*), the beautiful is that in which the creative will itself reflects its own shadows, objectifies itself, and is the self-consciousness of the pure will. What Boehme calls 'the groundless' (*Ungrund*), the shadow that is reflected within itself, must be the consummation of beauty. Aesthetic intuition is not a passive intuition, but the self-consciousness of pure act itself. The content of the beautiful is only given in the horizon of pure behavioral subjectivity. That which is constructed in the a priori of pure activity must be pure activity.

Moral behavior may be considered to exist only in the abstract relation between man and man, but a merely formal good will is not the true good. By inclining only to the side of this kind of formal good will one can, on the contrary, fall into evil. True morally good behavior must be the development of the concrete person. Of course, the beautiful is not directly the good, and artistic creativity is not directly moral behavior. But only when we see things purely in the horizon of moral behavior do we authentically stand in the same horizon as aesthetic intuition, which sees the thing-in-itself apart from every utilitarian motive. We must regard our fellowman on this earth with the same disinterest with which we admire the stars in the heavens. Kant's 'kingdom of ends' is a work of art that moral behavior creates. Moral behavior that is truly autonomous and good in itself must be a creative act possessing its own content. When we enter into that content by the merely formal free will, it must immediately become heteronomous. It is sometimes said that the end of moral behavior is real, while the end of artistic creativity is unreal, but the reality of the objective world of morality is not the same as the reality of the world of natural science.

4

If we can consider the relationship between aesthetic intuition and moral behavior in the above way, I think we can find many indications to clarify the relationships between the objective worlds of art and morality from within Kant's discussion of the relation between 'mathematical principles' and the 'principles of dynamics', but by taking the schema of 'the will' in place of the schema of 'time' and by taking the world of culture in place of the natural world. In order to clarify this idea, let us further state Kant's idea developed in the beginning of his "Analogy of Experience." Empirical knowledge is knowledge that determines objective objects through perception. Experience is then the synthesis of perception; this synthesis is not contained within perception but, rather, synthesizes and unifies perception. The necessary relationship between one perception and another perception in the empirical world cannot be clarified merely by perception itself. The necessity of existence in space and time cannot be sought within 'apprehension'. However, despite the fact that experience is given by perception and that its relations are objectively expressed in 'time', 'time' itself cannot be perceived, and therefore the existence of things in 'time' must be determined by their unity in 'time'. In other words, the three modes of 'time' (*Mode der Zeit*) refer to the transcendental concepts that construct our empirical world. Kant considers duration, continuity, and simultaneous existence (*Beharrlichkeit, Folge und Zugleichsein*) to be the three modes of 'time', and by means of them he establishes the three principles of the duration of a substance (*Grundsatz der Beharrlichkeit der Substanz*), of continuity based upon the law of causality (*Grundsatz der Zeitfolge nach dem Gesetze der Kausalität*), and of simultaneous existence based on the law of mutuality or communality (*Grundsatz des Zugleichseins nach dem Gesetze der Wechselwirkung oder Gemeinschaft*).

That our experiential world is constructed by the synthetic unity of pure apperception is Kant's fundamental thought. The synthesis of apperception must be operative both in the depths of intuition and—even more—in the depths of imagination. Even space and time, which are considered to be the forms of intuition, must be derived from such a synthetic act of the pure ego. 'Time', which Kant considers to be the schema that unifies concepts and intuition, best manifests the creative act of pure apperception. Perception, which gives objectivity to our knowledge, is given by the form of 'time'— indeed, we may say that it is created by 'time' and that 'time' itself is not the object of perception. There is no creative act within the thing created; the self reflected upon is not the reflecting self. However, while that which has been created is not the creator, it is not something different from it, either. The created thing must reveal the shadow of the creator. The self reflected upon is not a thing, but must be the self. Therefore, the object is always incomplete and to be completed with respect to the act. For experience of the given to complete its own meaning, it must enter into a world of infinite development. It must enter into the world of existence, which is the object of thinking—that is, into a world of necessary relations from the world of perceptions, which are thought to be mutually accidental and complete in themselves. As the self is an infinite depth that cannot be attained, the world of existence must also be infinite. Just as the eye that has been turned toward the object in self-consciousness is turned toward the act itself, so, too, the eye of the creator, who is self-conscious of his own incompleteness in the created thing, is turned within itself, and thereby the world of reflection, which takes the act itself as object, is established. The world of 'time' itself, which cannot be perceived, is a world that takes the form of 'time' itself as object; that is, it must be a world of material power that cannot be perceived directly. Of course, for an act itself to function as object, it must stand in an even higher dimension—that is, in the will, the intentionality of the act underlying all acts. Even the physical world may be thought to be established in the horizon of the will, which unifies the direction of infinite 'time'. Material force is an objectification of the will. Even Kant's three modes of 'time' cannot be conceived merely as 'time' that flows.

The act of aesthetic creation is not an event in the natural world. Of course, it may be viewed in this way from the standpoint of knowledge, but, if we think in this way, the universal validity of the beautiful must be lost. In the horizon of a pure act of aesthetic creation, experience is grounded on an a priori different from that which constructs the natural world, and we construct a different objective world; in other terms, we construct the objective world of pure will in the intentionality of pure will and construct the world of culture different from, and of an even higher order than, the natural world.

It is not that we act in pursuit of pleasure under the domination of causality; if we consider that the actualization of universally valid values is cultural behavior, then the creative act of the artist, needless to say, must directly be cultural behavior. Conversely, the transformation of human life into art begins when man first constructs society and enters into cultural life. Moral behavior must be the pure transformation of human life into art. In this sense, both art and morality belong to the objective world of pure will as cultural phenomena. Therefore, the world of culture is constructed by the pure will, and we see things artistically, just as the empirical world is constructed by pure apperception. That is, aesthetic intuition corresponds to intuition in the empirical world—to what Kant terms "perception." The given, as an object of art, must be the given in the objective world of pure will. The object of painting must be given to the eye acting in concert with the hand of the artist. As the objective world of pure will there is nothing whatever that is not beautiful. Even in ugly and vulgar things we can discover profound beauty as expressions of human life.

However, as in Kant's statement that perception is constructed by the form of 'time' and cannot perceive 'time' itself, artistic objects are also given by the structure of pure will, but we cannot transform the will itself into art. Within the created there is no creator, and within the self reflected upon there is no reflecting self. Even the fact that we view reflections of human life in an artistic object does not mean that it is human life itself. Human life reflected in art is one-sided and incomplete. Nevertheless, even though the self reflected upon is not the reflecting self itself, the former is also not something apart from the latter; it is the product of the act of the self and at the same time is directly the act itself and must contain the development of an infinite self within the self of the present; in other terms, it must be a kind of productive point. We cannot perceive 'time' itself, but perception is given in the standpoint of the construction of the schema of 'time', and, just as the self reflected upon in self-consciousness is directly the reflecting self, it must also include the development toward the world of existence within it. Therefore, we must advance from the world of perception to the world of objects of thinking and must enter into the world of primary qualities from the world of secondary qualities. Similarly, in the world of the pure will we move from artistic intuition into the moral imperative by internal necessity.

Of course, when I speak in this way, I do not mean that morality develops from art. I only indicate the profound and essential relationship between them. When in the above way we move from the passive to the active intentionality of pure will—that is, into the dimension of the self-consciousness of the creative act itself—the modes of pure will must become the principles that construct the moral world, just as the three modes of 'time' construct the fundamental principles of the world of existence. The moral world is a world constructed by the will and is the objective world of pure will; it is Kant's 'kingdom of ends' established by the relationship between person and person. In this moral sphere there is no such thing as substance or cause. It is the world of pure act, in which one act gives rise to another. In the horizon of the will, the dark shadow that is latent in the background of the schema of 'time' must vanish completely, for the will unifies both content and form, as the act underlying all acts. We may be able to term this the communality (*Gemeinschaft*) of acts. However, this is no merely static simultaneous existence, for the three mutually contradictory modes of 'time' rather disclose their internal unity in the will.

5

Needless to say, the end of moral behavior must be the actualization of a certain ideal. What has moral value is our decision, our actual practice. Mere motive cannot have moral value. Such things as the realization or actual practice of one's end must mean that behavior is constructed by the categories of space, time, and causality and that it is manifest as fact in the world of existence; in other words, behavior must mean the moving of this objective world of reality. In this way, the way we must act in a certain manner from a moral standpoint opens up before us as an incontrovertible, rigorous imperative. We must follow it, and if we do not, it is evil and sin.

In contrast to this, the creative intentionality of the artist may be an event in the world of existence, but it can be thought that the end of artistic creation is the product of the subjective imagination, which is not real. Poetry and painting thus reflect only one aspect of human life. They offer no criticism of moral good or evil whatsoever; even evil things can become beautiful as objects of art. In moral behavior duty faces the self as a unique duty that must be followed, whereas we can find infinite beauty in an object. In the beautiful we are free. Art ultimately cannot avoid a playful mood.

When I say, then, that the content of the good and the beautiful are the same in quality, I mean that both belong to the content of the pure will. The horizon of pure feeling and the will not only transcends that of conceptual knowledge but even functions contrary to that of the feeling of pleasure and pain. Happiness and unhappiness are nothing more than generic concepts of feelings reflected upon; when creative feeling loses its own content and stands under the control of concepts, it can be thought merely to seek happiness and avoid unhappiness. Pure feeling or will, as the act underlying all acts, possess their own positive content, unanalyzable into intellectual content. Therefore, with respect to the objective world of knowledge, pure feeling or willing are creative. The transcendental nature of aesthetic content and the content of the moral imperative are given thereby.

Of course, the goal of moral behavior may be thought of as real and that of aesthetic creation as unreal; but in painting there is a beauty peculiar to painting, and in sculpture there is a beauty peculiar to sculpture, and it can be thought that even in the beautiful there is distinctive content, depending on the differences in sensory qualities. I acknowledge completely such an idea, but at the same time I cannot help recognizing some internal unity among the various arts. Indeed, I view the various arts as expressions or aspects of one multidimensional and infinitely rich aesthetic world that follows the special characteristics of its sensory material. I think that even the objective world of morality merges internally with this world as the objective world of pure will. The experience in which the sculptor faces his marble with a chisel, or the painter his canvas holding a brush, can be thought to be very different from the moralist expounding precepts or the legislator making laws. However, the sculptor, painter, and moralist are each constructing worlds of pure will. Even the objective world of art is not merely sensory, as is usually thought, for in art an ideal world is included within sensory images. In respect to poetry, which particularly treats the world constructed by 'reproductive representation' (*Nachvorstellung*), its nonsensory and more abstract nature is clearly discussed in Meyer's *Das Stilgesetz der Poesie*. The end of the moralist and legislator is the construction of an ideal society. Moral behavior must be an act of aesthetic creation, constructive of cultural society. If not, and if motives are the only good, one can only fall into a moral subjectivism in which everything is good. Whence, then, arise the distinction between art and morality and the difference between beauty and the good?

The physical world is given by experience, but it is not experience precisely as it is. The colors or sounds directly experienced are not immediately the qualities of things. Of course, even in present-day physics there may be no one who thinks that things exist apart from sensory facts. However, the physical world begins by selecting and constructing sensory facts from a certain standpoint. Poincaré's concept of 'law' (*loi*) is made from the relationships between crude facts. His 'principles' (*principes*) are further constructed in order to unify laws. The construction of knowledge in this way means advancing to the construction of one unified physical world. The truth and falsehood of physical knowledge must be decided by the teleological unity of this kind of physical knowledge itself. Even physical knowledge must advance infinitely. If there is no absolute truth, there can be no absolute falsehood. However, we are able to establish the imperative of physical knowledge from the end of physical knowledge itself. If not, physics cannot be established. That which indicates the direction of physical knowledge must at the same time be the a priori that constructed the physical world at the outset. The end is fixed by the very first a priori, and its end lies in its beginning. Therefore, the advance of knowledge must be infinite.

If we insert a stick in water, it seems to be broken at the water's surface. We are forced to say that the stick, seen only with the eye, is broken. However, when we appeal to the tactile sense, we immediately know that this is an error, and we can know that the reason this must be so depends upon the laws of refraction of light. When we say that the stick *seems* to be broken, we already have assumed the standpoint of cognition. Of course, if we say only that the stick seems to be broken, this is nothing more than knowledge of fact. But if we say that, even in other cases, this stick must be this way—that the stick *is* broken—then we already have unified and universalized a fact by the concept of substance. At such a time we have already entered into physical knowledge. The fact that this judgment is mistaken is proved from this standpoint, and at the same time the event requires explanation as a physical phenomenon from the standpoint of physical knowledge. If this fact is not explained, then it must remain as a problem of physical knowledge.

Now, from the above idea, let us reconsider the relationship between artistic and moral objects. As a pure expression of life, everything is beautiful and good. When we see things with a pure heart, there is nothing that is not beautiful and good. To view things with a pure heart means to view them in the horizon of pure will. This is also why artistic description transforms ugly and evil things into beauty. Even those things that we normally think of as evil, if viewed merely as such, have value as expressions of the internal necessity of human life. Nietzsche states that everything that has value is formed through evil. It is the same as our being able to say that the stick in the water is broken just as it is. That a certain will can be thought to be evil means that it is conceived within a hierarchy of the will that arises from relationships with others. As the mere given of the will, there is neither good nor evil; everything is an expression of beautiful life. However, when the will advances to the world of the construction of the will itself—that is, to the world of self-consciousness of the will—good and evil separate; the former must be sought and the latter rejected. In the standpoint of physical cognition, the judgment that the stick is broken must be an error. Just as reality and unreality, truth and falsehood, are decided by principles based on the three modes of 'time', so are the good and evil of behavior decided by the moral law based on the modes of pure will. Kant's moral law is this kind of principle that constructs the 'kingdom of ends'.

If I merely say that the stick in the water seems now to be broken, then it is a truth merely as something expressing a perceptual event just as it is. All empirical learning would seem to be constructed on the basis of such factual knowledge. If we say that this stick is broken in a universal sense by using the concept of substance, then at this time we fall into error. The pure demands of the heart are all beautiful and good—indeed, there is not yet the distinction between good and evil, beautiful and ugly. But when, on the contrary, we try to overlook our relational existence with others and insist upon certain egotistic demands, then every demand becomes evil. Why do they become evil? Just as truth and falsehood are distinguished by the standpoint of consciousness in general, so must this be distinguished in the standpoint of unified consciousness. But morality differs from nature. It must mean that each act, as a free, personal act, unites with the divine will. A certain desire can be regarded as good or evil, not as a mere impulse of nature, but as the construction of a personal a priori. The impulses of nature do not directly become my motive. For them to become 'my motive' must depend on the choice of my free will. When natural impulse moves the self as natural impulse, then the behavior of the self has no ethical significance. For a certain natural impulse to become 'my motive', it must vanish into the innermost depths of the self and again appear within the self, just as a curved line encircles an infinite point and appears again.

Now I think that when an impulse of nature once disappears within the self as nature in this way, to reappear as a personal phenomenon, it must come to possess the meaning of aesthetic content. Many past ethicians have not paid attention to this point. If we consider our desires to be merely natural and to directly move the self, the fact that the self conforms to them must mean that it is completely heteronomous and that the good will is completely formal. But formal will cannot give any content. Utilitarianism gives content of behavior in this way. For impulsive content to move the self directly from within the self itself as the content of moral behavior, it must be created as personal content—that is, it must be spiritualized. Natural demands, on the contrary, are the means of spiritual content and its expression.

Even the sexual love between a man and a woman, as it is directly transformed into something beautiful, possesses ethical significance as an end in itself. If not, it can only have the meaning of merely ephemeral pleasure or of some such utilitarian act as that of preservation of the species. The rituals of ancient man are not mere customs that have been handed down from generation to generation; they also aesthetisize man's natural impulses. To explain how we can clarify what should be done in a certain case, we must reflect upon the matter itself objectively, entirely apart from utilitarian considera- tion. We must reflect upon the matter itself in the transparent mirror of the sincere heart. We must look upon things with the same attitude as the artist looks upon things; as the artist lives within things in themselves, so, too, must we live within interpersonal situations in themselves. We may say that this kind of attitude means to strain the ear truly to catch the voice of conscience. There is a saying that the adult does not lose the heart of a child, and I think there must be an aesthetic, childlike attitude in the moral sage. The aesthetic spirit, such as is expressed in lyric poetry, must be one keynote of the moralist.

Thus, the given as the content of the moral will, which is an expression of the pure will, must be a sincere personal content given in the form of aesthetic intuition. We can say that, as pure intuition, everything is beautiful and good in the broad sense, but when we have advanced to the world of existence constituted by the unity of pure apperception from the world of perception, good and evil di- verge, just as truth and falsehood diverge in the direction of the con- struction of the transcendental will. We construct perception as the schema of pure apperception. But, just as 'time', which cannot be per- ceived as itself, constructs the empirical world, so does the pure will construct the objective moral world, which is a unity as an infinite ought that can never realize itself. Our unique direction is deter- mined, and the unique moral ought "You must act in a certain way" is established from the total unity of this world.

Perhaps the given of the pure will, such as expressed above, cannot yet be termed either aesthetic or moral content; it may simply be considered to be personal content that can develop in either way. Of course, if we consider it analytically, such content becomes the beautiful by uniting with the creative act of the artist and again may be considered to be good or evil as the content of moral behavior. However, personal content, given in such a sense, must mean the given with respect to our intellectual standpoint. In this sense it is neither good nor evil, neither beautiful nor ugly. However, the given in the intentionality of the pure will—that is, the given with respect to behavioral subjectivity—must contain development in some direc- tion. In this sense, it is the beautiful or the good. When the act sees itself as object in the intentionality of behavior, it is aesthetic intuition, and when it reflects infinitely upon itself, it is moral behavior. That which is given to the painter or sculptor is given to his eye and hand as one organic experience and is the content of life that moves transintellectually. Precisely the content of this life must be the material constructive of the world of culture, which is the objective world of the pure will. Of course, the content of life that the artist sees is simply the content of life latent in the depths of space, and the creative act of the painter or sculptor is nothing more than the activity of formation of eye and hand.

However, the form that the artist sees is not simply form; it must be the expression of life. Self-consciousness of life itself, which is the constructive principle of this kind of sensory world, is also moral content. The fact that life proceeds to form life itself as its own goal is moral behavior. That the will, the act underlying all acts, which is the unity of all acts, reflects internally—the fact that it constructs its own world—must mean that it unifies the content of all acts and must construct a unique, objective world. Here I think there is a kind of transition from Leibniz's world of the possibles to the world of actuality. Infinite possible worlds, as the union of eternal truth, can be thought to be in the knowledge of God, and one of them is selected by the will of God, so that the uniquely actual world is created. In artistic intuition, potential human life, which is reflected from various perspectives, is determined from the unified standpoint of the totality of human life; when unique and actual human life is established, there appears the unique world of duty: "You must act in a certain way." Just as factual truth is unique and immovable, so moral duty cannot be a playful mood, in that it is an absolute imperative. When the creative act returns to itself and finds an objective world complete in itself, there is established a unique, infinitely unattainable world.

6

The above ideas simply express a part of a way of thinking that attempts to clarify the fact that both art and morality belong to the objective world of the same pure will and how the two are distinguished and related. Each of the arts, as a reflection of pure human life, is a fact of human life complete in itself, just as the stick in the water is thought to be broken and the heavens are thought to revolve. However, in the objective world that is constructed by self-consciousness of the a priori itself, constructive of such fact and complete in itself, art is nothing more than an incomplete and accidental fragment; the given is not complete. The world of the act that finds completion in itself must be the infinite ought; and the self that reflects, in contrast to the self that is reflected upon, is always an infinite ought. Herein lie the distinction and contrast between art and morality. Our moral society is the aesthetic creation of God, who eternally resides beyond the process of completion. The content of human life, seen from the horizon of behavioral subjectivity, must be either good or bad, just as the content of our knowledge in the horizon of cognition must be either true or false. The fact that the concept of good differs from the concept of beauty and takes existence as its end, arises from the fact that a unique, objective world is required as transpersonal subjectivity. In the plane of consciousness in general, the world of existence is given by the unity of relations. Because the horizon of transcendental will is inclusive of that of consciousness in general, the good must be conceptual, and moral behavior must be real. As Bergson states, in clashing with the real world, we must proceed to abandon most of our innately rich personal potential. However, by doing so we construct the person of God, who transforms reality itself into person.

Chapter 11

Law and Morality

1

We usually take the so-called world of nature to be the only objective world. But the world of nature constructed by cognitive subjectivity is not the only objective world. Volitional and active subjectivity are at the ground of cognitive subjectivity. That which is truly given directly to us is the objective world of the will. This objective world of the will lies at the ground of the objective world of knowledge. The world of cultural phenomena should be sought here. The objective world of the will appears through our will—indeed, it is a world that appears through our behavior. In the horizon of pure artistic creation the objective world of art appears; in the horizon of pure moral behavior the objective world of morality appears. Each appears as an objective world of the free self that transcends and internally includes cognitive subjectivity. Just as there is a relationship between perception and empirical knowledge in the empirical world, so in the realms of art and morality is there something similar to the relationship between the world of the given and the world of construction in the objective world of the free self. The realm of law is the first stage of the world of construction of this kind of transcendental will—that is, the first stage of the world of morality. Law has no value in itself. Only if it has value as a means of another, or—at any rate—if it has cultural value in itself, can law exist in this sense.

Among students of law there are different opinions concerning its essence, but I think that in order to respect and obey the law as the obligation of men who have free self-consciousness and in order for the law to have authority for us, law must have value as an end in itself. If this is not so, law would merely be a means of happiness, and it could not require any absolute submission on our part. Of course, many present-day laws have merely utilitarian ends. Again, there are many that have been created for the sake of some social class. However, setting aside for the moment the rightness or wrongness of content, the formal will in itself, which honors law in itself and obeys the law for its own sake, must already have personal content and cultural value. The very fact of obeying given laws presupposes this kind of personal significance. It can perhaps be said that a law that has no moral content has no value at all. But I think that obedience to law is not merely for the sake of morality; it has cultural value in itself. Depending on the way of thinking about it, submission to the authority of inscrutable content, in one aspect, has a religious meaning and has independent significance, in contrast to merely subjective morality. The moral law can be said to fulfill its meaning by having a transcendental foundation, as well.

We only stand in dread of the vast powers of the external world, which are unrelated to the personal unity of the self, but we cannot help being overwhelmed by infinite awe at great personal power. The concept of infinite respect for law must be one of awe for the transcendental will that has an infinitely deep root in the unity of the person. Not only does the transcendental will transcend and internally include consciousness in general, but also, because it has its own objective world, the construction of such a world must be the end of the will in itself. The will does not follow law in this intentionality for the sake of any other purpose; it follows it for its own sake. Law in this objective world of the will is different in essence from natural-scientific law; we can say that it is grounded on a deeper foundation. It is thought that the world of culture develops from the natural world, but the natural world is nothing more than a shadow, in which the transcendental will is reflected within itself. The transcendental will that transcends time, on the contrary, includes it internally as one process of its self-development.

2

There is volitional and active subjectivity in the inner depths of intellectual subjectivity. The world of the free self opens up when we enter into this standpoint. The aesthetic world is established—for example, the world of painting, as the development of pure visual perception, and the world of music, as the development of pure aural perception, come into being—in this horizon. However, the worlds of law and morality appear in the direction of the self-consciousness of the will itself, which is the act underlying all acts. These worlds appear as the content of the synthetic and constructive act of the will. With reference to the world of empirical knowledge, I think it is comparable to the empirical world, which Kant considered to be established by the principles of dynamics. The pure self, the standpoint of synthetic cognition, is the reflective direction of the transcendental will; and hence law and morality, as spheres of positive content of the transcendental will in itself, lie at the foundation of the world of existence that is established in this horizon. In other words, we may think that these two spheres are two sides of reality established by the same horizon.

In the intentionality context of the will, the given is not a mere object of knowledge but must be an object of the will. Water not only is a colorless, transparent liquid, but also something that quenches our thirst. As pragmatism states, all knowledge can be thought to have a practical meaning. However, to consider knowledge to be practical already creates an opposition between knowledge and the will, making the former follow the latter. But in the horizon of the even deeper will, knowledge is included within the intentionality of the will. When we completely transcend the plane of knowledge and include it internally, we directly see the object of the will in the background of intellectual objects themselves. In the horizon of artistic creation, colors in themselves and forms in themselves become the objects of the will; we see personal content even in the background of the qualities of water. However, although we may be able to personalize perceptual content in the horizon of art, we can neither personalize the objective world of thinking nor recognize personal meaning in the background of the real world. The realms of law and morality are established when transcendental consciousness opposes itself, and they recognize personal significance in the background of the real world itself.

Law and morality are processes of the divine act, which personalizes all reality. The objective world of law only appears as we transcend nature in the standpoint of the free person. In this world we see personal relationships between one thing and another thing, in the sense that each thing belongs to someone. Things have inviolable rights as expressions of the person. Things do not merely exist; they enter into the processes of personal development. Hegel states that in human rights freedom has obtained the form of immediate existence (*Das Recht ist zuerst das unmittelbare Dasein, welches sich die Freiheit auf unmittelbare Weise giebt*).

A legal society is established as we enter into the life of the self-conscious will from the life of nature. If we think that the natural world is the only world, such a society can even be considered to be artificial. But as we see the will as a deeper reality, we can enter into an even profounder world of reality thereby. In this world, everything arises as the object of desire and has reality as the possession of some person. A mere natural phenomenon does not have reality in this intentionality. When someone develops a wasteland so that the area belongs to that person's property, the temporal event of thus opening up the wasteland has reality in this place. Satisfaction of desire in this case must be recognized by a common will. We live by being recognized in the common will. Here the idea of the imperative of following law for its own sake arises. Even perfect moral behavior is not simply submission to conscience but involves following this kind of objective law. However, at the point where morality and law differ, law means the inclusion of irrational elements as its content; its content is accidental with respect to form. Therefore, law can be thought to be merely formal. There is something similar to the relationship between physical law and perceptual content in the relationship between the contents of law and desire.

3

Mere thinking and cognition are not identical. Knowledge is established from the union of concept and intuition. According to Kant, we obtain the objectivity of knowledge through a union of the categories of the understanding with perceptual content. I think that this way of speaking presupposes the self-consciousness of the will that unifies thinking and intuition. Pure will must thus be the foundation of experiential knowledge. For example, the category of force that constructs the so-called objective world is a projection of the will. However, the will internally includes the world of this kind of knowledge and at the same time possesses its own immediate world. This world is constructed by the categories of free will; each given element in it is impulsive as a structure of the will. In knowledge, it can be thought that we obtain objectivity through uniting with the objective world of the will as its concrete foundation, while in the will we attain that objectivity through the will's returning to itself by taking itself as end. In other words, it becomes objective through becoming pure activity, as the fusion of subject and object. Art, which can be thought to purify impulse, and law and morality, which rationalize the natural desires, are their own pathways to this goal.

Knowledge can be thought to become objective by uniting with empirical content. But that content can in no way avoid being external in reference to form. In this case, form and content must be unified in a standpoint of an even higher order. In the objective world of the free self we become objective as we find universal ideals within specific desires—that is, by finding the universal within the specific. We acquire objectivity through the fusion of form and content, by such opposition's being extinguished. For example, perceptual experience does not attain such unity in a physical explanation but attains pure unity of form and content in artistic creation. Artistic creation is also an act of transcendental will in such a sense, but transcendental will, which includes reason within itself as the infinite act underlying all acts, cannot discover itself in the partial, objective world of art, for the will must possess a direct, objective world of itself. The realms of law and morality are constructed herein. In art, the will possesses its own world by transcending the world of existence; in morality, the will constructs the real world by including it within its own world.

Just as reason stands over against empirical content in empirical knowledge, so does law oppose impulsive content in the objective world of the will. In empirical knowledge form and content cannot unite internally; in the objective world of the will the object is the act, the act is the object, form is content, and content is form. The very fact of being conscious of impulse does not occur in the intentionality of mere knowledge but in the intentionality of the free self, which is the act underlying all acts. Kant, too, has stated that the very understanding of law directly becomes the motive of behavior. Without reason there is no consciousness; phenomena of consciousness are established by containing the shadow of reason, which is the act underlying all acts. In the objective intentionality of the will, law and impulse, form and content, do not have to oppose each other, as the rigorous ethicians think. The moral law and the content of motive must be one as phenomena in the objective world of transcendental will. If we attempt to explain morality only in terms of one of these, we can only come up against an unbridgeable chasm. The essence of morality lies in positive volitional content, which unifies them. Perhaps there may be some who oppose such an idea by pointing to the clash between natural impulse and the moral law in many actual cases. But do not such people think of law only in the sense of the laws of the natural world? In the laws of nature things move according to law, but in the world of the will law moves of itself: law is the thing, and the thing is law. They both move of themselves.

For the objective worlds of knowledge or feeling to possess a transcendental quality and to be universally valid for us, they must possess their own positive content; in other words, their a priori must be creative in themselves. Only in such a case can it be thought that our acts conform to them. When an object is external to the act, it cannot become an imperative for the act. The fact that the world of mathematics and the world of physics become imperatives of the cognitive act must be so for this reason. If we say that our will is entirely formal and possesses no content whatever or that it is indifferent to any content, we are free to do anything at all, for the objective imperative would cease to exist. But as an object of moral behavior arises by the creation of the a priori of the will, there must be a world of positive content of the will in itself, for the autonomy of the will is established thereby. In this sense, moral behavior in many ways resembles the creative act of the artist, and moral society is a work of art created by free will. However, the point at which it differs from the physical world is that it is object *qua* act as the objective world of the will.

For example, such a thing as a family as a moral reality must be grounded on personal unity. It must be an end in itself, as a reality constructed by free will in itself. We cannot view the fact that the family system developed out of religious significance as a simple causal relationship. However, the family is not merely a group of people unified by austere duty; it must be a unity of love possessing positive content. Indeed, at the foundation of familial unity there must even be dark, instinctive demands. The family functions as a moral reality by spiritualizing the dark forces of life, just as painting and sculpture beautify the female body. Moral reality creates and constructs that which has been given through the flesh, through the a priori of free will, and thereby the body is spiritualized and spirit made incarnate.

I hold that the creative direction of the transcendental will is pure love. Transcendental will on the one hand must be the pure sentiment of duty and on the other must be pure love. The family or the state, as pure moral realities, are the positive content of transcendental will created through pure love. The morality of the state and the family cannot rest merely on tradition, for within them there must be the content of pure feeling. If feeling does not possess its own content in the transintellectual standpoint, then we can say, as Kant held, that adulteration of feeling makes the will heteronomous. However, in the same way that primitive life creates living matter, pure love is the force of spiritual life that creates infinite personal reality. This very content must become the end of the autonomous will itself.

From the standpoint of the so-called psychological individual, law, as something based on external authority, cannot avoid being external to us. When individuals are born into a society that has already been constructed by objective spirit, the legal system of that society looms before us as an external authority that should not be violated. We can think of it both as incomprehensible and as suppressing our freedom. However, when we say that we respect the law, it is not utterly external to us. Even though we might fear something wholly external, we could not say that we respected it. When we have lost respect for law, we must seek authority within the self. Moral motives arise when we have found an infinitely profound internal authority transcending nature within the self. However, moral motives that are contentless and merely formal cannot avoid being subjective. We first unite interior and exterior in an objective object created by the moral a priori, and true moral behavior can only be conceived as an end in itself. In the content of transcendental will that is thus infinitely creative and exceeds our own preconceptions, we cannot help recognizing an infinitely profound external authority. We can also think of the moral law as given by God, as the ethicians of divine authority state. This is also the reason we must think that the content of morality is given by history. But, of course, infinite content is not external to us. It is a realm created by the moral self latent in our own inner depths. We can have both infinite respect and infinite love for such a realm.

4

Needless to say, knowledge is based on transcendental forms, and we can think that knowledge acquires objectivity by uniting with content—that is, by becoming particularized. Moral behavior is good neither by according with merely formal morality, nor merely because its motive is good. Content becomes perfect good behavior by according with it. Just as we must take individual facts as our point of departure in order to construct empirical knowledge that has content, moral behavior must also take facts that are actually given as its point of departure. Since every ideal produces a practical value by uniting with actual facts, even if there is an ideal that is good in the case of *A*, it can be thought to be bad in the case of *B*. Aesthetic creation does not take any abstract ideal as its foundation; it is the same as seeing the light of the aesthetic ideal in the inner depths of concrete actuality. Of course, when I say that moral behavior must take actuality as its point of departure, I do not mean to neglect universal ideals; I mean to idealize given actuality, to see actuality as a unity of infinite possibilities. However, its unity is not a mere infinite sum. Its reality must have positive content as an unattainable limit that cannot be exhaustively analyzed into potentials. Seen from this standpoint, the universal becomes the means of its development. There can be no will from the mere universal; the will begins and ends in the will itself.

Of course, formal law, which takes the person as end in itself, must become the basis in moral behavior. Moral behavior must take this law as power and must be able to construct actuality in the content of the transcendental will—indeed, it must be able to see profound reality at the foundation of actuality by standing in this intentionality. In this sense, I think, the laws of the natural world and moral laws differ in essence. In physical nature, universal laws are precisely nature, and specific content is analyzable into universal law. In contrast to this, the moral law must be a quality identical with practical law, and it differs from other practical laws only in the fact that this law is an end in itself. On this point it can be said instead to have the same nature as the laws of the natural world. The content of the end in itself is given by regarding actuality as the actual process of the transcendental will. In knowledge the particular is considered to be contained within the universal, but in the will the universal is contained within the particular. The content of the creative will appears when the content of moral behavior functions in the dimension of pure reason. However, because it is the content of the transcendental will, it is a norm and at the same time law.

I cannot help thinking that here there exists an intimate relationship between the content of moral behavior and historical content. Needless to say, there is no culture without historical development. If natural phenomena are real in space, cultural phenomena are real in time. Spatial content constructs the material world, and temporal content constructs the cultural world. On this point, cultural phenomena are identical in essence with biological phenomena. Without temporal development there is no life. Even in the case in which new culture arises by sweeping away an older culture, the past culture is not completely lost. Even reforms that arise from the same motives and thoughts do not produce the same culture. Seeing red and blue is not the same as seeing white and blue. There is a difference between spiritual and material phenomena. Dynamic ideals appear in the unity of space. Of course, even a historical fact makes no difference at all to nature; rather, the essence of nature is to be independent in the parameter of 'time'. As far as nature is concerned, a foundation stone that records the date of an old palace is no different from a stone by the wayside. In this sense, even historical facts must disappear without trace and be unreal in the course of time. However, historical facts differ from individual imaginings, which come into being and vanish like dreams. They are objective in the sense of belonging to the objective world of consciousness in general. On this point we can again say that they are the same in essence as natural phenomena. This kind of subjective and transindividual objective world can be considered to exist only in the standpoint of the transcendental will. The content of objective spirit develops in history. 'Time' that has no content constructs the natural world; 'time' that has content constructs history. For the above reason we must always discover the content of moral behavior within history.

The laws of empirical science have universal validity, but it is generally thought that this kind of law does not exist in morality. However, let us scrutinize this idea further. Why are the laws of empirical science considered to be objective? The empirical world must be constructed by what Kant terms synthetic principles. Synthetic principles are created by the unity of the categories of the understanding with 'time', which is the form of intuition. This unity, according to Cohen, is established by the unity of consciousness. But I think that the form of the will, which is the act underlying all acts, must be considered in order to call the form of knowledge objective, by virtue of its uniting with content. The union of reason and perception is only possible in the horizon of the will. Our experience is a kind of volitional act, and we can think that the objectivity of empirical knowledge is based on the transcendental nature of the will. However, as in Kant's statement "time itself does not move," the direction of reflection and the direction of creation unite in the will. Even if we consider individual, personal consciousness, our consciousness preserves past experiences, while at the same time being creative at each step. On the one hand, it must be considered to be repeatable; on the other hand, it must be considered to be unrepeatable.

The world of nature is nothing more than the reflection of the transcendental will. When through Kant's concept of synthetic principle we construct a given experience as the empirical world, we enter into the objective world of transcendental will and proceed to reflect in this standpoint. 'Time' is the form of experience that is a pure experience that flows; it is the form of the pure act itself. To reflect upon 'time' is to stop 'time'. We can transcend 'time' and deal with it freely by recollection. The freedom of the will is grounded on the freedom of such recollection. We feel a bottomless freedom in this horizon; we can even believe that we have free will that is without cause, without law, and wholly arbitrary. However, when we attempt to act in the standpoint of this freedom, we feel conflict with the powers of the self. Fichte's concept of *Anstos* (shock) upon the self may be such a thing. However, it does not come from without with respect to the will; it must be a projection of the will itself. Every act is determined by the content of the act itself. Something that comes entirely from without to a certain act must be nonbeing with respect to this act. The fact that the act is determined by its own content in this way —in other words, that the act is self-determining—must be reflection.

When the transcendental will reflects upon itself and determines itself in this sense, the empirical world is established from the union of perceptual content and the forms of reason. The concept of a thing is established by stopping the time series, and causality is established by being a repetition of a time series. And we can think that the natural world is established by reflecting upon and uniting an unlimited number of such series. The fact that we are able to think that "time does not move" is possible only in the horizon of free will, which can transcend the category of 'time', and on this foundation the worlds of law and of nature are established. Because the world of nature is the world of law, natural law is objective in the world of nature. But, just as the will reflects—that is, is creative—in self-consciousness, it possesses a creative aspect behind self-reflection. The world of morality belongs to the creative world, to the world of positive content, of this kind of will. At the time we create the experience of actuality in the horizon of transcendental will latent in its background, we are able to advance in both directions of reflection and creation. By advancing in both directions in this way, actuality as the content of concrete will can be viewed as an abstract universal, on the one hand, or as a concrete particular, on the other. As the process of the infinite development of the concrete will, we see an infinite destination in either of these mutually opposing directions. We perceive an infinitely universalizing direction, on the one hand, and an infinitely particularizing direction, on the other. Particularization means the concentration of the meaning of the entire world at one point. It is behavior in the perspective of the entire world—that is, the transformation of the entire world into one meaning. The true particular must be that which has been determined in the whole— indeed, it must be that which internally includes the whole. Herein is established the categorical imperative which has content.

5

I think that a moral ideal crystallized in a certain society can be compared to a species of living things. Biological life is one vast flow. Even the fact that we can think of various species in the present simply means that one form of life is temporarily dominant. A certain form of life is not something merely repeatable, but something that develops and particularizes itself. Needless to say, life is a temporal reality. The past has not been lost in the life of the present, for life bears the weight of the past as it advances toward the future. But one form of life is decided not merely internally, but also in its relation with the external environment. Here the law of the survival of the fittest is applicable. A certain moral structure may also be decided by a similar method. The fact that things adapt to the external world to live must mean that those that are able to adapt the external environment to themselves survive. Yet, even adaptation of the external world does not mean that life transforms matter but simply that it unifies it teleologically. A teleological reality is established other than the reality of mere mechanical causality. A teleological a priori constructs its own independent, objective world. In this case it is not that a teleological a priori destroys the mechanical a priori, but, rather, that it transcends it, making it an element of itself as it constructs its own world.

If we consider that consciousness in general is the standpoint that constructs the natural world, when we say that we adapt to nature we may be able to say that we thereby internally include the standpoint of consciousness in general. When we transcend the plane of nature as simultaneous existence that can be repeated and include it internally, this becomes the temporal plane—that is, the plane of teleological unity. When the self reflects upon itself, it transcends itself and constructs personal history. In this sense, transcendence of the natural world and inclusion of it mean that the specific becomes real. The reality that is established by the category of 'time' must be something particular. Here lies the reason for moving from Spinoza's substance to Leibniz's monads.

Though I use the term *biological life*, as above, it is no longer as a mere natural phenomenon but as it possesses its reality in the objective world of the will. However, biological life that is not yet self-conscious can still not possess its own objective world or its own reality. This is the reason that vitalism can be thought to be unscientific. Teleological causality, as natural science, can possess only the meaning of a regulative principle. However, in a phenomenon of consciousness we can for the first time say that we transcend and include the natural world within. The natural world is a product of thinking that has constructed immediate experience as the material. We can think of pure apperception, which may be termed the legislator of nature, as the situation in which consciousness within the self completely transcends nature and possesses its own world. Perhaps we may be able to explain biological life mechanically and completely reduce it to the natural world. But that consciousness of the self that is constructive of nature is irreducible to nature. Here the objectivity of nature disappears and the objective world of the free self is established—in other words, the moral world is established—and our life obtains true independence.

A certain morality crystallized in one society must be a biological species in this kind of world of life, in the teleological world. It must be a fixed 'type' of spiritual life. This kind of 'type' of spiritual life does not arise merely from internal necessity, as does a biological species, but it must stand in relation to the external world. In this sense, the principle of survival of the fittest can be said to be operative even within morality. But what would the moral external world be in such a case? Its environment in respect to the moral will is not mere nature. The true environment of moral will must be the world of personal will. In the case of *person* versus *nature*, the moral will has no function; there is only a utilitarian world. The world of the moral will must be an interpersonal one.

Of course, we can think that the kind of morality that is established and develops is decided by natural causality, as in natural selection of biological species. However, as Pascal states, even if the entire universe crushes us, because man knows this fact he is greater than that which kills him. Therefore, in the moral will it can be thought that we transcend nature and possess an objective world established by the will's own creation. Nature itself vanishes within it. We can thus think that the moral will includes its own environment within itself. As in self-consciousness, the act takes itself as object, and one act gives birth to another. We can think that its own environment is created within itself and that it particularizes itself within itself. The moral law in this way creates its own environment of itself and is a species of spiritual life that particularizes itself.

Therefore, the moral law, in one aspect, can be thought to be similar in essence to biological law. Universal laws cannot be established in the same sense as mechanical laws. If we consider something that follows universal law, as it might mechanical law, it is not life. We attain moral life only when we reverence and obey law. Just as causality yields the natural world, so does the moral law yield the moral world. However, the world of the moral will, differing from the natural world, is a world of individual reality. The universality of the moral world must not be an abstract universal, but a concrete one. The moral law is not a given merely to be followed; it is given to construct individual life by.

6

Previously, in chapter 10, I discussed the objective world of beauty and the given of the objective world of the good. Now I should like to discuss the relationship between the two in more logical terms. Perception is the material of empirical knowledge, but in its ultimate form it is not material. It must first be created in the form of law that expresses the relationship between fact and fact. True personal content that becomes artistic content must be created in the form of a norm in order to become content of the moral will. Just as perceptual content becomes the material of Poincaré's principle of physics in the form of law that expresses the relationships between facts, so does personal content become the content of the self-conscious will in the form of norms. The content of the self-conscious will must not be impulsive, but normative. As Kant states, it is the will that understands law and acts from law. Just as perceptual content in the plane of consciousness in general is conceptual, so must impulsive content in the horizon of the will in general also be conceptual. Conceptual content is content that appears in the horizon of the infinite act underlying all acts—that is, in the reflective intentionality of the transcendental will. That which becomes the content of the moral law must be sincere, personal content. If not, the will does not avoid being heteronomous. In this sense, artistic intuition becomes the given of the moral will. However, for it to become content of the moral will, it must be unified in the horizon of the synthetic will; it must be unified in a completely personal system. Just as the given is that which has been sought and must be thought to include the form of thinking within the form of intuition, so can artistic intuition be thought to exist in the horizon of the transcendental will and include the form of the will within itself. However, the self that has been reflected upon is not directly the reflecting self. Between them we must recognize a difference such as that between the self itself and the shadow of the self.

As has been said, we can think that the relationship between perception and empirical knowledge is analogous to that between aesthetic intuition and the moral will. But, just as perceptual content can be thought to be entirely unanalyzable into conceptualized empirical knowledge, so can the content of aesthetic intuition also be thought to be deeper and richer than the content of the moral will. The moral will encounters endless opposition; and there is something unknowable at its foundation—some kind of intuition. However, in this case it can no longer be said to be aesthetic content; the intuition can be thought to be religious content.

Chapter 12

The True
and the Beautiful

1

On the one hand, we cannot help thinking that the true is the beautiful. We cannot recognize artistic value in what is artificial and created, no matter how skillful it is. But, even in the case of a dreamlike fairy tale, so long as it has artistic value, we cannot help recognizing some kind of deep truth of human emotion and nature. Of course, though I speak in this way, I do not mean to confuse the beauty of human emotion with the beauty of art. No matter how evil human emotion is, it can become an object of art as the truth of human emotion. Although the false has no artistic value, even the false sentiments of the artist can become an object of art. I believe we can say the same with respect to art that takes nature as its object. Something that has artistic value does not allow of subjective artificiality; it must be the objectively given, in some sense.

On the other hand, however, we can also think that the true and the beautiful must always be distinguished. Something true is not necessarily beautiful and vice versa. For example, there may be something symmetrical and beautiful—even musical—within a mathematical truth. But there is a difference in essence between a mathematical truth's being beautiful and its being true. We may think that it is even more difficult to recognize aesthetic feeling within the truth of natural science, or truth within such a thing as music. How, then, should we understand the relationship between the true and the beautiful?

2

I shall first consider the difference between formal beauty and beauty that has content. A unity of a manifold, or a symmetry, are examples of purely formal beauty without relation to sensory content. However, in considering the problem in this way, content means intellectual content and not aesthetic content. Content in such a sense is, needless to say, unrelated to aesthetic value and is accidental. Yet we cannot think that formal beauty has no content because of the distinction between form and content in this kind of knowledge. In my opinion, there is no beauty without content; in the beautiful, there must be an internal life that can be expressed, and the expression of pure internal life is always felt as the beautiful. If we understand the essence of formal beauty in Kantian terms, it cannot be said to be mere formal beauty, as Kant himself thought, but, rather, must express the content of our pure rational life. Must we not see a spiritual act of the power of the understanding as the expression of the content of the act itself, which reflects from the standpoint of the act underlying all acts? Formal beauty must be a kind of beauty having content in such a sense. Various kinds of contents of life derive from our various intentional acts, and various kinds of aesthetic beauty similarly derive from these acts.

If the plastic arts take space as object, then space must be considered to constitute content in the plastic arts. We can think that such a thing as color is external in reference to it. Indeed, the conceptual content of the image of the Madonna or of the Greek goddess Venus may be thought to be entirely external to the aesthetic content. However, the plastic arts cannot then be arts of formal beauty. If we consider the matter in Fiedler's terms, the plastic arts are expressions of our pure visual perception, and that which constitutes the content of the plastic arts must be the content of pure visual perception. The objective world of pure plastic art comes to appear in the standpoint of pure visual perception as we break through the web of concepts. Things come to live, and space is filled with life in this intentionality.

Life is the fusion of subject and object, appearing when the self becomes thing and the thing becomes self. In this sense, color constitutes the content of the plastic arts as long as it can be unified within the intentionality of pure visual perception. Even religious content can be given physical form through the depths of the person of the artist. Especially in poetry, which can be considered to be an expressive art, as Meyer states, everyone will recognize that conceptual content directly constitutes its internal content. I thus hold that there is no distinction between formal beauty and beauty that has content within the beautiful, for I think that everything can be called beauty that has content. However, are there not various distinctions within artistic content? Generally speaking, the distinction between form and content may be thought to be one that has shifted a distinction of intellectual content to aesthetic content.

3

If the beautiful, in the above sense, possesses various contents, what is its relation to intellectual content? In the visual act there is the beauty of the plastic arts, and in the aural act there is the beauty of music, and if these aesthetic experiences have specific experiential content, then we cannot help thinking that there is some kind of internal relationship between intellectual and aesthetic content. For example, such a thing as symmetrical beauty may not be thought to be the same as beauty of form or beauty of sound. As its beauty becomes deeper, one kind of beauty possesses aesthetic content that cannot be exchanged with another. If the creative act of the artist is a constructive act, constructing something objectively, then that constructive act must follow the objective laws of experience. The plastic arts must follow the laws of visual experience, and music must follow the laws of aural experience. We can even think that aesthetic content possesses particular content by being controlled by these laws.

In establishing the relationship between colors or sounds, we must depend upon visual or aural perception. In the plane of judgment, the truth of sensory knowledge is established in the form of judgment. We can regard such a thing as a 'color entity' (*Farbenkorper*) as this kind of system of relations. Anything that possesses even the slightest visual perception, such as the truth of representation itself, may be considered to be truth that everyone must recognize. Concerning the fact that we can change sensory content into the form of judgment, we may be able to say that our free self is the act underlying all acts and reason is the direction of its determination, whereas will is the direction of its development.

Hegel, in the introduction to his *Philosophy of Right*, also considers thought to be the reflective direction of the will. We can think that construction of sensory truth means changing the content of a partial act into the content of the standpoint of the act underlying all acts and viewing it thus. Reason, which is the reflective direction of the intentionality of the act underlying all acts, changes the content of the act into the content of the self and constructs its own objective world. In this way, a world of universally valid objective truth is constructed with respect to each individual subjectivity. But, viewed from another aspect, the contents of seeing or hearing are reflected upon in the standpoint of reason, while still having their own contents as creative acts; they possess their own positive contents that cannot be analyzed into intellectual content. The creative act of the artist, which can be considered to be the expressive movement of pure sensation, expresses this kind of content.

Of course, the above two directions are mutually opposing ones. But, in establishing empirical knowledge, universal reason must follow the particular act. The particular that internally includes the universal must first be constructed before reflecting upon empirical content and the construction of universal truth. Seeing or hearing in actuality constructs such experience. By acting, we are able to include the universal within the particular. The act of artistic creation is also nothing other than an advance in the direction of such particularization. It can thus be thought that the true and the beautiful come together and the beautiful is present in the background of the true. The act of artistic creation is not merely the construction of things subjectively; it is the seeing of things objectively, the discovery of profound reality. In things there is always a gap between the above direction of creation and the direction of reflection, but in the self it is clear that these two directions are internally one. Of course, when I say that the self proceeds to create itself, I do not mean that it is directly an act of artistic creation. That which creates the self is rigorous moral behavior. The act of artistic creation in things becomes moral behavior in the self. But both of them are the same intentionality. When the internal union of both of these directions is broken, we can think that this becomes the act of artistic creation.

Needless to say, when sensory experience becomes the foundation of truth, or when the particular includes the universal, that particular is not the particular considered in formal logic. It must be a unity, a particular unity in the horizon of the will that transcends reason. Knowledge acquires objectivity by advancing in this direction. In this sense we can say that the beautiful is at the foundation of the true. A kind of aesthetic intuition is operative at the foundation of the conviction of empirical truth. We may thus say that the true is grounded on the beautiful. There is no content of beauty that goes against empirical truth that is affirmed in the standpoint of consciousness in general, for aesthetic intuition internally includes reason and is the direction of infinitely individualizing it. To lose the objectivity of knowledge means at the same time to lose the objectivity of beauty. Universal truth becomes the condition of the establishment of the content of beauty, but universal truth is not directly the beautiful.

The content of beauty must always be individual. Even in the case of truth, the more it becomes individual, the closer it comes to becoming aesthetic content.

Of course, it can be thought that the individual and the universal never completely merge: the beautiful is always the beautiful; the true is always the true. Each of these directions acquires its internal unity in the standpoint of religion, which is truly the self-conscious horizon of the act underlying all acts. In the religious intentionality, the directions of individualization and universalization come together; the true becomes the beautiful, and the beautiful becomes the true.

4

We usually distinguish between perception and thinking. However, on what points do these acts differ, and on what points must we view them as the same? Thinking distinguishes content that has been given by perceptual experience and is not a mere formal act of classifying things. Thinking possesses its own content. Mathematics can be thought of as the object of pure thinking. Furthermore, we can think, as expressed above with regard to thinking, that thinking, if seen as the reverse side of the will, is a creative act in one aspect. We can think that it creates its own world of reality. The world of the free self is created by thinking reflecting on itself. On the contrary, even perceptual experience is not merely passive, nor is it a merely static intuition. As a pure and direct act, the act reflects on itself; it is Fichte's *Tathandlung*, in which one act gives birth to another. The fact that we proceed gradually to view things more profoundly is the same as that we proceed gradually to think of things more profoundly. The world of visual perception is linked to visual perception, and the world of thinking is linked to the world of thinking. Even if each act takes itself as object, each creates a complete world in itself. A visual act does not develop by making the representation of color itself its content but, rather, advances by directly continuing a prior act. The painter and sculptor think with the eye, and the philosopher sees with his mind. As Plotinus states, thinking is seeing.

In what sense, then, can perception and thinking be distinguished? For what reason do we think that in perception the transition from act to act is immediate and unconscious, whereas in thinking there is a gap between acts and the transition is conscious? I think that we shall be able to understand this if we consider thinking to be the reflective direction of the will, which is the act underlying all acts, and by viewing it as the horizon of free unity with respect to every act. Every experience in its pure state may be viewed as a projection of the will as a pure internal continuity of acts. But in the horizon of the self-consciousness of the will, which is the act underlying all acts, we can view it as the object of the act itself. Thinking, as the reflective direction of such a standpoint and as its determinative act, is independent and free with respect to all acts and is able to be unified. Because the plane of representation transcends and includes that of sensation and the plane of recollection does the same for that of representation, they are independent and free with regard to their content. We can view the plane of thinking as the ultimate, in this sense. Representation is not a continuity of sensations. Seen from the plane of sensation, there is a gap between them. We may say that that which is unconscious as the unity of sensation becomes conscious as representation. We may say that what was unconscious in representation becomes conscious in memory.

However, I think that in every kind of experience there is both knowledge in the reflective direction and knowledge in the creative direction in which the act sees itself. This distinction appears as the distinction between eternal and factual truth. When the perceptual act discriminates color and form, they are, of course, still not distinguished in the form of judgment. But, needless to say, this distinction becomes the foundation of the judgment that red differs from blue. I should like to regard such intellectual content as eternal truth in the perceptual world. The 'color entity' can be considered to be a system of universal truth based on such intellectual content. In order to discriminate red from blue, perceptions of red and blue must be reflected upon from the standpoint of perception in general, which synthesizes the two, so that perception can be considered to reflect upon the content of perception itself. It may be said to be judgment and not perception. But that which aligns two colors in the present and discriminates them must be a visual perception.

Perhaps one sensation and another sensation may directly be different from one another. However, two things that are independent of one another cannot be entirely distinguished from one another. To discriminate the two, there must a totality that synthesizes and unifies them—indeed, the two must be seen as the differentiation and development of this totality. This kind of discriminatory act is what the psychologist calls the act of sensation. It can perhaps be thought that all sensory acts are the same. Of course, we can recognize an act of sensation as the standpoint of sensation in general, but concretely each act of sensation must be a particular. The act of sensation has this kind of discriminatory direction and at the same time

has the content of a constructive direction as a continuity of pure acts
—that is to say, it has an intellectual direction and at the same time a
volitional direction; and the full realization of the latter direction
can be thought to comprise the contents of the plastic arts. In this
direction we can say that we have factual truth in the world of perception. The psychology of 'structure' (*Struktur*), as Dilthey terms it,
is established in this perspective. There is artistic truth in artistic reality; the unity of truth and beauty appears in this direction. Psychological truth can be thought to be contained within artistic beauty.
Cervantes' *Don Quixote* and Shakespeare's *Hamlet* can be thought
to be individual artistic creations and at the same time psychological
'types'. Of course, artistic content is not directly psychological truth.
Artistic content cannot be reduced to intellectual content; we must
say that it is concrete as it is. However, just as the universal is discovered by the physicist from actual empirical truth, so, too, is intellectual content contained within artistic content, and a kind of
psychological knowledge can be thought to be objective through this
standpoint.

5

To clarify this point, let us examine reality, or factual truth.
Reality can be regarded as the objective world of the will. The actual
world, as distinguishable from the potential world, must be constructed in the standpoint of the a priori underlying all a priori,
which unifies infinite truth. The monad is created by the will of God.
The objectivity of knowledge in the Kantian sense, as expressed in the
thinking of the present-day Southwest school, not only has universal
validity but must be sought in the union of the form and content of
knowledge, and such a synthesis is only possible in the standpoint of
the act underlying all acts. Objective knowledge can be knowledge of
reality in this sense. Factual knowledge must be knowledge of reality
in this sense, and the will must be intellectual content that has reflected upon itself. Of course, the will cannot exhaustively reflect
upon itself. That which could do so cannot be termed the will. The
thing in itself is the infinite destination of the will itself, which cannot be attained by knowledge. However, factual truth established by
being reflected upon within the act itself can be thought to arise in a
standpoint that is opposed to merely objective eternal truth. The
concept of a Leibnizian monad, or of historical knowledge in the
Southwest school, is established in the intentionality in which the
act reflects within itself. The universal that is the foundation of his-

torical cognition is not the same as the universal of natural-scientific knowledge.

If we consider factual truth or historical knowledge in the above way, I think we can regard them as contents of behavior. There must be an active universal at the foundation of intellectual content as described above. It must be considered the content of something moving, of something acting. Of course, intellectual content that has already been reflected upon cannot directly be termed the content of something moving or acting. However, something moving or acting is not contentless. We activate the content of 'time' as the content of the self. There is no content apart from this content. Our moral behavior establishes historical fact as content. We advance as we take such knowledge as content. Intellectual content in which the transcendental will reflects within itself becomes historical knowledge, and the development of the transcendental will reflected within itself becomes historical knowledge, and the development of the transcendental will becomes moral behavior. Historical truth and moral truth are two sides of the same coin. Of course, considered from the standpoint of subjective good, it cannot be thought that there is an Idea of the Good behind history. However, let me digress a moment to recall Hegel's idea of world history. Hegel thinks that the rational will, the concrete good, is most powerful, and this kind of active good —that is, the development of the providence of God—is world history, and he states that the truth of that which is true is the created world.

In sum, the content of world history can be considered to be the content of the moral will, and the content of structural psychology can be considered to be the content of aesthetic creation. The true is established through the beautiful and the good, and the beautiful and the good are established through the true; the true, the good, and the beautiful exist in the same direction. To speak about the experience of visual perception, a color entity expressing various kinds of relations of color in a merely abstract way can be compared to the system of pure reason in the experience of thinking. Just as we have the world of empirical reality in the plane of thinking, so, too, does visual experience have its own real world. Just as empirical facts are transformed into laws and become natural-scientific truths, so is the content of visual experience transformed into law as a kind of psychological truth. However, just as we have the world of factual truth, the world of history, in the sense of the unique actual world in the plane of consciousness, it can be thought that we have the world of individual fact in the creative horizon of the plastic arts, and even in the plane of visual perception. Aesthetic content that is unique occurs only once in the world of perception. Just as historical cognition can be thought to be knowledge that is a unique event and at the same time to include infinite eternal truth within itself, we can think that eternal truth is contained infinitely within a work of art.

Chapter 13

Truth and Goodness

1

I have discussed the unity of the beautiful and the true in the horizon of the transcendental will reflecting upon its own content. Now I should like to examine the relation between the true and the good, based on the same idea.

I should first like to consider truth in knowledge. If we follow Rickert, a universally valid content of knowledge is thought to be truth, and universal validity is thought to be identical with objectivity in knowledge. Opposing the correspondence theory, he thinks of knowing as a form of construction. Now, it may be appropriate to think in these terms in the standpoint that takes the cognitive object as the imperative; however, if we follow this position to its logical conclusion, the various a priori of knowledge become independent of each other, the unity of knowledge ceases to hold, and we are forced to fall into a confusion of values. Hence, I wonder whether there is not a meaning beyond that of mere universal validity at the point where Kant seeks the objectivity of knowledge in the union of the categories of thinking and of perception. When mathematical knowledge is established by the fusion of the categories of thinking with pure intuition, we can say that the latter is more objective than the former as a concrete totality. But, as Kant states, mathematical knowledge expresses the potentiality of experience and is neither knowledge of things nor empirical knowledge. Objective knowledge is established by the union of intuition which has content.

Now, what does it mean to say that thinking unites with intuition, and how is this possible? Intuition is not, as is usually thought, a passive state. Intuition in such a sense is the product of thinking. Thinking cannot acquire anything at all by uniting with it. Intuition that has been truly given must be an act of the fusion of subject and object that is dynamic in itself. In this sense, the fact that thinking is able to unite with intuition means that it returns to its own foundation. This is the reason that mathematics possesses objectivity as the concrete foundation of logic. However, reason is only one aspect of the self and not its totality. The form and content of knowledge are first unified, and we truly attain to objectivity in knowledge in the horizon of the will, which, as the act underlying all acts, unifies all acts and becomes their concrete foundation. In the above way, the various a priori of knowledge are unified, the goal of knowledge is determined, and knowledge acquires objectivity in the horizon of the a priori underlying all a priori. As Plato thought long ago, the Good and the Beautiful are at the foundation of the true.

Since knowledge is established by some a priori and knowing means constructing by virtue of that a priori, truth must be an imperative with regard to our cognitive act. If the cognitive acts of every man have transcendental value as their immanent meaning and are established by reflecting it within the act, its imperative can be said to be universally valid. However, when we say that knowledge means that the cognitive act follows an imperative, there must be a distinction between the cognitive act and the imperative. If we say that knowing is construction, then there must be that which constructs and that which is constructed. And if the cognitive act is merely the development of the a priori itself, then the irrational and error would vanish—indeed, there would be no way for consciousness of the act even to arise.

When subject and object oppose each other, if the known is merely something complete in itself and if consciousness is merely something like a passive mirror, then there is no way for the opposition between subject and object to arise. In the latter opposition there must be contradiction and conflict, at least within the systems given. Even if there is not a contradiction and conflict between systems, when a certain system proceeds to determine itself, we can see an opposition between that which determines and that which is determined. However, something that moves and determines itself must be that in which its final end is present at the outset and that in which the a priori itself is productive. Simply moving from within is not directly consciousness. Even though the given is that which has been sought and our world of cognitive objects is rational, it cannot be said that it in itself is conscious. A point on a curve, physical force, and biological life can each be thought to be productive in itself, but it cannot be said that they are conscious of themselves. In systems that are merely developmental in themselves there may be differences of degree of completion, but there is no opposition between the irrational and the rational, and the distinction between truth and falsehood cannot be established. An imperative is meaningless in this instance.

If subjectivity were thus something that constructs knowledge from only one a priori, there would be no such thing as error, even though there were differences of degree of completion. Error arises from a confusion of a priori. For error in this sense to arise, there must be a free unity of a priori in the horizon of the a priori of all a priori. Knowing must mean recognition of an a priori in this horizon. The fact that knowledge attains its goal—namely, the truth—not only implies a purification of a priori but must also mean attaining a unity of a priori. The question "Is this true?" is established and decided in the horizon of the a priori of all a priori. Knowing is constructing. The true significance of the position that knowledge acquires objectivity through union of form and content lies herein. That truth is a universally valid imperative for us must mean that we, having infinite a priori of cognition in the intentionality of the a priori of a priori, follow our own internal unity.

Assuming a certain a priori, it can be thought that truth is decided thereby. But if there is nothing else that decides what kind of a priori we must take, then truth is merely artificial. In this case we are forced to think like the pragmatist, or, if not, that truth is merely a kind of scholar's play. If there is such a thing as the 'will to truth', this must mean that it is the will that combines and unifies different a priori. Hereby we are able to escape from the pragmatist's position. In establishing the objectivity of knowledge, this will must be transindividual and objective. If knowledge is established merely in the horizon of "*if* I take such an a priori," then we cannot establish the objectivity of knowledge. Of course, we cannot clarify all the a priori of knowledge nor construct their system, but knowledge presupposes the ideal of some final unity. The pure objectivity of knowledge, which does not allow the least element of subjectivity, must be based on such an ideal of knowledge, itself. Even in the case in which a judgment on the basis of a given a priori is recognized as true, the possibility of an opposing judgment based on a different standpoint can be thought of. Moreover, by negating it, truth can be recognized; in other words, truth can be established by one perspective's being negated from another. The imperative must be the individual will following the transindividual will. Only when the will confronts itself, is there the meaning of an imperative. The various a priori of knowledge are born from cognitive will and must be unified within it.

In the above terms, I hold that the objectivity of knowledge bears witness to the fact that knowledge returns to its source and unites with true reality. However, true reality is not a world constructed by cognition; it is not an objectified world but must be one in which one act gives birth to another, a world of an infinite continuity of acts themselves. It must be a world in which construction (*Bilden*) is reproduction (*Abbilden*) and vice versa. We can apprehend such a world of true reality—the world of concrete reality—in our immediate experience of self-consciousness. In self-consciousness the fact of facing toward the unobtainable thing-in-itself must mean uniting with the thing-in-itself. The function of knowing itself is knowing, and the object of cognition lies within the act itself of cognition.

When a cognitive act as a shadow of the pure self proceeds to construct a system from a certain a priori, it does not possess its goal in that system but possesses its true goal within the act itself. The goal of cognition lies within the world of the cognitive act itself. That which opens up before us as imperative must be the content of such transcendental will. That which suppresses it must also be the will. The goal of knowledge does not lie in construction by an a priori, but in the fusion of subject and object. When it proceeds to construct according to an a priori, it can never depart from the standpoint of the opposition of subject and object. The opposition of subject and object signifies the subjectivity of knowledge. To eliminate subjectivity in knowledge, there must be fusion of subject and object—that is, they must become one act. This does not mean that the distinction of subject and object disappears, but that the contradictions and oppositions of subject and object become unified content just as they are.

The fact that we can think that physical knowledge is more objective than mathematical knowledge, in the sense of its being knowledge of that which is real, lies in the fact that it is the content of the act underlying all acts, which is the standpoint of this kind of fusion of subject and object. In purely mathematical knowledge the self stands wholly outside of knowledge and cannot reflect itself in the objective world of mathematics. However, because physical knowledge, as the content of the act underlying all acts, takes the fusion of subject and object as its end, we are able to reflect and see the self within the physical, objective world. Materialism arises in this way. Even if we do not go so far as materialism, natural-scientific psychology already indicates this trend.

Of course, we cannot completely attain the fusion of subject and object by such a process, but I should like to point out that there are two meanings to the objectivity of knowledge. When we stand in a given a priori, we already function in the dimension of the transcendental will. But that which determines the objectivity of the a priori must be the a priori of all a priori. It must be transcendental, volitional subjectivity, or subjectivity as behavior. If we do not allow such a position, we cannot clarify the question of why physical knowledge is more objective than mathematical knowledge. Perhaps it may be thought that such a horizon is a transintellectual one and not that of knowledge, but concrete knowledge is always grounded in such a horizon.

That which we usually think of as factual truth based on intuition must basically arise in the horizon of the a priori of all a priori, as I have stated above—that is, in the intentionality of the act underlying all acts. Intuition is not merely the reception of intellectual content but must be construction. This is the reason that it can be thought that knowledge that has content is more objective than merely formal knowledge. In the intentionality of behavioral subjectivity various sensory acts are unified transcendentally and various empirical contents are subsumed objectively, and thereby the worlds of force and reality are established. The a priori of force must be one category of behavioral subjectivity. Every a priori of concrete cognition is given in this standpoint. Of course, even knowledge established by such a priori is directly objectified and becomes internal truth. Natural-scientific law is truth of this kind. In reference to this, the content of behavioral subjectivity itself can be thought to be an unobjectifiable transcognitive world. But behavioral subjectivity objectifies the content of itself; yet, before the self has its own content and objectifies that content, it must first reflect upon itself. Truth that has been objectified is established by the truth's objectifying itself. In demonstrating a physical truth, we must first clarify the fact that the self exists in the world of truth.

A physical experiment in a dream cannot demonstrate a physical truth. The self that establishes physical truth must be the historical self. The true reality of this kind of self is established only by reflection upon itself. Even if we are able to think of a mathematical problem in a dream, this does not negate the fact that it is a mathematical truth. However, even if a physical experiment in a dream conforms to truth, we cannot say that it is physical truth. For it to become an eternal truth as a physical truth, it must first be reflected within the active self as the content of the active self. It is not that it is the content of the dreaming self but must be reflected as the acting self. Therefore, I think that in physical truth there is a significance beyond that of the mere imperative of thinking. The content of active subjectivity must be the content of that which acts; and the content of that which acts must be the content of reality. Herein must lie the meaning of becoming truth by reflecting reality. The ground of factual truth is not given merely as an imperative but, rather, lies in its being a partial reproduction of reality. Factual knowledge is not established merely by logical judgment; active subjectivity is established by reflecting upon itself. In such a case judgment is simply a form of self-reflection and a means of reflecting the self. It is not that thinking includes behavior, but that behavior includes thinking. Thinking is the reflection of behavior, and behavior develops by thinking of itself. In this sense, factual truth becomes truth by virtue of advancing to the concrete from the abstract.

As I have stated, the concept of truth is not exhausted by mere universal validity but acquires its objectivity by the fusion of subject and object, which is the end of knowledge. The true reality of the fusion of subject and object is a self-conscious system such as Fichte's *Tathandlung*. Knowledge becomes objective by reflecting the shadow of reality as its reflective direction. Perhaps some may say that it is impossible for knowledge to reflect true reality because the self cannot reflect upon itself. However, the reflecting self and the self reflected upon are not different things; there is no wall between them. Therefore, in factual truth a fact proved as fact in the intuition of the actual self becomes universally valid. Even the natural world is established by the a priori of the self-consciousness of the will, and the uniformity of nature is established thereby.

Of course, nature that has been objectified is not the self-consciousness of the will itself. We must find the content of a self-conscious system itself in historical knowledge. In the intentionality of historical cognition we can infinitely approach concrete knowledge as the fusion of subject and object. Natural-scientific knowledge, on the contrary, becomes abstract, universal knowledge. From the perspective that takes that which has been objectified as real, it may be thought that such an idea makes the subjective objective. However, the reality of the objective world must be established by the reality of the act that infinitely objectifies itself. If we view the truth of knowledge as eternal truth, then the truth of factual knowledge may be thought to differ from it in essence. But in the sense that they both must be recognized in the standpoint of consciousness in general, we can say that they are both truth in the sphere of cognition. It is merely that they differ in a priori and in significance as forms of cognition. In the former there is the a priori of mere thinking; in the latter there is the a priori of the will, which includes thinking. Eternal truth is established by consciousness in general, and factual truth is established by including it. The former, which is included in cognitive subjectivity, may be thought of as repeatable, while the latter, which transcends and determines it, can be thought to be unique. The fact that truth can be thought of as transcending cognitive activity simply means that it transcends the psychological act that has been objectified.

It goes without saying that knowledge cannot be established apart from cognitive subjectivity. Eternal truth is established by cognitive subjectivity's determining itself, while factual truth is established by the self's being determined. Of course, we can think that every truth is established as the self-determination of a system and that each truth is a unique entity in that system. In the standpoint of mathematical thinking, a relationship between given numbers becomes a unique fact of the mathematical world. The reason that we think of it as eternal truth is that we are able to think in an even higher standpoint. Factual truth can be thought to be unique as cognition in the highest standpoint, in this sense.

2

What is the content of the good? If we speak from the position of the formalist, then moral good is completely formal. However, formal morality without any content whatsoever cannot avoid being subjective. It does not provide any direction at all, in the case of actual practice. The truly universal must include a principle of particularization within itself, and truly objective morality must objectively stipulate the content of behavior. We are not free apart from content; we become free by finding the self within content. We only attain true freedom when we submerge our entire self within the objective.

How can we find the self within the objective? If the objective is mere nature, then, however powerful it is, we cannot find the end of the self within it. The self can have the pride that it is a 'thinking reed'. The end of our moral behavior does not come merely through being a complete reality or the cause of the universe. The flaw of pantheism lies therein. In order to truly find the end of the self within the objective and to submerge the self within it, the objective must be the foundation of the self and a spiritual reality. Even our subjective demands are not the artificial products of the self. All our impulses and demands can be thought to have an objective foundation. However, the self is not their mere synthetic unity. These demands, on the contrary, are established by the unity of the self; the self discovers its end in the unified content of itself. We cannot help thinking of such a thing as Hegel's objective spirit—that is, of recognizing the objective world of personal content as the foundation of the self. Our self is established by this foundation and finds its end in it. Formal morality is the condition of the establishment of such an objective world; it is the passageway, as it were, into this world. All desires are purified and made moral by entering through this passageway.

Good behavior is such a thing as the above; the truth of knowledge, as also stated above, has meaning as a reproduction of reality itself. If good behavior and the truth of knowledge, as described above, have meaning as reflecting reality itself, then we can find the unity of the true and the good by taking the reality of objective spirit as medium. Knowledge of the self itself is the essence of spiritual reality. This fact of self-knowledge is activity and development. We can think that we attain to the good by knowing the true reality of the self. Of course, there is a great discrepancy between the truth of fact and the good of behavior. However, even in the case of considering the mere factual world by applying the forms of space and time, we must recognize something moving in a certain direction at its foundation. The unique and immovable world and factual truth are established by it.

This is the reason that 'time' can especially be considered as the category of reality. When 'time' has attained some content, it becomes the world of force, and that which is self-conscious of that content becomes the world of history. That which for us is thought to be an objective good that everyone must recognize and obey must be the direction of this kind of objective world itself. The direction of the advance of true reality must be precisely the end of our behavior. Of course, we cannot think that our goal lies within nature when various human desires are opposed to the dispassionate laws of nature. However, even if nature is the only reality, as the materialist thinks, not only must we follow it, but we can also think that we are able to follow it. If we consider the matter more thoroughly, our desires are also phenomena of nature, so that we can erase this conditional aspect of the problem. Even if we do not go so far as the materialists do, when our self becomes something utterly powerless—that is, when the volitional self is eliminated—anything still remaining as the self would only be a self that knows in a passive way.

The good of the intellectual self must be to know the truth. Truth is the good, and error is evil. The philosophy of Spinoza, which culminates in the theme of 'intellectual love', best clarifies this point. On the contrary, when the self is considered not only to have independent reality over against nature but also to have something irrational and unanalyzable by reason at its very core, the end of the self, as I stated above, cannot be found in the objective world of cognition. At times nature is a means for the self, and at other times it becomes an obstacle to the self. However, in such a case, what is the self that has independent reality over against truth or nature? Even if the goal of the will lies in pleasure or happiness, as the hedonist maintains, impulse or instinct must first be given in order for there to be pleasure or happiness. Pleasure or happiness can arise as satisfactions of impulse or instinct. However, if we think in this way, the self must be submerged again within the objective world of cognition. Can we, on the contrary, consider the self as completely contentless? The self must be satisfied with any content whatsoever. Thus, can we consider such a thing as a rational unity of desires that are given to be the activity of the self? There must be rational content given for us in such a unity. Even if there is such a thing as mere logical law, we can say that there are objective laws that the self must follow. However, the self itself is lost, whether that which is cognized as objective content is considered to emerge within the self or to come from without, and whether following the objective is considered to mean following the end of the self itself or following the objective.

Let me turn to this question of internal or external origin. If cognition is entirely restricted to what is termed the ego, how can we know the exterior of the ego? The perspective that can distinguish the interior or exterior of the self must be one that transcends the two and includes them internally. Even if we cannot see an external obstacle, we must recognize it as external, and, when we know that we are closed off by an obstacle, we have already transcended it, as Fichte states. To know the infinity of the heavens depends not upon visual perception, but upon thinking. When we regard the thing-in-itself as the limit of cognition, this means that we have attained a standpoint beyond cognition. When Kant considers the thing-in-itself to be the limit of cognition as something unknowable, cognition means empirical knowledge. Kant thinks there is no objective knowledge without union with intuitive content. When we know the limit of the cognition in the form of judgment, there must be something beyond the cognition in the form of judgment. Men often say that this is still not knowledge. However, factual knowledge is established by it. Intuition prior to judgment cannot be said to be undifferentiated or unclear. Judgment is simply the articulation of it in terms of categories. This does not mean that the prior content of intuition becomes clear when it is thus expressed in the form of judgment, for the clear content was there from the beginning. We can demand universal validity by judgment, but, in order for the judgment "this thing is red" to become universally valid, one's own intuitive content must be objective. Of course, sensory content of my experience of red may differ from that of others. I cannot compare my sensation with that of others. However, if there is not some place wherein we share in the area of sensation, then we can only fall into solipsism.

It goes without saying that we cannot demand universal validity in knowledge that comes from experience. However, if there is no objective foundation in sensory content, it becomes meaningless to say that knowledge becomes objective by acquiring sensory content. The fact that we possess an empirical world would be entirely an accident. A world restricted to within my consciousness is no different from a dream. The fact that knowledge acquires objectivity by uniting with sensory content depends on transcending the sphere of cognition of the self thereby. It depends on our possessing an objective world at the foundation of sensation. The concept of force unites the worlds of the self and the other, and thereby the contingent is transformed into the necessary. We are not free, even in such a thing as mathematics, which is thought to be purely rational. However, since the self is free to think of mathematics or not, it can be considered the conscious content of the self. Hence, we may say that it is transindividual as a pure object, but it is subjective as conscious content. In sensory experience alone we possess no such freedom. We can only make sensory experience free to a certain degree by volitional action. Here the distinction between the interior and the exterior of consciousness arises. That which opposes our will is thought to be the reality of the external world, and it is thought that we possess an objective world externally. In other words, the distinction between the interior and the exterior of consciousness and also the relationship between the self and other are established in the a priori of the will. That which thus becomes the limit with regard to the objective world of knowledge is nothing other than the objective world of the will. In the objective world of the will we possess the ultimate limit of all knowledge as the world of the fusion of subject and object. That which is considered to be the external world and objectivity with respect to the self is nothing other than a profound depth of the will.

If, with Spinoza, we consider the essence of the self to be simply reason, then knowing is our ultimate satisfaction and becomes the highest good. If, with Kant, we distinguish cognitive from volitional subjectivity, then truth and the good differ from one another. However, cognitive subjectivity is one aspect of volitional subjectivity, and, hence, the dimension in which the transcendental will has reflected upon itself within itself must be the realm of truth and the world of reality. There is nothing that, while being true reality, is not good, and that, while being good, is not reality.

The reason that it is thought that reality and the good oppose each other is that we do not recognize the will in the background of sensory experience. Just as it can be thought that we transcend the consciousness of the self and enter into the objective, spiritual world of the union of self and others by recognizing the will behind it, when the objective world is established by the world of thinking's uniting with the world of sensation, the subjective self and the objective world oppose each other. But, just as it can be thought that since there is the eye there is the world of color and form and since there is the ear there is the world of sound, so, too, that which stands in opposition to the self is again the self.

In the horizon of the active self we can thus subjectify objectivity and objectify subjectivity. The self and the nonself are unified in the horizon of the active self; there is nothing that further remains as the nonself with respect to the active self, for self-conscious behavior takes itself as goal, and there is fusion of subject and object in this intentionality. In the horizon of such an active self we see a world of eternal and imperishable material force that has transcended 'time'. 'Time' is nothing more than the form of our cognition, and force is independent of time and place, for the a priori of the will, which causes the establishment of the world of force, transcends the plane of knowledge and includes it internally. Without time and space there is no force; force exists by appearing within 'time' and 'space', but force must be something that cannot change according to 'time' and 'space'. 'Time' and 'space' are nothing more than means of the manifestation of force. When we have further penetrated to the horizon of the fusion of subject and object, to the intentionality of active self-consciousness, we see an imperishable, eternal beauty in the background of reality. Not only is the beautiful without relation to 'time' and 'space', which are the forms of our cognition, but it transcends material force and cannot be affected by it. However, without things there is no beauty. Just as force appears in the union of 'time' and 'space', so, too, does beauty appear in the combination and union of things.

Perhaps someone will say that beauty is merely a phenomenal aspect of things. Beauty is simply the content of the objective will in the background of perceptual reality. When we have truly penetrated to the active horizon of the self, we see a world of eternal and imperishable good in the background of material force, in which every-thing that is real is the content of the self. It is thought that because beauty is phenomenal it is unrelated to 'time' and 'space', while be-cause the good is diffused throughout 'time' and 'space' and includes them, it is truly eternal and imperishable. There is no material force apart from 'time' and 'space', but there is also no 'time' and 'space' apart from material force. Apart from force, then, 'time' and 'space' are in no way different from something like a series of numbers. Of course, we may be able to imagine the forms of mere 'time' and 'space' apart from things. But, for them to become real, they must unite with experiential content. In contrast to physical time and space, mere formal 'time' and 'space' lose their reality. Kant also states that, while 'time' seems to flow, 'time' itself does not move. The reason we can think that the mode of 'unmoving time' is the form of reality is that it embraces the mode of 'time that flows'. This is the reason we can think that the world of force is eternal and imperishable, in contrast to the world of consciousness. However, in contrast to mere 'time that flows', space becomes the external world; but in 'concrete time' space becomes one of its modes. The material world, which depends upon the form of 'unmoving time' and which confronts the phenomena of consciousness that are considered to be established by 'time that flows', can be thought to be the external world. The direction of 'time that flows' becomes unreal, and the direction of 'unmoving time' be-comes real. But in the standpoint of 'concrete time'—that is, in the standpoint of the will—that which is objective is the self. At least, we are able to see this clearly in impulse.

Impulse is objective, but at the same time it is subjective. The reason that impulsive content can be thought to be subjective just as perceptual content is subjective, is that it is partial and impure. Im-pulsive content latent in the background of perception, once it has been purified, becomes artistic content. While it transcends 'space', 'time', and force, it is expressed by them. The eternal nature of beauty can be recognized by them. The content of the good, because it embraces the plane of consciousness in general, in the sense of being self-conscious content of the will itself, not only transcends the tem-poral course of the entire universe but also becomes its foundation. That we say that the realms of beauty and the good are more real than the world of material force may seem strange. But if the world of force is nothing more than a projection, in which the transcendental will reflects itself within itself, then true reality is only the develop-ment of the will itself. Force appears through 'time' and 'space'; simi-larly, the good appears through force. However, just as 'time' and 'space' are imaginary apart from force, so is force imaginary apart from self-conscious will. It has been thought that we emerge from matter and return to it. But apart from sensation there is no matter. That which can never be eliminated as reality lies only in the development of the universal spirit, which has appeared as our own experience. If we consider that such spiritual content is the content of the good, then we can think that the ideal of the Good is at the foundation of reality.

That which is conceived as the external world in opposition to the self is not strictly opposed to the self. It is simply the objective world of the will. We can unite with this world through behavior. The goal of the will lies within the will itself, and we can arrive at the standpoint of the fusion of subject and object through self-conscious behavior. In contrast to this, there is nothing that is further able to be established as the external world. The category of the power of the understanding and perceptual content unite under the a priori of the will. When the so-called world of experience is established by the category of understanding and perceptual content uniting under the a priori of the will, we enter into the objective world of the unity of self and other.

However, the empirical world is a projection of the will in which the will reflects itself within itself. When the will is self-conscious in its own standpoint, the facts of the empirical world become the expression of the self. It is the body that first transforms our will into direct expression in the empirical world. In the body, subjectivity and objectivity are internally united. In the body, which is unified by the a priori of the will, the objective worlds of knowledge and the will intersect. Apart from the body there is nothing that we can call the self. The self is a 'sublimated body'. The worlds of fact and truth unite through the sense organs; similarly, the worlds of reality and of beauty and truth unite through movement. As our self is the fusion point of various worlds, so, too, is our body the fusion point of various worlds, and we are able to enter into various worlds by taking it as a point of departure. When we enter into the objective world of the will through the body, which, because it is the foundation of the self, must be recognized as the condition of the establishment of the self and at the same time as unknowable by us, then the world of the self and the world of things are in opposition.

In sum, only to the extent that the body is not purified as the self is the world of things in opposition to it externally. In such a case, if we view the matter from the standpoint of the self, the world of things becomes a world of means. The world of things enters into the scope of the self as far as the movement of our body extends. We can think, as does Bergson, that our consciousness accompanies it as far as this kind of movement extends. In such a case, knowledge possesses merely utilitarian significance. However, when we deepen even further the significance of the body as an expression of the will, we are able to enter into a realm beyond knowledge through the movement of the body. We enter into the volitional realm that constitutes the background of the empirical world.

We can think that the creative act of the artist is something that possesses this kind of meaning. The artist sees through a fusion of eye and hand. The world he sees is not a mere world of cognitive objects. Bergson distinguishes between instinctive and intellectual life and states that in the former the parts of the body are at the same time mechanisms. The creative act of the artist also resembles this in one aspect. In instinctive life, things are the self; means and goals fuse. That which confronts the self is not a thing. There is only the expression of one life in unison with the self. But in the creative act of the artist, physical movement is internally purified through discipline, and at the same time even those things outside the body are direct expressions of the life of the self. Artistic discipline—that is, the purification of physical movement—means subsuming the standpoint of knowledge within that of the will. Moral behavior is another instance of this. In moral behavior we attempt to purify the whole self. We do not only purify the conceptual self through the purification of motives. The good is not merely motive but must also be good action. As Hegel states, without great and violent passion (*Leidenschaft*) there are no great men.

But it is the religious dimension that goes to the very essence of this standpoint. In this dimension, there is nothing that is not an expression of the self. Reality is that which moves in itself. We know reality through moving. But, while that which moves as object is a projection of the moving self, knowledge of reality is knowledge of a deeper self. Our self does not lie merely within consciousness, for if it does, it is not the self. When the dynamic self, the self that is the foundation of infinite reality, reflects upon itself, interior and exterior oppose each other, and consciousness of the self is created. The self is the problem given to itself to be overcome. Purification of the body through behavior means to unify the self. Interior and exterior fuse and become one act when there is movement *qua* consciousness, the intentionality in which the self discovers itself. Our losing the self objectively does not mean losing our individuality. The self does not cease to exist. We discover infinite good and sadness beyond

Spinoza's 'intellectual love'. To enter into the realms of Beauty and Good, we must pass through the gateway of truth. Within the gate lies eternal and imperishable true reality. On this side of the gate the self that we see within consciousness in general is nothing more than a shadow of a darker instinct.

Bibliography

Nishida Kitarō zenshū [The complete works of Nishida Kitarō], ed. Shimo-mura Toratarō et al., 19 vols., 2nd ed. (Tokyo: Iwanami Shoten, 1965–1966), comprising:

Zen no kenkyū [A study of good], 1911;

Shisaku to taiken [Thought and experience], 1915;

Jikaku ni okeru chokkan to hansei [Intuition and reflection in self-consciousness], 1917;

Ishiki no mondai [Problems of consciousness], 1920;

Geijutsu to dōtoku [Art and morality], 1923;

Hataraku mono kara miru mono e [From the acting to the seeing], 1927;

Ippansha no jikakuteki taikei [The self-conscious system of the universal], 1930;

Mu no jikakuteki gentei [The self-conscious determination of nothingness], 1932;

Tetsugaku no kompon mondai [Fundamental problems of philosophy], 1933;

Zoku tetsugaku no kompon mondai [Fundamental problems of philosophy, continued], 1934;

Tetsugaku rombun shū, I–VII [Philosophical essays, I–VII], 1937–1945.

Primary Sources in Translation

"Die Einheit des Wahren, des Schönen und des Guten." Translated by F. Takahashi. *Journal of the Sendai International Society*, 1940.

A Study of Good. Translated by V. H. Viglielmo. Tokyo: Japanese Government Printing Bureau, 1960.

Intelligibility and the Philosophy of Nothingness. Translated with Introduction by R. Schinzinger. Honolulu: East-West Center Press, 1966.

Fundamental Problems of Philosophy. Translated by D. Dilworth. Tokyo: Sophia University Press, 1970.

"The Problem of Japanese Culture." Translated by Abe Masao. In *Sources of Japanese Tradition*. New York: Columbia University Press, 1958, pp. 858–872.
"Religious Consciousness and the Logic of the Prajnaparamita Sutra." Translated by D. Dilworth. *Monumenta Nipponica* 25, 1–2 (1970): 203–216.
"Towards a Philosophy of Religion with the Concept of Pre-established Harmony as Guide." Translated by D. Dilworth. *Eastern Buddhist*, New Series 3, 1 (1970): 19–46.

SECONDARY SOURCES

Arima Tatsuo. "Nishida Kitarō: The Epistemological Character of Taisho Japan." In *The Failure of Freedom: A Portrait of Modern Japanese Intellectuals*, Harvard, 1969, pp. 7–14.
Callaway, Tucker. "Nishida's Philosophy of Nothingness," *Japan Christian Quarterly* 27 (April 1961): 124–127.
Craig, Albert, et al. *East Asia: The Modern Transformation*. Boston: Houghton Mifflin Co., 1965, pp. 544–546.
Dilworth, David. "The Initial Formations of 'Pure Experience' in Nishida Kitarō and William James." *Monumenta Nipponica* 24, 1–2 (1969): 93–111.
———. "Nishida's Early Pantheistic Voluntarism," *Philosophy East and West* 20, 1 (1970): 35–49.
———. "The Range of Nishida's Early Religious Thought." *Philosophy East and West* 19, 4 (1969): 409–421.
———. "Nishida's Final Essay: The Logic of Place and a Religious Worldview." *Philosophy East and West* 20, 4 (1970): 355–367.
———. "Nishida Kitarō's Philosophy of the *Topos* of Nothingness as the Negative Space of Experiential Immediacy." *International Philosophical Quarterly*, December 1973.
———. "The Phenomenology and Logic of Interpresence in Watsuji Tetsurō and Nishida Kitarō." *The Japan P.E.N. Club Conference on International Studies*. Kyoto, November 1972, pp. 1–18.
Kim, Ha Tai. "Nishida and Royce." *Philosophy East and West* 1, 4 (1952): 18–29.
Knauth, Lothar. "Life is Tragic: The Diary of Nishida Kitarō." *Monumenta Nipponica* 20, 3–4 (1965): 335–358.
Kōsaka Masaaki. "Nishida Kitarō's *Zen no kenkyū*." In *Japanese Thought in the Meiji Period*. Tokyo: Pacific Press, 1958, pp. 484–494.
Noda Matao. "East-West Synthesis in Kitarō Nishida." *Philosophy East and West* 4, 4 (April 1954–January 1955): 345–359.
———. "Modern Japanese Philosophy and the Philosophy of Kitarō Nishida." *Proceedings of the Eleventh International Congress of Philosophy*. Vol. 12. Brussels, 1953, pp. 263–267.
Piovesana, Gino. "The Philosophy of Nishida Kitarō, 1870–1945." *Recent*

Japanese Philosophical Thought, 1862–1962: A Survey. Tokyo: Enderle Bookstore, 1963, pp. 85–124.

Piper, R. F. "Nishida, Notable Japanese Personalist." *Personalist* 17, 1 (1936): 21–31.

Shimomura Toratarō. "Nishida Kitarō and Some Aspects of His Philosophy." Translated by V. H. Viglielmo. In *A Study of Good*. Tokyo: Japanese Government Printing Bureau, 1960, pp. 191–217.

Takeda Hiromichi. "Nishida's Doctrine of Universals." *Monumenta Nipponica* 23, 3–4 (1960): 497–502.

Takeuchi Yoshinori. "Nishida's Philosophy as Representative of Japanese Philosophy." In *Encyclopaedia Britannica*, 1966 ed., vol. 12, 958–962.

———. "The Philosophy of Nishida Kitarō." *Japanese Religions* 3, 4 (1963): 1–32.

Viglielmo, V. H. "Nishida Kitarō: The Early Years." In Donald Shively, ed., *Tradition and Modernization in Japanese Culture*. Princeton: Princeton University Press, 1971, pp. 507–562.

Waldenfels, Hans. "Absolute Nothingness: Preliminary Considerations on a Central Notion in the Philosophy of Nishida Kitarō and the Kyoto School." *Monumenta Nipponica* 21, 3–4 (1966): 354–391.

Index